The American
Television Critic

The American Television Critic

A History

Melissa Crawley

McFarland & Company, Inc., Publishers
Jefferson, North Carolina

ISBN (print) 978-1-4766-6936-6
ISBN (ebook) 978-1-4766-2903-2

LIBRARY OF CONGRESS CATALOGUING DATA ARE AVAILABLE

British Library cataloguing data are available

Front cover images © 2017 iStock

Printed in the United States of America

*McFarland & Company, Inc., Publishers
Box 611, Jefferson, North Carolina 28640
www.mcfarlandpub.com*

To Tom Hill,
whose observation that I had the writing voice
of a columnist started me on this TV critic path.

And to Helen, Elle and Charlie,
the best four-legged officemates a writer could have.

Contents

Preface

As a TV critic, I receive a steady stream of emails every day from television network publicists. The people over at PBS think I'll be very interested in their latest documentary. The men and women at the major networks want me to know that last night's screening of their new cop drama was a big hit with 18- to 35-year-olds. Do I want to join a conference call and interview the star of a new situation comedy on Fox? Or maybe I'd rather speak to the latest reality TV winner or loser? The publicists who flood my email inbox every day hope to guide my choices so that I might guide your choices.

Whether or not I persuade you to watch or avoid a show depends on so many factors that it's not a real goal. You know what you like so my intention is to share why a show delights me or leaves me feeling uninspired in a way that makes you consider something new or different about your viewing experience. It's a desire that comes from knowing that while TV has its lows, its highs are there too, waiting to be discovered. From the complex dramas to the laugh-out-loud situation comedies, from news to sports to documentaries to movies, television is everything. It is part of the fabric of life.

Having spent a few years exploring the work of my predecessors and colleagues for this book, I discovered that it is respect for the small screen that unites all of us. Our critical voices are unique and our stylistic approaches vary, but what we all have in common is awareness that television is not the "idiot box." Rather, it demands that its viewers be active participants, that they seek its many moments of excellence and recognize the cultural conversations it starts. Guiding those conversations with sharp insight into the way television as a creative product, as an industry and as a technology shapes everyday life are the critics.

1

This book chronicles those who celebrate the best that television has to offer and challenge it when it fails to reach its potential. It is about influential men and women who have sought respectability, struggled to define their professional practice and debated their role. Throughout their history, journalistic TV critics have been gatekeepers, advocates, agitators and promoters. Not every critic is all of those things but most are more than one, making a single definition of "TV critic" elusive. It is an idea that contemporary critics embrace as they accept that both television and those whose job it is to write about it represent a variety of voices, all being heard, and some louder than others. This book charts the development of an active, impressive and unsettled profession whose future, like that of television's, is full of possibilities.

Introduction:
Aren't We All TV Critics?

TELEVISION IS ALL AROUND and everywhere, ready for viewers to engage with it on their own. It is a direct art form with familiar stories that are designed to be relatively open for interpretation and easily accessible. It requires little mediation to be understood, so for many, deferring to "expert" opinion is unnecessary. In other words: Aren't we all TV critics? It's a question that has its roots in a fundamental way of thinking about art and how it's judged. Among critical traditions, popular writing about television occupies an uncertain place.

Art and literary criticism use measures of "high" and "low" to determine what is worthy of analysis. The objects studied are not expected to reach a wide audience. The criticism is specialized and often exists as meaningful on its own. Television criticism (here defined as that written by journalists in print and online) does not follow strict distinctions of taste, is aimed at a general audience, appears in mainstream outlets and does not depend on elite knowledge to be understood. In addition, TV critics have a relationship with their readers, their employers, the artistic communities who create television and the business interests who keep the industry running, making their status as cultural authorities more ambiguous than those in other critical traditions. While this ambiguity may lead some to dismiss their expertise, the people who write about television shows play important roles in how those shows are circulated. TV critics are intermediate consumers, mediators of audience response and meaning-makers who offer ideologies that validate certain programs as art.

Hundreds of critics reach thousands of people every day with TV columns and online sites that do more than list program schedules. Their coverage of the creative and business aspects of the industry is the major source of information that connects the viewing public in a discourse about television. The critics who write for the popular press and for online publications may not convince viewers to watch or avoid a particular program but they enrich the debates surrounding shows. They help audiences understand why television means what it does within communities and societies. They give viewers different ways to engage with the series they love or thought they hated. TV critics recognize television's role as an art form and as an integral part of everyday life. They influence how audiences share their views on a pervasive medium.

While academic television criticism teaches students how to become informed "readers" of TV "texts" by learning and employing a set of critical tools, the best popular television criticism, while less methodological, aims for a similar outcome. It describes, interprets and evaluates visual and sound style, production techniques, narrative devices, and representations of different races, ethnicities and sexualities. Its goal is to broaden the way audiences think about what they watch. Understanding how the best critics talk about television matters because their reviews are much more than simple judgments of taste. They create frameworks for how audiences interpret television's diverse meanings and, ultimately, help to create more critical viewers.

Talking Television

This book is the first to cover American critics from the early days of television to the present. Organized chronologically, it uses their writing as a new way to explore the social and cultural impact of television. Whether they are praising or discouraging programming trends, educating readers on production techniques or ratings, analyzing narrative or gender representations or weighing in on policy decisions and funding issues, their work represents more than a consumer guide. It is a rich and overlooked part of television history that offers a valuable way to think about American culture and its relationship to the small screen.

TV history is used to frame the study but this book is a selective rather than an exhaustive account of television through the years. Each chapter highlights some of the programming trends, policy decisions and technological changes that had audiences and critics talking. Threaded throughout is the critics' work, both as it appeared in daily review columns that focused on specific programs and longer essays that went beyond assessing shows. The picture that emerges is one in which critics are more than witnesses to television's creative, technological and industrial transformations. They are active participants in the debates that surround those changes.

One of the challenges in exploring a subject as large as the development of popular TV criticism is deciding on what to include and exclude among a vast body of work. Popular criticism is in newspapers, magazines, websites and blogs, daily and weekly. Several critics, including a few who have won the Pulitzer Prize, have published collections of their columns while some have written books that explore one or more television shows. Examining all this material would be impossible for one researcher so the choice of which critics and publications to focus on came down to practical considerations of access. The majority of critical work referenced here was published in larger circulation newspapers and magazines and heavily trafficked websites and blogs which all offer easily searchable archives. These sources are also the most influential in terms of reaching the biggest number of readers. The work of critics with large readerships was chosen because it is a logical way to narrow a very wide field while also providing the readers of this book with an introduction to those who have, in both the past and the present, made their voices heard the loudest.

Chapter Outline

Chapter One begins with the 1950s when editors hastily assigned staff, many of whom worked as theatre critics, to evaluate television. As they were unsure how to comment on the new medium, much of their early work did little more than describe programs. The exception was several first generation critics including *New York Times* journalist Jack Gould and his contemporary, John Crosby, who wrote for the *New York Herald Tribune*. The work of Gould and Crosby, as well as several others in the 1950s, demonstrated the potential of popular TV criticism to influence viewers, policy makers and industry leaders. Valued by the networks for legitimizing the new medium in its infancy, the 1950s critics covered in this chapter were influential cultural intermediaries. Gould's work, in particular, had its greatest influence from 1947 to 1961 when it covered the "Golden Age" of television. This sway changed, however, with the quick social uptake of television and the establishment of regulatory norms.

Chapter Two looks at the 1960s, a time of social and cultural upheaval where the one constant was television. Shows featuring friendly Martians and lovable country bumpkins distracted audiences from the turbulent events happening outside their doorsteps but the formulaic programming pushed critics to question the networks' ability to responsibly balance the public interest with commercial interest. The critics' harsh responses to the networks' broadcasting strategies caused tension and the networks, no longer needing the critics to strengthen their credibility, reduced the press critics' role. As a result, they became more valued as promotional agents, a change that would lead to less ambitious work and calls to re-evaluate and formalize the profession.

Chapter Three turns to the 1970s when a generation of TV journalists who came of age during Watergate demanded a shift from the "soft" news approach of the 1960s to a more "hard" news focus. Unlike their predecessors, most reviewers who started their TV writing careers in this decade were trained as journalists and rejected the networks' control of information through press releases. The result was criticism that was not afraid to upset network executives. Chapter Three will also discuss the creation and impact of the Television Critics Association. Founded in 1978 by journalists demanding the end of network controlled press junkets in favor of press tours that featured panels and conferences, the TCA became instrumental in legitimizing the profession by providing more opportunities for critical coverage.

Chapter Four covers both the 1980s and 1990s when technology and the multichannel environment changed how viewers watched television. No longer restricted by a network's broadcast schedule, audiences had the power to delay their viewing, jump between stations and bypass network shows for specialized programming that suited their interests. Increased competition, fragmented viewership, network mergers and new audience measurement techniques all contributed to changing the business of television. Critics were again prized as promotional agents who helped viewers find programs but their work also echoed that of their predecessors in the 1950s, as the value of programs underwent a transition. The wider field of programming choices led to a shift in the economic logic of the industry so that lower ratings were accepted in exchange for a higher ranking among certain profitable demographics. Many critics distinguished the shows that appealed to those valued demographics as different from the rest. The notion of "quality" television was once again part of the critics' conversation with one important difference. Rather than trying to discredit the critics for being out of touch with the programming desires of the public as the networks did in the 1950s, in the 1980s and the 1990s the industry supported the quality discourse because it helped to legitimize television among a lucrative demographic.

Traditionally the domain of newspapers and, to a lesser extent, magazines, TV reviews discussed a limited number of shows upon their debut with no comprehensive coverage of a series over time. A significant shift took place in the twenty-first century as websites and online versions of print magazines and newspapers gave TV critics the opportunity to review many shows and cover them weekly. This change is the focus of chapter five. The saturation of programming combined with the endless space of the Internet not only lifted the limitations placed on critics by column space and gave them more to talk about but also increased their contribution as cultural agenda setters. TV review websites began to generate buzz.

While the Internet enabled critics to reach a wider audience and to engage in lively debates with their readers, it extended the same benefit to anyone who wanted to talk TV. Passionate viewers employed by recap sites summarized every episode of a series in painstaking detail hours after it was broadcast. The landscape of TV criticism was changing but not all agreed it was for the better. Chapter Five looks at these debates.

Chapter Six explores the work of contemporary critics. A complete account of everyone writing in the new millennium is a book in itself so the chapter offers a detailed overview of those who are widely read or most well known. As critics were no longer seeking legitimacy among high art commentators or debating public service versus promotion, their professional discussions focused on the most effective way to serve their readers. Some believed readers benefitted most from detailed episodic reviews. Others preferred close readings of narrative, performance and production. All infused their analysis with valuable insight into television's cultural and social impact.

The book concludes with a brief summary of the development of popular TV criticism in America and suggests that it continues to evolve, as its practitioners seek new ways to talk about their practice and their role in a pervasive medium.

In Search of Television Criticism

Television critics are men who report traffic accidents to eyewitnesses.
—JACKIE GLEASON[1]

Comedian and actor Jackie Gleason was not alone in his feelings about the men and women who reviewed his programs. For some scholars, cultural commentators and viewers, TV critics represent a distraction between the creators of a program and the audience to whom they speak directly. This is partly due to television criticism's complicated role within the overall critical tradition. Before we begin, it's important to look at how their work fits within the broader concept of criticism as well as to discuss useful ways to think about their influence. Borrowing concepts from media and communication studies, this section and the one following it briefly address those ideas in order to create a more complete picture of the television critic's development.

Critics are in a unique position to discuss a medium that impacts almost everyone but this pervasiveness comes with a price. The disadvantage of TV being embedded so deeply in everyday life is that it is often considered a "lowly" cultural art form. The primary challenge for television critics seeking legitimacy is that unlike their counterparts who write about elite art forms, the TV critic's role is less institutionalized. In elite art subjects, universities offer formal training in criticism and define the criteria for analysis, which is then used to make evaluative comments and arrive at a value judgment or a type of universal truth. In those high art fields, agreed upon experts have the authority to criticize a cultural object and audiences defer to their expertise rather than make independent judgments. In the non-elite, popular world of television, viewers make choices about the programs they watch without referring to critics. In addition, television studies, once a marginalized field in higher education, is a discipline with a relatively short history.[2] Without a recognized set of evaluative criteria or institutional support, TV critics are often thought of as fellow viewers expressing an opinion, making it difficult for them to be considered valuable experts.

Yet critics whose cultural authority is more accepted because they rationalize or intellectualize traditional forms (a ballet, an opera, a painting) within institutional frameworks also give interpretations that make use of opinions. As one drama critic has suggested: "Criticism lives on opinions. Opinions are the electricity of the mind. 'What do you think?' Is there a more profoundly social question than that?"[3] The act of passing judgment on cultural objects is virtually impossible to separate from the act of giving an opinion but it is in this obvious relationship between evaluation and personal taste that TV critics are most easily dismissed. The reasons for this lie in the complicated status of popular television criticism. While TV critics are part of a long critical tradition, they are perceived as operating on its fringe, commenting on a medium that lies outside the traditional artistic domain. Some scholars and cultural commentators suggest that the role of the critic in a non-elite art world such as television is in fact unnecessary.[4] However, others propose that the approach to judging elite art forms is not dissimilar to that used in evaluating popular art forms because they both rely on emotional as well as intellectual judgments. Sociologist Herbert Gans argued: "I use the term aesthetic broadly, referring not only to standards of beauty and taste but also to a variety of other emotional and intellectual values which people express or satisfy when they choose content from a culture, and I assume, of course that people apply aesthetic standards in all taste cultures, and not just in high culture."[5]

Similarly, television studies scholar Horace Newcomb suggested that in basing their standards for evaluation on how well a program satisfied the viewer's desire for an emotional reality, critics applied a "popular aesthetic" or a standard that reflected how a show reached a degree of emotional authenticity for those watching it.[6] Following this argument, the critic's job of evaluating television with a popular aesthetic is a valid alternative approach that recognizes the emotional criteria applied to the judgment of all art forms while also acknowledging an important way that engaged viewers experience the medium.

Complicating matters even further for the TV critic is the nature of the industry. Television represents an articulation of popular values, symbols and myths but its creative products are also designed to reach demographics that appeal to advertisers. While the TV landscape is more fragmented than it was in the past with subscriber supported networks and online streaming services not always using profits as the primary consideration when choosing which shows to broadcast, ideas for programs on advertiser supported networks are still vetted and screened for their commercial viability. As a cultural product whose artistic properties are often outweighed by its commercial mandate, much of television's value lies in how successful it is as a profit earning form of entertainment. This puts television critics in an unusual position. Unlike their colleagues in the high arts, they do not have many chances to review the work of groundbreaking creators or discover promising new talent. They do not publish their comments in elite publications for "connoisseurs." Their writing is circulated in the mainstream for a vast, diverse audience and does not require specific intellectual training or an exclusive vocabulary.[7] All of these factors contribute to the perception that the cultural authority of TV critics is less certain than those who cover "high art."

The scope of television also impacts the critic's job. TV is drama, film, music, dance, news, sports, education, game shows, reality shows and advertisements. It is networks, celebrities, ratings, regulations, economics and politics. Ideally, TV critics are expected to write about all of these areas, unlike their colleagues in other critical traditions. As communications scholar Hal Himmelstein suggested, television critics face unique challenges:

> Those critics of television, unlike their fellow travelers engaged in evaluating the more traditional art forms of literature, theater, visual arts, music, and film, find themselves faced with a singularly challenging task—for they must examine not only works of television art in isolation, but they must also consider television's presence in the world as an economic institution of considerable influence; television as a technology constantly impacting on a substantial number of cultural issues including the directions and pace of social change; television as a barometer of the status of subcultural group relationships to a dominant culture's control of information processing and dissemination; and television as an institutional mechanism.[8]

Covering television, in all its forms, is a broad task that separates its critics from a traditional notion of what it means to analyze an art form.

The operational complexity of the industry is another factor that adds to the critic's hard to define status. Many powerful decision makers run television: network executives, advertisers, writers, directors, producers and the audience. The location of critics in this list is difficult to place because their power is always shifting. Audiences read a review to decide whether or not they should invest their leisure time in watching a show. Industry players read a review hoping that it will predict a show's commercial success. The danger is that an insightful analysis may benefit the audience but alienate the industry side and vice versa. Critics depend on the business side of television for advanced screenings and interviews with the creative community. They have to nurture this relationship while simultaneously creating a respected status among their readership. Not alienating the industry or their audience can be a difficult balancing act.

Understanding the Critic's Influence

> Good criticism of any kind—of movies, ballet, architecture or whatever—makes us think, feel, respond; if we then agree or disagree is less important than the fact that our faculties have been engaged or stretched. Good criticism informs, interprets, and raises the ultimate questions.... The critic induces us to think, to widen our horizons, to open yet another book, to reconsider a snap judgment, to see something from a loftier vantage point, in historic perspective, and using more and truer touchstones.—JOHN SIMON[9]

Film critic John Simon may or may not have had television in mind for his "whatever" category but his point about the characteristics of good criticism applies to the medium nonetheless. Good TV criticism educates and evaluates while prompting viewers to consider how its programs and structures impact their immediate environment and the wider cultural landscape. Yet rarely do viewers credit TV critics for impacting their ideas about the industry or influencing their program choices. Most critics would agree that they have little to no persuasive power when it comes to convincing their readers to watch or avoid a show. There are, however, a few ways to understand the influence they do have.

One way is to place them within the circuit of cultural production,[10] a model that lays out the relationship between producers and consumers and identity and meaning within society. Within this framework, producers encode products with particular meanings but these meanings are not received passively. They are not fixed or singular but rather actively made in the consumption of a product. In television, for example, the creators, writers and directors of a show have certain meanings in mind for their program. A show might be intended as a commentary on society's preoccupation with surveillance but a viewer might overlook this meaning in favor of something that resonates with them more strongly. The idea that consumers of a media product or, in this case, viewers of a TV program, reach their own conclusions regarding its meaning goes beyond earlier communication models that stressed one way communication from senders (the creative people behind a show) to passive receivers (the audience). The circuit of cultural production suggests that while certain forms of representation are produced, receivers of media messages actively interpret them based on their experiences. The critic's role in this lies with his or her position in the circuit. Critics sit somewhere between production and consumption because they engage with both those who produce, create and distribute television's products and the audience who receives those products.

Another way of looking at this is that meaning is produced in relationship to how media forms reference other media forms. Media and communications scholar John Fiske called this intertextuality, or the connections between media products or texts.[11] These connections operate horizontally and vertically. Horizontal intertextuality exists between primary texts. In the case of television this is a program or a series. The connections are genre or characters or content. Vertical connections, on the other hand, are the connections between primary, secondary and tertiary texts. Secondary texts make specific references to primary texts while tertiary texts refer to the forms of meaning produced by an audience. A review of a television show is an example of a secondary text while conversations between family and friends, fan mail or gossip referring to that show is a form of a tertiary text. The concept of intertextuality proposed that a viewer's understanding of an individual media product was partly shaped by his or her experience of other related products. One of those related products is the critic's review.

If a viewer reads a review of a television show that evaluates that show in a specific way—it could take a feminist approach to talking about the female lead, for example—he or she might use this model (possibly without realizing it) to form his or her opinion of the show. The review then is part of the process of how meaning is created. Like reviews, advertising and publicity are also secondary texts that shape a specific view of a show. In this case, the goal is to attract audiences and ratings. A critic's review may work for or against this goal. The review may also become part of the tertiary text. For example, it could influence conversations viewers have about the show with their friends.

Critics are not unaffected by the media texts that swirl around television. Gossip, public discussions or publicity campaigns might influence how they judge a program but those judgments are also personal. Like viewers, critics have specific tastes and values that are formed by their education, their upbringing and their social class.[12] All of these factors play a role in how they write about television. Critics then shape meaning and are shaped by it within the endless circuit of culture.

One final way of thinking about the influence of television criticism is the idea that reviews are also "paratexts." Related to the notion of intertextuality, paratexts exist in the space between a media product, its audience and its industry. Drawing on the work of Gerard Genette, media scholar Jonathan Gray argues that press reviews are examples of critical paratexts that either try to "deflect readers from certain texts or to infect their reading when it occurs."[13] As paratexts, TV reviews prepare audiences for shows but they do more than tell viewers what to expect. They also provide the early framework through which viewers will examine, react to, and evaluate what they are watching. For Gray, critics are privileged paratextual creators and their reviews, particularly the ones prior to a television show's release, are able to "catch the audience at a decisive pre-decoding moment, just as the text is being born."[14] Not all critics have the same reach and not all audiences read reviews. However, a review, once released, still has the power to establish frames for how viewers should watch a show, if they should watch it and what it might mean.

CHAPTER ONE

Sound Meets Sight: The 1950s

EVEN BEFORE TELEVISION WAS an experimental, working technology in the 1920s and 1930s, the press was imagining its possibilities. Writing in 1900, columnist Charles H. Sewall described his vision for televising an event worldwide in a piece for *Harper's Weekly* called "The Future of Long Distance Communication." In it, he imagined a marching band in New York City watched by an audience in China. It would take awhile for television to catch up with Sewall's imagination but less than two decades to capture the attention of journalists across the country whose writing would quickly spread awareness about the new technology.

In 1928, General Electric demonstrated what a mechanical television system could do with a forty-minute broadcast of a one-act play called *The Queen's Messenger* to an eager audience of reporters gathered in the hallway of its station in Schenectady, New York. The review by Russell Porter, "Play Is Broadcast by Voice and Acting in Radio-Television," made the front page of the *New York Times*. With more demonstrations and experimental licenses given to stations broadcasting in the northeast, Chicago and Los Angeles, the spectacle of television was a news story that soon became a hot topic in the press. Reporters made predictions for this wave of "radio movies" in papers from New York to the Midwest. The *Utica Observer* envisioned a future where "motion-pictures by radio may become as effective in keeping people home as the automobile has been for taking them away"[1] while the *Milwaukee Journal* suggested that "the mechanical age we brought is hustling us. Now it is movies by radio in the home."[2] Helped along by enthusiastic press coverage, the excitement over television was also thanks to an extensive public relations campaign. In 1938 alone, the Radio Corporation of America (RCA) held 134 press conferences to herald the coming of television. Throughout the 1920s and 1930s, however, the press would also be disappointed as economic and technological issues lead to TV's regular postponement. An ambitious visionary with an astute understanding of public relations finally fulfilled the promise of all those press conferences. His strategy? Upstage the president at the 1939 World's Fair.

While Philo T. Farnsworth, the inventor of an all-electronic TV system, made discoveries that were more groundbreaking than those achieved at RCA's first research laboratory in New Jersey, it was RCA president David Sarnoff who launched TV in America. The RCA exhibit at the 1939 World's Fair was TV's coming out party. Instead of waiting until the official April 30 inauguration day to launch RCA's service with a broadcast of the president's opening ceremony speech, Sarnoff and public relations executive Edward Bernays came up with a plan. Sarnoff would hold a preview event at the RCA exhibit. The promotional telecast featured Sarnoff standing behind a podium draped with an RCA banner. In a speech that lasted about ten minutes he expressed his thoughts on the power of the new medium: "And now we add radio sight to sound. It is with a feeling of humbleness that I come to this moment of announcing the birth in this country of a new art so important in its implications that it is bound to affect all society. It is an art which shines like a torch of hope in a troubled world. It is a creative force which we must learn to utilize for the benefit of all mankind."[3] With one brief speech, Sarnoff guaranteed that it was his words and image rather than President Roosevelt's that became the defining moment of television's beginning in American culture. What Sarnoff could not have realized was how quickly his enthusiasm would spread.

Television Meets Its Audience

If the 1930s represented television's introduction to the American public and the 1940s began the courtship, the 1950s cemented the romance. Americans embraced television in a surprisingly short amount of time. It took just ten years to reach thirty-five million households. In comparison, the telephone took eighty years to reach a similar saturation. The car needed fifty years to achieve it and radio did it in twenty-five.

Within a generation from Sarnoff's broadcast in 1939, television was in over 90 percent of all American homes.

By 1948, the television audience began to take shape as the medium cemented its move from a technology to a consumer product. Due to the Federal Communication Commission's (FCC) freeze on television licenses in late 1948, a situation that lasted for more than three years, television was primarily in New York and Los Angeles with each city having seven stations. While some cities including Austin, Texas, and Portland, Oregon, did not have any stations most cities had one. As a result, it was easy for the industry to monitor the impact of the medium. The effects were significant. In 1951, almost all television cities reported a 20 to 40 percent decrease in movie attendance.[4] Sports events, restaurants, nightclubs and even public libraries all felt the impact as attendance dropped. People were staying home to watch television. When the freeze ended, a more favorable regulatory climate enabled broadcasting to spread across the nation. Small town and rural residents joined the ranks of urban viewers and television quickly became an integral part of even more citizens' lives. Marketed as a domestic appliance, it promised to open the family home to entertainment and educational possibilities while also creating a new togetherness.[5]

For some viewers, the new medium's possibilities offered a positive, even life-altering experience while others thought of it in less celebratory terms. In a survey conducted by social research scholar Gary Steiner in 1960 and published three years later, one passionate viewer had this to say: "TV is wonderful—just wonderful. Why, TV has brought me the whole world. I just love it. I love everything. I love to see our President.... And I love the stories and the westerns. I just love every minute. It's the most thrilling thing of my life."[6] Another offered a dire prediction: "TV engineers are going to roast in hell till eternity as a result of what they have done."[7] Some social critics seemed to agree, particularly when it came to children. Citing television's potential to harm childhood development; one social critic suggested, "No Pied Piper ever proved so irresistible."[8] Discussing the situation in a piece for the *New York Times Magazine* called "A Decade Since *Howdy Doody*," on September 21, 1958, reporter Dorothy Barclay wrote that many believed early children's programming would create a generation of kids who, dazzled by the screen, would become passive, "immovable objects." Steiner's study of viewer attitudes toward television noted, however, that the celebration and the condemnation of TV represented extremes. He discovered that the typical viewer watched for 3.5 hours per day out of habit more than dedication and there was very little evidence showing an extreme response: "He is not overwhelmed by what he sees, nor is he bored or disgusted."[9] Yet, when viewers were asked to describe what happened when their sets didn't work, the responses were dramatic: "We went crazy.... We couldn't do anything. Didn't even try to read a paper. Just walked around brooding." "When it is out of order," said one viewer, "I feel like someone is dead." Another declared: "I nearly lost my mind. The days were so long, and I just couldn't stand to miss my continued stories."[10] Habit, need, blessing or curse, 1950s TV successfully implanted itself into the fabric of daily life. As media historian Gary Edgerton notes: "It was both adaptable and revolutionary, to be both a technological marvel that fascinated and a piece of bulky furniture that talked incessantly. TV became the center of the urban and suburban household, the reliable children's babysitter, the harried housewife's friend, the sports buddy of the exhausted husband."[11]

It was not too long before newspaper editors started to pay attention to the medium's growing influence. While some refused to cover television because they feared it as competition, the majority understood the benefit of not ignoring the medium and assigned reporters, most of whom were the arts and entertainment critics, to the television beat. By the mid–1950s, reviewing was widespread in daily newspapers while space devoted to television increased 500 percent between 1953 and 1955. In 1958, almost 80 percent of American daily newspapers with a circulation over 50,000 employed television editors and the content they covered borrowed heavily from popular radio shows since they naturally benefited from the transition to a visual medium. Throughout the early years of the 1950s, television lured radio stars away from the airwaves. George Burns and Gracie Allen made an easy transition; bringing characters they fined tuned over twenty-five years in vaudeville and radio to the small screen. The transition of *Amos 'n' Andy*, one of radio's first big hits, was less successful, however, as the show's characters and stories lead to charges of racial insensitivity. Telecasts of sporting events routinely brought in the largest viewing audiences with NBC's *The Gillette Cavalcade of Sports* becoming the first successful long running commercial network TV show in 1944. Boxing was extremely popular, leading a reporter at the *Philadelphia Daily News* to declare: "The winner—Television!"[12] Baseball although slightly less successful due to TV's technical limitations, still earned coverage. Reviewing a college game, a critic for the *New York Times* claimed it was well executed but the players looked like "white flies running across the 9-by-12 inch screen."[13] A reporter for *Variety* had a more positive reaction, deciding that the telecast of the 1947 World Series made television better than radio broadcasts and even "better than a seat on the first base line" at least when it came to dramatic moments.[14] Viewers also watched cops as dedicated professionals on *Dragnet*, slice-of-life situation comedy with *The Goldbergs* and *I Remember Mama*, soap operas, *The Lone Ranger*, the superstar of children's television, *Howdy Doody*, and *Texaco Star Theater*'s Milton Berle, who quickly became the king of sketch comedy.

Most of television's afternoon programs during those years were designed to reach a female demographic or as *The Reporter* television critic Marya Mannes put it, designed "to make life tolerable for the woman over forty who seems to need certain attentions denied to her elsewhere."[15] Mannes was referring to the show *Ladies Date*, one of many, she noted, with a formula that consisted of making women laugh, flattering them and offering them gifts. Another show called *Here's Looking at You* featured a male host named Richard Willis who gave advice to women on their appearance. Mannes noted that along with comments like "I don't see a thing the matter with your nose, dear ... you're just conscious of it," Willis' most repeated advice was that a particular hat was unsuitable.[16]

Cooking programs featured prominently on the schedule and Mannes described her impressions of them in the same February 17, 1953, column: They consisted of attractive women with constant smiles who created elegant dishes in tidy kitchens and displayed embroidered mats crafted by *mountain people*. They also helpfully pointed out that serrated cake knives could also be used for fish. Mannes' *only* complaint with cooking shows was that their hosts worked with flawless equipment and behind-the-scenes help. Her assessment of the show *Bride and Groom*, while maintaining her sarcastic wit, was more thoughtful. Despite loathing the fact that she was watching couples share their courtship stories before being publicly married and then sent on a honeymoon paid by the show's sponsors, the couples, she observed, appear to be genuinely moved by the experience. It was "a triumph indeed of human innocence over commercial exploitation."[17] Mannes was also concerned with the abundance and quality of commercials on her television set and shared a few thoughts with her readers in a March 2, 1954, *Reporter* column titled "Those D—n Commercials." After a day spent watching commercials that happened to be interrupted by programs, Mannes offered her report. She had little patience for men who wore white coats and pretended to be doctors and those who wore overalls and assumed the status of workmen. She disliked advertisements where women were depicted smelling or stroking their wash because laundry was "not a sensuous experience." On her list of commercials she could watch without boredom were ones that featured animation with jingles that she described as cheerful and silly but most importantly, quickly over.

She ended the piece with suggestions on how sponsors could make their ads more useful to viewers, namely, remembering that the audience was not a group of fools that needed to be told the same message multiple times. Mannes was a clever critic but she did more than entertain her readers. In these and other columns, she urged them to think about the ways in which the "new and miraculous medium" of television was being used.

For Walter Annenberg, the miraculous medium was the key to expanding his family's publishing business and his decision made a lasting impact on both television and its critics. Using a Philadelphia area publication called *TV Digest* as a starting point, Annenberg decided to publish a national television magazine that would include features and local listings. *TV Guide* began in 1953 and quickly expanded across the country with regional editions. The magazine went beyond the fan approaches of its competitors and became both an advocate for the burgeoning television system and a critic of its shortcomings, often urging readers to support quality programs that were struggling to gain an audience. Striking a successful balance between appealing to the public's viewing tastes and urging television to reach its potential, *TV Guide* achieved wide popularity. Its writers and editors including Merrill Pannitt, Sally Bedell Smith, Neil Hickey, Frank Swertlow and Cleveland Amory offered a combination of features, interviews and investigative reports. Over the years, noted specialists and media practitioners contributed think pieces. Notable writers and cultural commentators including Betty Friedan, John Updike and Gore Vidal found large audiences for their work in the magazine. At its height in the late 1970s, *TV Guide*'s circulation reached close to twenty million copies per week. Annenberg's foresight created a respected venue for TV criticism that continues today.

In the 1950s, both journalistic and cultural critics spoke out about the new medium, either praising television for its ability to bring society together or declaring it a disruptive force that was threatening social harmony. Committees formed to study the "problem" of television, namely its focus on sex and violence, which some believed was the cause for the rise in juvenile delinquency. Bawdy jokes and stories, along with low cut necklines became a target. The president of Boston University told the 1950 graduating class: "If the television craze continues with the present level of programs, we are destined to have a nation of morons."[18] Others sounded more dire warnings. On December 27, 1952, *Chicago Daily News* TV critic Jack Mabley published a story on the front page of the paper with the headline "TV's Holiday Fare for Kids: It's Murder." Mabley reported that a group of parents who decided to monitor Chicago television stations for depictions of violence over a four-day viewing period counted seventy-seven murders and over fifty shootings in addition to kidnappings, fist-fights, robberies and knifings. He followed the story with a series of articles on excessive violence in children's programs that lead to angry public debate. Concerned parents, pastors, city councilors and even Chicago Police Commissioner Timothy O'Conner expressed opinions that TV violence had real world implications. O'Conner said he was convinced that there was a relationship between television programs and the rising crime rate.[19] In fact, juvenile crime had not risen in Chicago during this time. The year it peaked was 1945, long before television arrived in the city.[20] The controversy over televised violence that Mabley's articles generated during the winter of 1952-1953 resulted in a Chicago City Council recommendation that urged local stations to self-police their output. Mabley was dissatisfied with this legislative version of a scolding but at least one important point was made thanks to his efforts: TV and its critics were capturing the public's attention.

While some of the public was busy (or not) worrying about television's depiction of sex and violence, others were concerned with a more ominous threat. Communist forces took control of governments in Europe and Asia and some Americans began to worry about the potential threat to the U.S. government. Eventually, writers and actors in film and radio were black-listed and television was not far behind. *Red Channels*, a booklet containing 151 names of entertainment personalities suspected of having ties to the Communist party, was published as a guide for network executives and sponsors who used it to quietly keep the named performers off their shows. While it was devastating to those it affected, blacklisting, for most viewers, was an industry issue practiced quietly behind the scenes. They wanted entertainment from their television sets rather than disturbing news.[21]

Critics of the 1950s

The first generation of TV critics faced a public climate of wonder and fear over the new medium. Television was both praised as a unifying cultural force and blamed for destroying the social fabric so the critics' role was an influential one. Favorable show reviews made TV credible and assisted in its social uptake. Several New York City–based critics quickly rose to prominence including Jack Gould, John Crosby, Marya Mannes,

Harriet Van Horne and Robert Lewis Shayon. Their work was clever and astute and importantly had the advantage of appearing in the newspapers and magazines of TV's broadcasting center.

From the mid–1940s to the late 1950s live dramas broadcast from New York City, using actors from the city's renowned theatre scene, occupied much of the production schedule. Written by aspiring playwrights, including Paddy Chayefsky, Rod Serling, Reginald Rose, Horton Foote and David Shaw, the productions dominated what came to be called the Golden Age of television. Because the stories, characters and themes changed each week, audiences had one chance to see live anthology dramas before they disappeared forever, generating the excitement of a weekly opening night. Viewers were caught up in the immediacy and spontaneity. Twenty-one million TV homes viewed the first live performance of *Peter Pan* in 1955.[22] The impact on the critics' practice was significant. Live dramas demanded reviewing styles that went beyond description. Critics had to make their reviews mean something to those viewers who missed the performance.

Each of the first generation critics had a unique critical voice. Some, like Mannes and Van Horne, were often witty and occasionally sarcastic. Others, like Shayon, took a more serious tone but all approached TV as a medium with great potential and were not afraid to challenge its shortcomings. Gould and Crosby's work in particular would have a lasting impact on the industry as they went from the industry's advocates to two of its most prominent detractors.

Jack Gould started his career with the *New York Times* as a theatre critic. In 1944 he became the paper's radio news editor and reviewed a production of *The Boys from Boise*, a musical comedy that he called "a valuable and important step toward television's own self-sufficiency."[23] He wrote short program reviews during the week as well as a regular column for the *Sunday Times*, which was either a longer, more detailed review of a show or a commentary on a broader issue facing the industry. As television started to make its mark on cultural life, so too did Gould's coverage of the new medium. In his three decades as a columnist, he demanded positive culture outcomes from television and was not afraid to chastise it when it failed his expectations. His body of work, from his early championing of live television drama to his chastisement of the networks for failing to cover politically significant events, was an insightful commentary on what he believed television was and was not doing for American society.

Gould's fellow critic and main competitor was John Crosby, who was a reporter for the *Milwaukee Sentinel* in 1933 before moving to the *New York Herald Tribune* where he worked from 1935 to 1941. He left the paper and after five years with the Army News Service during World War II, Crosby returned and began his role as the *Herald Tribune*'s radio-television critic, a position he had until 1965. His column was syndicated in 1949 and was carried by twenty-nine newspapers with an estimated readership of four million. Turning to television in 1952, his commentaries were quickly distinguished by their wit and refinement.[24]

Despite being outnumbered by their male colleagues, a few female critics also rose to prominence during this time. Marya Mannes, a social critic as well as a theatre, radio and television critic wrote for the magazine *The Reporter* from 1952 to 1963 where her work included articles, essays and reviews. Her 1958 collection of essays, mostly from her years at *The Reporter*, was titled *More in Anger: Some Opinions, Uncensored and Unteleprompted*. The title was a fitting description of Mannes's critical voice. Whether she was writing about social issues or reviewing a television show, she was not afraid to be outspoken. She also appeared on various television programs, leading fellow critic Gould to write: "her sustained acerbity is one of the attractive adornments of contemporary criticism."[25] She wrote several books including an autobiography, two novels and a volume of satiric verse. An anthology of her writing titled *The Best of Marya Mannes* was published in 1986.

Mannes' contemporary, Harriet Van Horne, along with Gould and Crosby, attracted a wide following for her television criticism. She began her career as a columnist writing about radio in 1942 for the now defunct *New York World-Telegram*. In 1947, she turned her attention to television and by 1967 her criticism was published in the *New York Post* and syndicated by both the *New York Times* Syndicate and the *Los Angeles Times* Syndicate. In an October 13, 1945, *Collier's Weekly* column called "Views Coming Up," she described TV as a "fluid medium, intimate and directly expressive" and predicted that within her lifetime it would be "the greatest force for world enlightenment and freedom that history ever has known." While she believed that the medium would mean ideas would cross boundaries, her later work suggested she found that most of these ideas fell short. Reviewing *The Occasional Wife*, a show broadcast during the 1966-1967 season on NBC about a businessman who makes a deal with a woman to pretend to be his wife in order for him to get ahead at work, she wrote that the series "may amuse your dotty old Aunt Susie but its ineptitude will be painful for the rest of the family."[26] Her reaction to NBC's spin-off *The Girl from U.N.C.L.E.* was not any kinder. The show, she declared, was "violently sadistic and altogether repellent."[27] In a September 9, 1968, column in the *New York Post* titled "Female Firebrands," she had a harsh reaction to the protest staged by the group New York Radical Women against that year's Miss America contest, questioned their femininity and suggested that they had been "scarred and wounded by consorting with the wrong men." Van Horne's strong opinion about the group's action and the women's liberation movement in general took the focus away from a critical assessment of the broadcast. While she offered her thoughts on the show's limitations, suggesting that its garish focus on physical beauty above all else made a sad social statement, her personal attacks on the women were a surprising departure from her usual focus on a program's highs and lows.

In the mid–1970s she was the contributing TV columnist to *New York Magazine*. Her thoughts on two made for television movies reflected her tough-minded approach. Comparing them to junk food, they were both trash TV.[28] One of the films, titled *Secrets*, about a woman who is sexually promiscuous, was tedious and crude but she noted, "if nymphomania is your cup of TV, don't miss it."[29] Not every program was a target of Van Horne's caustic wit. She praised another made for TV movie, this time about the life of Senator Joseph McCarthy, naming it one of the best movies for the small screen.[30] In a review of NBC news magazine program *Weekend*, she offered her thoughts on how the show helped television reach what she felt was its most powerful potential, which was "dropping the veil of make-believe and showing us life." Broadcast news was a particularly comforting source where viewers could encounter authentic people who were dealing with relatable problems including crime and even bad weather.[31]

Van Horne would eventually turn her attention to topics beyond television, writing her *New York Post* column three days a week on anything that interested her. In 1972, she published a collection of those essays under the title *Never Go Anywhere Without a Pencil*. Most of the collection did not cover television but the columns that focused on it were clever and funny. In one, she discussed the Reverend Billy Graham's appearance on the show *Laugh-In*, which he quickly followed by a prayer gathering in New York. She wrote: "Having seen *Laugh-In*, I must confess I'd rather hear Dr. Graham jesting about sin than crying, 'Woe unto sinners!' If that prejudice puts me a little short of the glory of the Lord, so be it."[32] In another piece she described her exasperation with politicians, as she watched them while preparing dinner: "The evening news once more is curdling my sauces and burning the biscuits.... I can't even mince a mushroom without catching the President or some member of his family in another whopper.... By 7:15 every night I'm either shaking my wire whisk as Spiro Agnew or wiping the gravy off Senator Fulbright."[33] It was Defense Secretary Melvin Laird, however, that made her really angry. Taking exception to what she viewed as Laird's deceptive reply to reporters' questions about the military build-up in Laos, she suggested that he (through the power of TV news) had revealed the weaknesses of the administration's handling of public information regarding the military. Noting that Laird's surly exchange with reporters weakened the credibility of the Pentagon, perhaps to the department's surprise, she warned that the inability to convincingly lie will incite the public to action.[34] The column ends with a critical and humorous take on the White House's efforts to re-make Nixon's image as an intellectual by giving reporters a list of the books the president would be reading during a trip to the Virgin Islands.

Van Horne is credited with saying that she got into television criticism "the day they invented it." In the late 1960s and into the 1970s, she remained a prominent critic among her male counterparts even as her focus shifted away from television. Throughout her twenty-year career of reviewing television, Van Horne may have found with few exceptions, little to praise about the small screen but underneath her sharp and often tough-minded assessments she recognized that television was a significant cultural force.

Another critic who recognized television's social power during this era was Robert Lewis Shayon, who became a proponent of TV's educational possibilities and the first television critic for the *Christian Science Monitor*. Shayon was well known for writing and producing radio programs in the 1940s including the *You Are There* series for CBS, which was made into a television series hosted by Walter Cronkite. After leaving the *Christian Science Monitor*, Shayon joined the *Saturday Review* as its television critic, a post he held for more than twenty years. In 1950, Shayon's name appeared in *Red Channels* and the broadcasting industry blacklisted him, prompting his career in print journalism. He was the author of several books including *Television and Our Children* (1951), an early look at the impact of television on young people.

For industry leaders, most of whom read the *New York Times* and the *New York Herald Tribune*, Jack Gould and John Crosby were, as an April 15, 1957, article in *Newsweek* called them "Big Men on the Paper." The article suggested that they were particularly influential among their bosses in the editorial room because the power players at the networks respected their opinions. While their influence was not about impacting viewer numbers for a particular show, it was significant nonetheless. An article in *Television Magazine* explained it this way: "Even though the network brass are aware that their Nielsens are not likely to fluctuate a bit because of a critic's opinion, they wait breathlessly for The Word from the men who write the reviews."[35] The word from Gould proved very influential in 1956 when he reprimanded the networks for failing to broadcast the meeting of the United Nations Security Council as they discussed the Suez crisis. In a column titled "Disgrace of the Networks: Chains Ignore Session at United Nations" from October 31, 1956, Gould wrote that the industry had made a travesty of its duty to serve the public. Then he wondered how the country could appreciate the seriousness of world affairs when so little was permitted to disrupt broadcasters' allegiance to commercial interests. Gould's son, historian Lewis Gould, recalled that "Disgrace of the Networks" lead to an outpouring of public support for his father's opinion and caused network executives to change their programming.[36] The change would not last but Gould's words made an impact.[37] His work also made a difference in 1961 when a New York station decided to cancel a dramatic show called *The Play of the Week*. Gould urged his readers to save the show, instructing them to give meaningful assistance by sending a postcard to the station. Viewers, he pleaded, must also help.[38] The viewers did and the program continued for over a year.

Gould's influence was also felt in more subtle ways. His columns covering the blacklisting of television professionals alleged to be communists, beginning with the firing of TV actress Jean Muir exposed the harmful effects that unsubstantiated charges had on people's lives and careers.[39] A series of columns addressing the quiz show scandals that would eventually uncover Charles Van Doren's rigged performance on *Twenty-One* became a platform to address broader issues involving ethics and corruption in the media as well as an indictment of the industry's commercial imperative. Gould argued that the scandals were not about the individuals involved but rather the impact that television had made on the relationship between everyday life and consumerism. He suggested that the medium had regularly turned all things and all viewers into tools of merchandisers.[40] Gould was not the only critic talking about the controversy. In a November 14, 1959, column, "The Scandal," Crosby echoed his competitor's sentiments, commenting that the quiz show scandal caused a moral decay that had far reaching consequences for the industry. Advertisers were stifling the truth and corrupting television's leaders. He suggested that anyone with idealism and creativity could either not find work in television or had left the business for other, better opportunities. While the dark side of television's commercial imperative was not a new topic for critics, Crosby and Gould's coverage of the quiz show scandals gave the subject the attention of powerful voices.

Gould and Crosby were also important advocates for quality children's programming. Gould used his columns to criticize the networks for shows that he considered to be too violent, too dependent on commercialism and too bland. In his view, the problems with children's television had been a conspicuous failing of the industry for several years because network executives did not trust creative teams to plan imaginative programming for the younger generation.[41] He accused television executives of hiding educational programs by airing them in marginal timeslots and demanded a crucial turnaround of policy.[42] For his part, Crosby blamed the networks' lack of creativity and its refusal to balance series like *Roy Rogers* with *Mr. Rogers*. It was, he argued, their obligation and their main offense was disregarding it.[43] He also pointed to educators' lack of interest in participating in television's potential for educational programming. Commenting on the FCC's hearing to reserve 20 percent of the VHF television band and thousands of stations in the UHF band for educational use, he argued that the country's educators were not against television but rather indifferent to it.[44] He accused them of walking away from what he admitted was a difficult task—making educational subjects as "arresting as Milton Berle"—so that they could forever condemn television for its materialism, its impact on youth and its mediocrity.[45] He ended with a call to his readers to write the FCC in support of the cause.

Both Crosby and Gould covered Edward R. Murrow but it was Gould, who, according to his son Lewis, played a small but definitive part in the esteemed journalist's difficult relationship with CBS in the late 1950s when he published a front-page story that angered Murrow and precipitated his departure from the network.[46] Gould, however, also identified with Murrow and often praised his impact on television.[47] He called Murrow's program *See It Now* a remarkable and powerful illustration of how television could work as a tool of journalism, "lifting the medium to a new high in maturity and usefulness."[48] Describing *This Is Korea, Christmas 1952*, a film about life on the front lines of the Korean War that was broadcast on *See It Now*, Gould declared that it was one of the best shows ever broadcast and a "masterpiece of reportorial artistry."[49]

Crosby also praised Murrow and his work on *See It Now* calling the series highly profound.[50] In a 1951 review, he described Murrow's coverage of American soldiers in Korea as affectionate and educational.[51] For Crosby, Murrow's choice to concentrate on the everyday activities of infantry soldiers rather than the violence of war demonstrated that he understood what television was capable of achieving in the field of news.[52] Watching American soldiers eat and sleep, gamble and joke captured "the humor of an essentially unhumorous occupation, the humanity of an essentially inhuman profession."[53] When CBS canceled the show in 1958, Crosby was highly critical of the decision: "*See It Now* ... is by every criterion television's most brilliant, most decorated, most imaginative, most courageous and most important program. The fact that CBS cannot afford it but can afford *Beat the Clock* is shocking."[54] While there was no evidence that Crosby and Gould's columns brought more viewers to Murrow's show, their influence as powerful critical voices added to its credibility.

One program that brought millions of Americans to their TV sets in the early 1950s featured a zealous senator and several gangsters. The popularly named Kefauver Committee hearings on organized crime were held in New York in 1951 and television cameras captured the action. Officially known as the United States Senate Special Committee to Investigate Crime in Interstate Commerce, the hearings were chaired by Tennessee Senator Estes Kefauver and attracted widespread public interest as an estimated audience of twenty million watched the proceedings. Critics quickly recognized the impact. In an April 7, 1951, column entitled "An Open Letter to the Television Industry," Robert Shayon claimed that the Kefauver crime hearings gave the public a thoughtful communal experience but they didn't know what to think about what they saw. The hearings, he suggested, were an opportunity for the networks to go beyond reporting and provide viewers with documentaries that analyzed the case in depth. He explained: "I want leadership and direction by the experts.... I want to know whether the Senate crime hearings were merely the unhappiest circus I ever saw— or whether this thing called television can really make a positive dent in our mores." Shayon's recommendation for television to not only document an event but to help shape public opinion about that event promoted the idea that television was more than pictures. It was a witness and a teacher.

Crosby's take on the hearings similarly recognized television's influence on viewers. In "A Jury of 20,000,000," published March 23, 1951, in the *New York Herald Tribune*, he argued that while the hearings were making an impact on both popular awareness and public development, viewers should also recognize that emotional responses to TV's images did not equal considered assessment. Having a careless response based on the physical attractiveness or the personal issues of witnesses, as he believed the public did during the trial, was not the same as judging the proceedings on what those witnesses actually said. While Crosby found value in television's ability to intimately connect the audience with events they would otherwise not experience, be they government hearings or the tedium of war, he cautioned his readers not to be seduced by TV's images.

Not all of television's images were seducing viewers, however, and in a 1948 column, reprinted in his book *Out of the Blue*, Crosby suggested that some national experiences have a way to go before the participants learned how to harness television's power. Commenting on the 1948 Republican National Convention he suggested that both the candidates and the reporters who covered them were going to have trouble with the intimacy that television created.[55] Throughout the convention's first day he wrote that there was a pattern of "nobody saying very much but always bringing the expectation that they might" along with an annoying amount of handshaking.[56] The lack of substance, he suggested, was the convention's failure rather than television's. Broadcasters brought viewers the hectic pace, the crowds and the chaos of the convention floor but little information thanks to a convention system that offered more style than substance.[57] Crosby concluded the piece with his trademark wit, describing the 1940 Republican convention as having vast stretches of broadcast time featuring an empty table flanked by two empty chairs. Eight years later, the 1948 convention had succeeded in placing people in the chairs. By 1952, he mused, the people in those chairs "may conceivably have something of interest to say."[58] More than anything else, Crosby's opinion about the convention may have had to do with his personal views on politics and politicians but the column also suggested that readers recognize television's value. Namely, that it gave them intimate access to experiences and that access came with a responsibility to be a critical viewer.

Beyond covering televised politics, Crosby offered his assessment of live television drama, a format he would remember fondly as indicative of TV's Golden Age. Reviewing the 1956 *Kraft Television Theatre* production of *A Night to Remember*, the story of the Titanic's sinking, Crosby described the play as paying great attention to detail and being flawless in its technical direction.[59] He was particularly impressed by the climactic scene, which had a crashing chandelier and used three thousand gallons of water, a feat, he was surprised, did not drown at least one actor.[60] Looking back on that column and another on *Playhouse 90*'s live production of writer Rod Serling's *Requiem for a Heavyweight* in a 1963 volume of essays, Crosby suggested that his reviews demonstrated how far television had come from the Golden Age. Unfortunately, it was "mostly straight down."[61] *Requiem*, in particular, stood apart in his view, for its emotional impact and for establishing a high bar for pace, direction, set design, casting and overall production values.[62] In an interview with *TV Guide* in 1973, he again recalled the impact of Serling's play noting that the decade's television did not generate the same level of excitement it once did, at least not about the writer of a TV play.[63]

While Crosby played his part in getting the word out about the value of live drama, it was Gould, who was perhaps the stronger advocate. Later, when more budget conscious filmed productions made in Hollywood replaced New York's live dramas, he was unapologetic about his preference. In his view, the immediacy of live drama generated an excitement that film or tape could not replicate and in an October 31, 1948, column titled "Matter of Form: Television Must Develop Own Techniques If It Is to Have Artistic Vitality," he urged those involved in live productions to embrace the benefits television had to offer as a medium distinct from the stage and the motion picture. What made television unique, he suggested, was its ability to create intimacy and immediacy on a level that was unimaginable before its introduction as home theatre. While *The Theatre Guild*'s first live drama production for NBC in 1948 "promptly fell on its art" due to what he thought was a clear unawareness of how to use television, by 1949, live productions started to meet Gould's high expectations.[64] A CBS, *Studio One* production of *Julius Caesar* had a "visual power and vitality that lifted television to the status of a glorious art."[65]

Gould's central argument regarding live television was that it had the power to dissolve the physical, emotional and intellectual distance between the viewer and the performance. In a 1956 column, he suggested that live drama bridges the physical and emotional distance between viewer and actor so that both those in the studio and those at home have a keen awareness of being in one another's presence.[66] Journalist and influential cultural critic Gilbert Seldes, who became the first director of television for CBS, made a similar case: "The tension that suffuses the atmosphere of a live production is a special thing to which audiences respond; they feel that what they see and hear is happening in the present and therefore more real than anything taken and cut and dried which has the feel of the past."[67]

For Seldes and Gould, the new medium's fundamental artistic strength was an immediacy only live programming delivered. By the mid–1950s, this strength was under threat from Hollywood created filmed dramas, which were increasingly appearing on program schedules. More cost effective than live productions, filmed programs not only lacked the immediacy so prized by critics but also the quality. The low budgets often meant they were not as well conceived as their live counterparts. Genre based thirty-minute telefilms, including Westerns, crime, science fiction and situation comedy did not compare to the larger budget, hour long, live network dramas and spectaculars.

Gould expressed discontent over what he saw as the network's primary mistake in a December 7, 1952, column where he made a plea for live drama, calling the networks' decision to broadcast more filmed productions the "colossal boner of the year."[68] He argued that the visual and aural components of films lacked the ethereal sense of depth and honesty of live TV and went on to comment that the 1952 season's trend of broadcasting films did not make sense and in fact, represented a backward approach that failed to use the most current and suitable method of transmitting pictures across the airwaves. Hollywood, Gould suggested, was producing run-down movies and "pedestrian little half-hour quickies" that were taking up too much space on even the best networks. In a final plea, he warned: "To regard television merely as a variation on the neighborhood motion picture house is to misunderstand the medium." A similar anti–Hollywood theme was evident in Seldes' comments in a *New York Times Magazine* article in 1954: "It is ungrateful to bring up such things, but the lack of pungent characters, of the excitement of discovery, all trace back to the principle of playing it safe by imitating whatever has been successful. This is the cynical method of Hollywood, which did more than television to keep the people away from movie houses."[69]

At first, the networks were equally anti-film and anti–Hollywood, a position that was at odds with their programming practices. *The New Yorker* quoted a 1953 memo from Pat Weaver, head of NBC, in which Weaver told his programming staff: "movies and radio point the horrible path that looms before us.... The conformity and carbon copy boys are hard at work. This is not satisfactory. Television must be the shining center of the home."[70] In a 1954 *Time* magazine article, NBC Vice President John K. West's echoed Weaver's position on film programming, albeit in a less delicate way: "Keep it the hell off the networks."[71] Despite the rhetoric, NBC and the other networks' opposition to filmed productions was primarily based on economic fears that their affiliates would strike independent deals with producers of filmed programming thereby selling commercial time directly to sponsors.[72]

By the mid–1950s, independent producers increased their efforts to challenge the network's economic power. Congressional hearings and senate committees were convened to reconsider regulatory practices. Faced with threats to alter their current business models, the networks used the critics' spirited defense of live programming to strengthen their arguments. In a 1956 hearing before the Commerce Committee, Sarnoff quoted Gould's views on live programming before telling the committee: "We shall continue our emphasis on live television.... We believe this is the way to maintain television's momentum and vitality."[73] Using Gould and other influential critics' positions on the aesthetic merits of live programming was an exercise in self-interest on the part of TV's power players but it also demonstrated the influence the critics had on an industry that wanted respectability.

The informal alliance between the networks and critics who privileged live productions, helped set the tone for public discussion of television throughout the early 1950s. When the unsteady partnership began to crumble in the second half of the decade, it caused a bitter rift. Critics, feeling betrayed by television's leaders for what they saw as a failure to protect its artistic merits and live up to its social responsibility, launched a contentious public debate.

It Was the Best of Times, It Was the Worst of Times

Critics, and network executives who were echoing the critics, might have praised live programming for its quality, but behind the scenes networks were always aware that they were in the business of selling audiences to advertisers. When Gould, Crosby and others celebrated live drama series including *Studio One* and *Playhouse 90* the networks were more than happy to use their critical praise to prop up their agenda in the face of regulatory pressures. Once those pressures were alleviated, industry players had less use for critics' thoughts on live drama, particularly when viewers started paying attention to shows like *The Honeymooners* and *I Love Lucy*. Part of the appeal of these family-oriented comedies for advertisers was that they showed the working class fighting for material fulfillment and advancement.[74] Characters proudly bought new furniture, celebrated job promotions and shared special moments together accompanied by Maxwell House coffee. Lucy and Ricky Ricardo bought a TV set, a washing machine and eventually, a home in the suburbs.[75] Their journey toward prosperity was a pattern followed by other couples all across postwar America. The optimism of the postwar years was reflected in single-family homes, full of children and modern conveniences. Viewers were learning to embrace consumerism and television helped make those economic goals legitimate. Live programming's darker themes failed to reflect this cultural shift and soon, critics began to grow weary of the genre's pessimistic storylines.

Part of what made live anthology dramas the darlings of critical commentary was the immediacy that the dramas created between the actor and the viewer. Most of the plays were not afraid to portray psychological naturalism or controversial themes. Where the majority of filmed series focused on external conflicts (other people are bad), live dramas concentrated on internal character conflicts but when these themes became routine critics noticed and the overall consensus was one of disappointment. Reviewing *The Remarkable Incident at Carson Corners*, a play by Reginald Rose broadcast in 1954, a *New Yorker* critic called Rose part of "the modern, beat-the-audience-over-the-ears school of playwriting." The work of these playwrights suggested that every bad action in a terrible world was the result of the "collective guilt of mankind in general and the 'system' in particular."[76] Shayon, wrote of an adaptation of Thornton Wilder's *Our Town*: "The video craftsmen have yet a deal of growing to do.... Their levels of conflict and thesis, their insights are far too cluttered with the immediate debris of life around them."[77] Both Crosby and Gould echoed their fellow critics' frustration. Crosby argued that a "literary neuroticism" was taking over the small screen with so many TV plays featuring anguish as the central plot point.[78] For Gould, the medium's main theme was quickly becoming a version of life was horrible because "a bunch of psycho-neurotics" had found it paid more to "work off their frustrations on a typewriter than on a couch."[79] The critics' negative opinions on thematic choices, however, didn't override their general support for the value of live drama over filmed programming. The most frequent reason they cited for the inferiority of filmed programs was that Hollywood lacked the creative vision that television production deserved. Crosby told his readers, "Hollywood's general effect had been toward the mediocritization of everything it has got its hands on"[80] while Gould argued that "what's lacking most vividly in Hollywood is a compelling incentive to be good."[81]

The sponsors had their own reasons for growing tired of live drama's take on life: the playwright's message was counterintuitive to their own. Media historian Erik Barnouw explains:

> Most advertisers were selling magic. Their commercials posed the same problems that Chayefsky drama dealt with: people who feared failure in love and in business. But in the commercials there was always a solution as clear-cut as the snap of a finger: the problem could be solved by a new pill, deodorant, toothpaste, shampoo, shaving lotion, hair tonic, car, girdle, coffee, muffin recipe, or floor wax.... Chayefsky and other anthology writers took these same problems and made them complicated.[82]

Afraid that live drama's dark storylines were driving away the viewer/customer, sponsors wanted happy endings and established celebrities. Along with their agencies, they became "increasingly intent on interfering with script matters, dictating changes, vetoing plot details."[83] The result was live series that incorporated more melodrama and spectacle. An article in the April 1957 *Sponsor* noted: "As the TV season proceeds, more and more dramatic anthology shows are relying on straight melodrama. Behind this trend is the conviction among Madison Avenue program experts ... that big audiences no longer are attracted by finely and soberly developed themes."[84] The change, however, did little to prevent the death of live dramas. ABC was the first to replace all of its live programming with filmed series in the 1955-1956 season. At the end of 1957, more than one hundred television films (telefilms) were on the air or in production, almost all were Hollywood made and the majority were episodic series.[85] By the 1959-1960 season, the number of live dramatic programs on all networks dropped to one.

While the shift from live to filmed series pleased sponsors, it created a hostile relationship with critics who grew increasingly pessimistic about the artistic merits of the new crop of shows. Commenting on the sorry state of father's in mid–1950s domestic comedies, Crosby said: "It's a tough rap we Pappas have to take—a single man can show signs of intelligence but the minute he spawns children he reverts to idiocy."[86] Reviewing the 1954 show *Bonino*, about a widower with several children, Shayon wrote: "Now there is only the stereotype of pater Americanus, well meaning, terribly stupid, and utterly inadequate in every department of life except his profession. Weep for Adonis!"[87] Of course, not every comedy suffered the wrath of the critics. Crosby liked *Ozzie and Harriet* because the dialogue felt realistic and the children characters were "not so all fired full of fresh air and wholesomeness that you'd like to kick them."[88] Shayon saw hope in *I Remember Mama* and cited it as an example that other domestic comedies should follow: "Within their proper sphere of entertainment the family situation comedies on the air could make a painless contribution if they would occasionally use their devices not as the end but the springboard for tender, true moralizing, the kind we get from *Mama*."[89]

The desire for the type of realism Shayon praised in *I Remember Mama* was shared among many of the top critics of the 1950s as they appreciated that an authentic storyline had the potential to communicate insight into the human condition. Shayon hoped that crime drama would stop using the criminal as a "rich whipping boy" and instead offer a few considerate and socially relevant statements about crime.[90] Mannes saw similar potential in depictions of American citizens' relationships with foreigners, if only programs like *Biff Baker, U.S.A.* would stop depicting

Americans as gullible and Europeans as more cultured, dangerous and morally bankrupt.[91] She urged her readers to watch the programs, often unsponsored and unnoticed, that attempted to depict an authentic experience that mattered.[92] Mannes and other critics writing in the 1950s were often looking for genuine, challenging shows that raised what they saw as poor program standards and spoke to the public's lived experience. Mannes found it in *Medic*, a program that took real medical cases as its inspiration. She told her readers that the show's writer was "able to build character and enlist compassion so that the realism of the operating room is preceded and given meaning by imagination."[93] She argued that the public needed *Medic* because it showed physicians as imperfect, capable of making mistakes and sometimes, "as unprogressive and profit-minded" as the patients they treated. Crosby had the opposite reaction, calling *Medic* "as phony as a three dollar bill."[94] Yet Crosby's condemnation of *Medic*'s unreality speaks to the same desire for authenticity that Mannes and other 1950s critics demanded.

Gould saw little to celebrate in the program schedule and continued to mourn the loss of live or prestige drama, blaming the networks for giving in to commercial pressures. Writing about the likely cancellation of NBC prestige drama *Omnibus*, he commented that the show had been an important symbol of a "venturesome spirit in an industry beset by many forces that dictate pursuit of safe and proven ways."[95] *Omnibus* and others like it including *Kraft Television Theatre* became casualties of the networks' pursuit of program homogeneity.

Crosby voiced similar concerns to Gould and by 1958, he was disillusioned and saw little to praise in programming. Fondly remembering the essays he could write on themes, acting styles and the other creative efforts of hour-long dramas, he lamented the move away from this type of criticism toward gossip, interviews, small talk and focusing on personalities.[96] He blamed television programming for what he felt was the poor state of criticism and remembering his days covering radio made the dire prediction that if television shows grew any blander, criticism of them would become as noncritical as radio coverage had been.[97] Pointing to the departure of several critics, Crosby then suggested in the column that the profession of TV critic was becoming outdated. Television eventually lost interest for Crosby who argued that the debates over critics' influence were inconsequential. In 1965, he left the *Herald Tribune* to write a column for British weekly newspaper *The Observer*, a position he would hold for ten years.[98]

Despite the tense climate between the industry and the critics, there

influence were inconsequential. Regardless of their re-commitment to reform, the networks were no longer in the business of taking chances. They were in the business of making money. The industry, as critic Charles Siepmann told the FCC in 1960, had undergone a "disastrous sea change," no longer seeing itself as responsible for public service.[3] If any network reformers were left, they had little chance of succeeding within a system that had fully embraced its commercial structure.

Critical discourse reflected these debates, as many journalists who covered television grew increasingly hostile toward the networks and their programming choices. On October 27, 1959, cultural commentator Walter Lippmann wrote a piece for the *New York Herald-Tribune* called "The TV Problem," in which he argued that the nation's most popular medium was a collection of social, moral, aesthetic and political difficulties. Lippmann's article ignited television's detractors who blamed it for everything from corrupting public values and harming children's development to destroying good taste and tarnishing the country's international image.[4]

Like Lippman, many TV critics began to doubt television's ability to balance aesthetics and market forces while responsibly guarding the public trust. They saw the networks as creatively bankrupt and went on the attack. Industry leaders responded with a deliberate effort to paint those critics as cultural elitists who cared little for the average viewer's tastes and in fact, were irrelevant to the audience's program choices.[5] As Gould and other critics' complaints about programming grew stronger, so too did the resolve of industry leaders to fight back. A 1956 article in *Sponsor* was one of the first to launch an attack, complaining that critics had done their utmost to spread panic as the TV season unfolded.[6] It used the high ratings of shows that critics disliked as an example of their poor prediction skills and irrelevance to a program's popularity. The idea that critics had no impact on persuading the audience to like or dislike a show soon became a common argument in industry responses. A 1957 NBC Research Department publication stated: "Once more the TV critics, both professional and amateur, are weighing the merits of the new season's programming and lashing out with adjectives like 'unexciting,' 'mediocre,' and 'unimaginative.' And again the public is ignoring these pessimists."[7] The public may or may not have been ignoring the critics but one thing was clear: the industry was in attack mode. A 1958 study of popular TV criticism reported the views of network executives who believed that the three most important critics were Jack Gould, George Rosen and John Crosby but the truth was that they were secondary to money and ratings.[8] One NBC affiliate made their feelings clear with a full-page advertisement in *Broadcasting*.

Titled "Malice in Wonderland," it was a crude drawing of a monster, labeled "TV Critic," holding an ax.

Primitive cartoon advertisements aside, the network response to critics' views of live drama's superiority over filmed product also had a more measured tone. In testimony to the FCC CBS President Frank Stanton suggested that "there were many turkeys in the good old days of live drama.... If these programs were to be put on the air today, we would be shocked at what we considered good programming."[9] An ABC programming chief made a similar argument, suggesting that live drama's time had passed: "I think it was great for the beginning of the medium but I certainly don't think there was enough product, enough production know-how and ability to program for the home.... Those shows didn't have any dimension, no movement—they were mostly talk. They were fine for their time, but not for today."[10] The idea that critics were out of touch with viewers' programming preferences quickly gained traction. Sarnoff told the National Association of Broadcasters (NAB) that critics' complaints were a way to impose their minority tastes on the public and their judgments about a show's mediocrity mattered little when the majority had chosen it.[11] One of those in the minority was Gould who was not spared the hostility in a 1961 article in industry magazine *Television Age*:

> The *New York Times*, for instance, has been close to carelessness in its reporting of television programs. The *Times* makes the primary mistake of assuming that American television viewers are *Times* readers.... It is probably that Jack Gould will despise anything that is popular.... He doesn't understand the work he is doing, ... the needs of the people for whom the bulk of programming is built. He doesn't give a damn for the public; nor a tin kopec for America's semi-literate multitude.[12]

Again, the argument established a contentious relationship between critic and viewer. Gould was a cultural elite who showed disdain for the democratic tastes of the mass audience.

Gould addressed the industry attacks in a May 26, 1957, column titled "A Critical Reply: An Answer to Objections Raised in the TV Industry to the Role of Critics Context Pavlovism Discouragement." In it, he argued that television executives must take responsibility for their programming choices because the medium was not a fixed or passive enterprise. It had the power to both raise and lower the public's tastes and standards. He commended the industry for broadening society's viewpoints but cautioned that it should also be aware that it had "a narcotic ability to deaden the national awareness of important standards and serious issues." Viewers, he argued, did not have the same opportunities as broadcasters and sponsors to make their thoughts known. Critics were their proxies and while they may not agree with each other's opinions on a program, they shared a common connection of "an independent opinion independently reached."

As for the charge of having elite taste, Gould explained that he applied the same test to every program he reviewed, asking himself what the show was trying to achieve and how well it was achieving it. Recognizing television's commercial imperative, he conceded that sacrifices in artistic quality will happen in an industry where market forces and cultural considerations formed an uneasy alliance but challenged the industry to see the bigger picture and avoid appeasement as a solution to the problem: "The fainthearted sponsor or a hesitant network chief need only ask himself where a policy of safety in sameness and mediocrity, if it is universally pursued, will lead." By 1966, Gould expressed a loss of interest in the medium, telling his wife: "I think I've just about had it.... I've run out of things to say and find myself repeating over and over."[13] Gould continued reviewing shows until 1971 when he turned his attention to only reporting about the industry.

The networks were busy trying to distance their viewers from those critics like Gould who had harsh words for less ambitious programming but they also had to fight a battle on another front. On May 9, 1961, Newton Minow, the new chairman of the Federal Communications Commission (FCC), gave a speech to the National Association of Broadcasters (NAB). In it, he challenged his audience to spend an entire day watching television:

> I invite you to sit down in front of your television set when your station goes on the air and stay there without a book, magazine, newspaper, profit and loss sheet or rating book to distract you—and keep your eyes glued to that set until the station signs off. I can assure you that you will observe a vast wasteland. You will see a procession of game shows, violence, audience participation shows, formula comedies about totally unbelievable families, blood and thunder, mayhem, violence, sadism, murder, western bad men, western good men, private eyes, gangster, more violence, and cartoons. And endlessly, commercials—many screaming, cajoling, and offending.[14]

What came to be called Minow's "vast wasteland" speech was more than a bad review, it was a warning to the executives of broadcast stations nationwide to limit the steady diet of formulaic programming they were feeding viewers and to take public service programming seriously: "For every hour that the people give you, you owe them something. I intend to see that your debt is paid with service."[15] A day later, on May 10, a story on Minow's address made page one of the *New York Times* and Jack Gould wrote a positive response. Other stories, columns, radio and television interviews and editorials followed for most of the year.[16] Thanks to the extensive coverage of Minow's remarks, the FCC was now known to millions of Americans and many of them started conversations about television's failures. Four thousand people wrote Minow, mostly in support of his address.[17]

Despite the public support and Minow's celebrity-like status, his demand for the networks to stop program hegemony was largely ineffective. Programming strategies, along with the economics and regulation of the industry continued in familiar routines, a fact that at least one network executive later confirmed: "I would say that to my knowledge, in the history of network broadcasting, no program appeared on the network as the result of any action taken by the FCC.... Programming decisions are made solely on the basis of circulation, demographics and for profit."[18] Broadcasters had even less to fear from the regulatory power of the FCC when Kennedy's reorganization plan of the commission was defeated in Congress. By 1961, Minow offered a few placating gestures to the industry and told *Variety* that the 1961-62 season was not a vast wasteland and advances were being made.[19]

One important impact of the vast wasteland speech was that it lent credibility to the growing number of researchers in the now developing field of communications studies. They began producing academic work that went beyond television's effects to include examinations of journalistic criticism.[20] A common approach in this early research was to analyze the content of critics' columns. Gould's writing was a popular choice for analysis as was the writing of critics from larger metropolitan newspapers including the *Los Angeles Times* and the *Chicago Daily News*.

Television in the 1960s

In the 1960s, professional critics were living in a tumultuous decade with one constant: television. In a role that became familiar, television played its part in distracting viewers from the turbulent events happening outside their doorstep. The medium changed the public's relationship with the presidency and became the primary source of news. John Kennedy's expert use of television lead to a new feeling of familiarity and interest among the public toward an American president and his family.[21] Television's powerful images brought the civil rights movement from the streets into suburban living rooms and those pictures would eventually become an important factor in building support for the Civil Rights Act of 1964, the Voting Rights Act of 1965 and other War on Poverty and Great Society legislation.[22] Ultimately, television took a nation to the moon and allowed it to collectively mourn its leader.

Much of the entertainment programming during the mid to late 1960s was light and uncomplicated. Viewers tuned into *The Beverly Hillbillies*, *Gomer Pyle, U.S.M.C.* and *Gilligan's Island* as well as more fantasy based series like *My Favorite Martian* and *Bewitched*. Situation comedies, adult westerns and detective thrillers let audiences escape the grim realities of real world events while series featuring professionals who served society including *Dr. Kildare*, *The Defenders* and *Ben Casey*, were popular with viewers seeking contemporary themes.[23] Network programming in the 1960s, despite the critics overall dissatisfaction, was a safe haven for many television viewers. Media historian Erik Barnouw explains that for many, TV was a mental refuge. Despite the occasional disturbing documentary, "evening television confirmed the average man's view of the world. It presented the America he wanted and believed in and had labored to be part of. It was alive with handsome men and women, and symbols of the good life."[24] Farcical or realistic, television programs were a way for many viewers to temporarily forget about the divided world outside their living rooms.

By the late 1960s, however, the escalation of the Vietnam War threatened to disrupt television's carefully constructed world of country bumpkins and friendly Martians. Labeled the "living-room war" by *The New Yorker* TV critic Michael Arlen because of the way it was presented to Americans—on their television screens, in their living rooms—the conflict in Vietnam was rarely a subject of critical discussion on primetime news broadcasts. When stories did appear on screen, they were carefully edited. Barnouw noted that in news broadcasts, a protest march "was likely to be covered with a shot or two of a bearded youth, as though to categorize it as a 'hippie' event."[25] Arlen recalled that television news coverage of the war "rarely furnished scenes of bloody combat, while at the same time, the nightly reports provided steady, filmic imagery that was bound to suggest, if not sustain, a positive, progressive approach."[26]

For television critic Neil Compton, a Canadian who reviewed American television, U.S. broadcast news coverage of Vietnam, while candidly discussed in American print media, was limited on screen. In a 1965 article in *Commentary*, he argued that a viewer who relied on the networks would have been much less informed than viewers in Canada, despite the fact that the time devoted to Vietnam on American television was greater.[27] Arlen agreed, writing in his "Living-Room War" column, reprinted in his book of the same name, that more than 50 percent of Americans might have been learning most of what they understood about the Vietnam War from television but that same percentage probably knew more about the weather forecast for major metropolitan areas. Ineffectual news broadcasts meant that the television audience understood "a good deal less about Vietnam than might be useful."[28] By 1966, the careful variations of the government line delivered by television newsrooms started to unravel when two prominent senators began publicly criticizing President Johnson's Vietnam policy. Due to their important positions, ignoring their arguments was not an option and CBS News broadcasted a thirty-minute interview program where they shared their viewpoints. Two years later, the shock of the 1968 Tet Offensive dissolved any remaining resistance from the executive levels of television news and reporters began more critical coverage of the war.

Primetime television, however, continued to keep audiences in a protective bubble. Cultural critic Josh Ozersky wrote, "few things are more striking, in retrospect than the sheer obliviousness of prime-time television in 1968 to the turmoil surrounding it in the real world."[29] This real world turmoil included the assassinations of Martin Luther King, Jr., and Robert Kennedy, riots in sixty U.S. cities following King's murder, clashes between police and protestors for four days in Chicago outside the Democratic National Convention and President Johnson's announcement that he would not seek another term. Add to this the escalation of the Vietnam War and many Americans sought out alternative forms of media that offered powerful messages ignored by prime time television. A subculture emerged who rejected commercial television as a symbol of the "establishment."

Yet, as Barnouw notes, the majority of Americans, during the 1966–1968 upheavals, were not participating in demonstrations, marches, or riots. They were going to work and relaxing in front of television.[30] In 1968, they were relaxing over a primetime schedule that was full of cops, cowboys and detectives but little violence thanks to congressional debates on the possible harmful effects of TV violence on children. The old argument that violence on crime shows was excessive and caused public harm was brought back by Senator John Pastore of Rhode Island, who lead the debate. While his findings were inconclusive, the networks feared he might suggest federal regulation so they voluntarily toned down the violence.[31] As a result, action on television was now more likely to be someone throwing a punch rather than shooting a gun.

Cultural relevance suffered a similar fate. If topical characters or contemporary issues were incorporated into primetime detective shows, they disappeared into well-worn crime stories so that their impact was minimal. Similarly, series that tried to appeal to the youth audience by tackling issues like rebellion, drug use and racial tension did so within traditional TV plots that maintained the status quo. The young, hip detectives of ABC's *The Mod Squad* were solving cases that reflected news headlines but they secretly worked for the establishment and legitimate authority always triumphed in the end. On other networks, the occasional drama series began with a rebellious young man who challenged society but more than likely ended with a conversation between the troubled longhaired youth and a wise, clean cut elder. With the exception of *The Smothers Brothers Comedy Hour*, it was business as usual for primetime television.

A left-leaning comedy variety show, *The Smothers Brothers* was a surprise hit for CBS in 1968. Using their ratings success for leverage, they pushed the boundaries with network censors. CBS affiliates grew wary, fearing viewer backlash and government penalties. The network started giving a closed circuit preview screening to the affiliate stations so the stations could decide if they wanted to broadcast that week's show. The system caused tension between the Smothers and CBS, ultimately leading to a clash over an April 1969 episode that the network claimed was not delivered in time for advanced screening by the affiliates. CBS took the show off the air, effectively firing the Smothers. Tom Smothers held a press conference for TV critics from New York, Boston and Philadelphia, who viewed the controversial April program and listened to the angry star share his feelings about the network. The majority of critics extended their support. In a column on the screening, Gould called the cancellation of the show a "silly and suspect move" and said the *sermonette* the network had challenged was hardly worthy of all the managerial anxiety it had caused.[32]

The cultural and political unrest of the 1960s, with the exception of *The Smothers Brothers Comedy Hour*, a few documentary programs and some late decade news broadcasts (particularly those that covered the war in Vietnam), was largely absent from America's television screens. For many viewers, the medium's happy families and by the book law enforcement officers who maintained social order were a welcome escape from the social and cultural revolutions that were collapsing the status quo.

Viewers may have used television to escape the cultural movements of the 1960s but the campaigns were an important backdrop to the press critics' re-evaluation of their practice. As leftist intellectuals began to defend the study of popular culture, more media courses appeared on university curriculums and the younger generation started to embrace the academic study of popular culture. As media scholar Lynn Spigel explained: "This elevation of popular culture as a form of intellectual currency was met by a more radical critique of the popular arts, especially television."[33] The advent of Television Studies as its own field reflected the significance of this intellectual project. The benefit for the critic, as Spigel noted, was twofold: "For the individual critic, academic Television Studies provided a defence against perceived disrespect and disenfranchisement from the system as well as the related desire to speak outside of the corporate discourse of PR."[34] The counter-criticism of television among leftist intellectuals, the perception of television studies as a serious academic pursuit and a new generation of critics who were unhappy with the move away from the reform minded criticism of their predecessors towards network guided coverage of celebrities and Nielsen ratings would lead to calls for professional reform. Of all the difficulties caused by the TV problem, the hardest one for the critics to solve was how to reclaim their legitimacy.

Critics of the 1960s

While television's commercial imperative was discouraging to influential East Coast critics including Gould and Crosby, several West Coast critics also challenged television's cookie-cutter programming and commercial focus. Two of the most influential were *Los Angeles Times'* critics Cecil Smith and Hal Humphrey. While their work focused on detailed reviews of programs and the entertainment community's role in the industry, they also criticized television's commercial mandate.

Smith began his career with the *Los Angeles Times* in 1947, as a reporter and feature writer, before becoming the paper's entertainment writer in 1953. From 1958 to 1964 he was a TV columnist and entertainment editor and in 1969 he turned exclusively to television becoming the paper's head TV critic, a position he held until his retirement in early 1982. Smith, who his successor Howard Rosenberg described as a "one of the giants in the business" and a "graceful writer" wrote radio plays and would go on to write fifty TV scripts after his service in World War II.[35] His work focused on television as an avenue for entertainment and he was an advocate for quality programming. He wrote that the beginning of his thirty-year love affair with TV began the day he bought a TV set after an editor asked him to write a story about the 1952 Republican National Convention.

Summing up his career, he said that television as both a medium of entertainment and as an art form had bothered, discouraged, confused and saddened him but also completely captivated him for thirty years. It was one of the greatest jobs in a "flea-bitten racket."[36]

At the center of filmed productions, Smith's coverage often included interviews with producers, directors and actors to whom he had close access. Dick Van Dyke recalls in his memoir that Smith was trailing him for a story during the taping of *The Dick Van Dyke Show* and used a great anecdote about Van Dyke's newborn daughter for his column.[37] In a review of *The Rebel*, Smith noted that he had a personal as well as professional interest in the show starring actor Nick Adams because during the previous year Adams had come to Smith's home with an idea for a TV western where a child was the hero.[38]

While Smith's work focused on television's creative community, it also addressed the issues that were troubling critics in the 1960s. In a column covering the debut of a new western series, he pointed out that actors were fond of declaring that it was the public's opinion about a program, not the critics', that mattered most. He countered that the voices that spoke the loudest were in fact those of the "manufacturers of unguents and deodorants and pills and those of the hawkers of such merchandise."[39] Smith's fellow critic Hal Humphrey, who wrote for the *Los Angeles Mirror-News* and later the *Los Angeles Times*, also featured the West Coast entertainment community in much of his writing. Humphrey was not afraid to offer harsh critiques or express a level of fandom for the programs he reviewed. In Sherwood Schwartz's book about *Gilligan's Island*, the producer noted that Humphrey's dislike of the show was strong and disturbingly consistent: "Hardly a week went by without some derogatory comment about *Gilligan's Island*. Even if he wasn't reviewing television shows that day he would find some way to drag an insult in by the heels, sometimes completely out of context to his topic.... It was though I was only producing the show to torment Hal Humphrey."[40] Schwartz recalled that when he asked Humphrey the reason for the negative comments, Humphrey replied that he thought the show was "an absolute waste of the airwaves."[41] Not a waste of broadcast space for Humphrey was NBC's 1962 series *It's a Man's World*, which he named the season's most original show before praising the writers and producers for doing what every creative team talked about but rarely did, built authentic stories and focused on character development.[42] An advocate for the show, Humphrey wrote that its merits deserved to be brought to the public's attention so they might discover it but also so the network would be convinced to support it.[43]

When the series was cancelled, he did not hesitate to get involved in the campaign to save it and urged his readers to write letters. Humphrey's belief in the power of the viewer was again evident in a 1964 column where he accused the networks of pandering to advertisers and blamed them for perpetuating viewer stereotypes where audiences were of two classes: "borderline morons ... or bored intellectuals."[44] Only when the industry rejected the idea that its audience was "a low IQ majority with a Jim Crow section of so-called intellectuals" would there be true advancement in television programming. Humphrey's challenge to the networks was that they recognize a layered and sophisticated audience that defied easy categorization.

Humphrey and Smith, like their East Coast counterparts at the *New York Times*, owed much of their influence to the large circulation paper that employed them yet other critics who wrote for underground papers during the 1960s also developed a following. One of the most well known was Harlan Ellison, the television critic for the *Los Angeles Free Press*. Ellison established himself as the anti-establishment critic with regular attacks on the industry and its programming in a column he called "The Glass Teat." A prolific writer, Ellison is the author of screenplays, teleplays, novels and short stories. A collection of his television columns from 1968 to 1970 was published as *The Glass Teat*, followed by *The Other Glass Teat* in 1975. For Ellison, television was a lens through which to view life and he was highly critical of much of what he saw. He wanted his readers to understand television's deeper social and cultural meanings and used his work to launch wider debates about the politics of race and gender. In the introduction to his book, *The Glass Teat*, he described the objective of the column:

> This column ... was born out of a need to examine what comes to us across the channel waves and to extrapolate from its smallness to the bigness of the trends or concepts to which it speaks. A situation comedy is not merely a situation comedy. It means something.... What does the acceptance of death but not sex on network TV tell us about ourselves and the broadcaster's image of us? How accurate is TV news reportage? Why is there so much bad TV and who is responsible for it? ... I am not really talking about TV here. I am talking about dissidence, repression, censorship, the brutality and stupidity of much of our culture.[45]

Ellison often reviewed shows as a way to interrogate society and culture. A review of episodes of *The Outcasts* and *The Mod Squad* lead him to conclude that both series were "bastardizations" that relegated the "black community to once again proselytizing the party line."[46] In another column, he argued that the unsettled times called for authentic depictions of heroes who were not predictable and boring. He explained that in a time of "fence-sitters, hemmers and hawers [and] bet-hedgers" what television needed to show viewers were men and women who had "something at stake, something to lose, something that can ennoble them for us."[47] Ellison's work was often a passionate plea to his readers to recognize television's impact and challenge the authenticity of its representations.

Whether working in Los Angeles or New York, the more influential critics of the 1960s were cultural intermediaries, a role that was strengthened immediately after the public outcry over the quiz show scandals but eventually grew weaker when network executives proclaimed them talentless hacks to counter their charges of low quality programming. By the mid–1960s, however, industry leaders changed tactics. Rather than try to tarnish critics' reputations, they attempted to distinguish serious criticism by relocating it from the popular press to university departments and peer-reviewed journals. In 1960, the CBS network lead the movement and commissioned articles for a quarterly magazine of television criticism. The project was never realized but it did become a book published in 1962 called *The Eighth Art*, edited by critic Robert Lewis Shayon. The network's attempt to flatter and showcase instead of "mocking the eggheads," resulted in a "new kind of critical elite which was singularly endowed with the 'purposeful' mission of knowing what constituted quality TV and knowing what constituted quality writing about it."[48] Quality criticism was therefore different than the criticism written by the popular press (despite including some of its writers). While CBS's attempt to control the climate of criticism was a way for the network to rehabilitate its corporate image, it was the only network to be directly indicted for its role in the quiz show scandals, its efforts made it one of the first to initiate what would become a recognizable academic brand of television criticism.[49]

The CBS project to transform television criticism from a journalistic practice to an academic discipline made an impact on press critics who began to rethink their professional approach, particularly in light of their changing roles. Despite their attempts to marginalize critics' cultural authority through campaigns to discredit them as snobs or to define quality TV criticism as a product of academia rather than mass-market publications, industry leaders knew that the critics were useful extensions of their publicity departments. As more critics accepted this gradual shift from public advocate to promotional agent, others called for an establishment of higher standards that would not only elevate the profession to a level on par with criticism of more traditional art forms but return it to its earlier public service mandate.

The Critics Look Inward

Part of the small group of influential critics writing for major metropolitan papers in the 1960s and 1970s, Lawrence Laurent was the *Washington Post*'s television-radio editor and syndicated columnist.[50] His work examined trends, reported on the relationships between federal agencies and the industry and reviewed programs. He covered the FCC's clash with a federal subcommittee over the role of government in broadcasting and discussed the commission's role in potentially changing cable TV.[51] He addressed the prime time access rule, how political campaigns were impacted by television and the challenges faced by public broadcasting.[52] He even poked fun at television personalities, including the Gabor sisters and Jerry Lewis and lightheartedly criticized viewers for finding it easier to complain about the lack of program quality when in fact they felt guilty about watching so-called trash.[53] In a piece for the *Journal of Broadcasting*, Laurent acknowledged the growing maturity of viewers who deserved a skilled level of critical coverage. He argued that no one had ever connected a review with the success or failure of a TV series—a small relationship between the two was possible but unlikely, yet the decade's television columnists still needed to recognize that their work had value and it lied in more than simple judgments.[54] Pushing his colleagues to raise their professional standards, Laurent was among those critics who were concerned with making sense of a dysfunctional relationship with an industry that was both discrediting and courting them. Publically, network executives did what they could to downplay the critics' influence over the audience. Privately, they knew they still needed the critics to publish and promote their broadcast schedules. Making the situation more complex were the dictates of being members of the press. As media scholar Lynn Spigel suggested: "TV critics were caught in the structural contradictions of a fully commodified public sphere. On the one hand, they were ideally supposed to operate in and through the utopian ideals of a 'free press'— a place where democratic speech and reason prevailed. On the other, they were expected to answer to market forces—readership statistics, advertising revenue, promotional activities."[55] This position, she argued, made them "especially vulnerable to charges of hypocrisy, and particularly in need of defense." As a result, a recurring theme in popular criticism was a call for higher standards that rejected the role of adjunct publicity agent. Laurent took it further, arguing that to be a *complete* television critic not only did one need to have "a respect and a love for the excitement and the impact of the combination of sight and sound" but also an understanding of the complexities of the medium: "This complete critic must be something of an electronics engineer, an expert on our governmental processes, and an esthetician. He must have a grasp of advertising and marketing principles. He should be able to evaluate all of the art forms; to comprehend each of the messages conveyed, on every subject under the sun, through television."[56] Laurent's vision for the model critic made the case that professional evaluations of television needed to go beyond discussions of programs and recognize its role as a technological, economic and social force. "The greatest fault of television criticism," he argued, "is that it needs a painful awakening to its awesome responsibility."[57] Gould also recognized the responsibility Laurent assigned to their profession and urged his fellow critics to stop making excuses for mediocre programming. He wrote that the most harmful influence a critic could have on the artistic standards of television was claiming that a show could be worse or was not too bad, considering what else was on.[58] The critic's job was not to rationalize but rather hold television to the same high standard as other art forms.

Struggling to define their role in the midst of a contentious relationship with the networks, first generation critics often argued that their main function was to educate readers on what constituted quality programming so that they would in turn desire it and the networks would provide it. As early as 1953, in an article for *Saturday Review*, Seldes suggested that if critics did their job, the public would demand better from the industry: "It is precisely the duty of a critic to be able to recognize inferior stuff, to make clear how he arrived at his judgments, and to impress himself upon the public so that in the end the managers of our entertainments will raise the quality of their output."[59] Marya Mannes echoed Seldes' argument but with a harsher opinion of viewers. She agreed that one of the functions of a critic was to establish a foundation of viewing standards from which viewers could build their own judgments, learning how to reject inferior programs and demanding better from the networks. This instruction was needed, she suggested, because people were "lazy" and would continue to "take poor stuff."[60] Lazy viewers or not, most critics analyzing their practice during this time saw their duty clearly. They were influencers and advocates for public taste. Crosby explained his view: "It's easy enough to criticize what's on the air, but I think one of the critic's main functions is to stimulate a demand for what isn't."[61] The idea of the press critic as the catalyst for quality shows appeared again a few years later, editorialized in the 1966-1967 issue of the *Journal of Broadcasting*: "The critic should be an interpreter, a collaborator toward achievement of ever higher standards and goals.... It is the job of the critic to hold up to us the vision of what "might be," and to redefine goals and standards in light of past achievement and future potential." In expressive language, Laurent argued that the critic should not only be incorruptible but also firmly "anchored in objectivity in a stormy world of special interests." The critic must "stand above the boiling turmoil" and "plunge into every controversy as a social critic and guardian of standards."[62] Laurent's ideal critic was a multitasking champion of quality.

While Laurent made a passionate argument for the idea that critics must be tastemakers, constructing hierarchies of what is and is not good TV, Mannes attributed the lack of quality programming to the snobbish attitudes of intellectuals who decried television's mediocre offerings when they should instead be leading its improvement. In a piece reprinted in Robert Lewis Shayon's book *The Eighth Art*, she argued: "If the best minds in the country had had the vision to think in the great terms which a great medium deserved, we might not have been deluged for the last ten years with the trivia, the relentless commercialism, the violence and the time-killing mediocrity which accounts for 80 percent of television programming."[63] Mannes' position was an interesting take on a familiar complaint from the critics. Where they frequently laid the blame for mediocre programming on network executives' pursuit of profits, Mannes cast a wider net. She suggested that quality TV was hard to find but it was not entirely absent. The problem was lack of support from a segment of the viewing audience who too quickly dismissed television as nothing more than popular entertainment. The intellectuals were not paying attention to the moments when television came closer to realizing its potential with innovative programming and network executives used that disinterest to justify their choices. No audience for shows outside the mainstream meant that a rerun of *I Love Lucy* was what the public wanted.[64] For Mannes, the critic should not be alone in the fight for better programming standards. Part of the responsibility for formulaic shows lay with the intellectuals who claimed to want more out of television yet failed to support the efforts it made.

Struggling to define their professional mandate, first generation critics were confronted with a new reality as the 1960s came to a close: previewing. The opportunity to watch a program pre-broadcast changed the nature of television writing because it emphasized critics' promotional value in bringing viewers to shows. Initially forbidden by the networks, closed circuit and taped television viewing was an occasional event held for critics at local stations. Increased pressure on the networks to make previewing a regular practice lead to hearings in front of Senator John Pastore's Congressional Subcommittee of Communications. CBS was the first to concede and in 1969, made it a policy to allow critics to preview the premieres of their major primetime shows. CBS was the top network during that time and while the preview decision might have been an opportunity to get ahead of negative reviews, Gould suggested other motivation. In an April 6, 1969, column, "The Critic May Have His Day," he wrote that the network knew previewing allowed the audience to make informed viewing decisions and was therefore a way to appease government concerns about content.

Bowing to federal pressures or hoping to avoid the possibility of negative reviews, the networks nevertheless understood the promotional value of previewing. No longer watching programs along with their readers, a practice that prompted Jackie Gleason to make his famous quip about "traffic accidents and eyewitnesses,"[65] the critic was now in a privileged position to influence those readers to become viewers of a particular show. The networks exploited the relationship, sending gifts and marketing materials along with opportunities to watch programs before they aired. They eventually started hosting events where they introduced new programs to a select group of invited critics who also had the chance to meet the celebrities and the creative teams who worked on the shows. On the surface, the events were mutually beneficial. Critics got access to more sources to assist them in doing their jobs. The networks may have benefitted from that access with more (positive) coverage of their programs. However, the gatherings rapidly took on the negative connotation of junkets due to the industry's excessive generosity. Extravagant accommodation and entertainment became the norm and networks disguised cash payments in the form of "laundry money" or "cab fare."[66] Professional standards suffered as critics made use of network prepared questions and written articles. The backlash was swift and some critics published scathing commentary on their colleagues' questionable conduct.

One of those who made his views know was Ernie Kreiling, a syndicated TV columnist. In what would become a manifesto for the profession and labeled the "Kreiling Thesis," he defined the critic's role with a familiar focus on raising viewers' taste levels: "The critic's goal should be to alert and involve the viewing public so it will demand the television fare that truly serves in its own best interest."[67] Summarizing his points in an article for *The Journal of Broadcasting*, Kreiling suggested that his fellow critics failed their readers when they perceived their role as entertainer: "If we aim primarily to entertain, aren't we guilty of exactly what we accuse television of: trying to reach the 'massiest' possible audience rather than striving to elevate the level of public taste and appreciation?"[68] Kreiling suggested that too many columns relied on personality notes and programming schedules, which were nothing more than free advertising space for the networks.[69] It was a problem of little concern to the television industry, a point *Variety* critic Les Brown made when he called for the medium to have a "respected jury." He argued that television, of all media, had the greatest need for a responsible viewpoint outside of its industry and it had the least because most broadcasters did not care if smart television critics were covering shows. They only saw their work as publicity outlets.[70] Kreiling agreed, adding that newspaper editors who were "duped into serving as the industry's principal means of promotion and exploitation" shared the blame.[71] Despite the problems, he was hopeful, noting that the quality of television criticism was making steady improvements.[72]

Less hopeful was *Chicago Daily News* critic Norman Mark who, several years after Kreiling's thesis, recounted a telling anecdote in an article for *Columbia Journalism Review*. Mark told the story of Jack Allen, a critic at the *Buffalo Courier-Express*, who attended a junket and then wrote a review of a show called *Apple's Way* in which he declared, "Many will learn *Apple's Way* and love it." The series, from *Waltons* creator Earl Hamner, Jr., was about a family surnamed Apple, who moved from Los Angeles to small town Iowa. Allen's reaction was notable for one reason: He had not actually seen *Apple's Way*. His confident judgment about a show he had never watched was printed weeks before the show premiered and at a time when even the actors did not know all the details about the series. Mark pointed out that Allen's work was only one example among several of the "not so bright writing" that came from network controlled press events.[73] It was a style at odds with the more serious approach taken by other critics. Mark explained that critics who wanted to know when a TV star's last trip to the East Coast was or other details of their personal life often clashed with their colleagues who approached the stars with more earnest questions like "the implications of gasoline usage during TV chase scenes in the midst of an energy crisis."[74] Mark's dissatisfaction with the junket atmosphere lead him to call for reform, suggesting that the only way for TV criticism to be as respected as film, for example, was for the trivial journalism practiced at junkets to be sincerely examined.[75]

The compromised atmosphere was troubling because it suggested that a professional approach to TV journalism was neither needed nor required. Overall standards began to slip and Mark gave an example of just how far they fell: "A real-life secretary who was about to portray a secretary on *Bracken's World* was asked how many words per minute she typed. 'Fifty words per minute,' she responded, but the reporter persisted: 'Electric or manual?'"[76] In his piece, Mark noted that not all work produced during junkets was as uninspired but he suggested that the majority of it deserved closer scrutiny. One of the problems he saw was the tight scheduling structure and mass press conference format imposed by the networks, which discouraged the independent effort that was needed to write first-rate criticism.[77] The other was the intimacy between the critics, the TV stars and the networks.[78] *Chicago Sun-Times* critic and Pulitzer Prize winning columnist Ron Powers agreed, suggesting that the networks were aware that fellowships developed, which potentially discouraged tough questions: "Nobody wants to be out on the fringe, asking the provocative questions. The very fact that we mingle with the subjects of the interviews over cocktails before and after the sessions discourages adversary questions."[79] Powers' view on the subtle yet detrimental impact of the junket atmosphere supported Mark's call for critics to stop allowing junkets to compromise their journalistic integrity. Both offered a far gentler scolding than fellow critic Gary Deeb who published a scathing commentary on the suspect journalistic practices. In a 1974 *Variety* article, Deeb blasted TV journalists who used network press releases in their entirety, calling them "fuzzyheaded boobs whose minds were sealed at birth," and "outright prostitutes."[80] He took provincial critics to task for asking celebrities they wrote about for autographs and gave a sarcastic example of the not so penetrating questions some asked of their interviewees, including a "quest for such trivia as the names, ages and middle initials of each of the subject's children." The blame for the sorry state of the profession, however, lied more with newspaper editors than with critics: "Most of these unprofessional hacks are merely products of foolish newspaper managements that demand—directly or indirectly—the TV beat be covered in a frothy, showbiz-y manner." Television, those editors and managers believed, was inexpensive entertainment that should not be considered too significant. The failure of the newspaper industry to recognize television's remarkable impact on the public was a disservice to readers who deserved more thoughtful commentary. Deeb also chastised newspapers that owned TV stations for not being critical of those stations but he saw hope for the future with the *New York Times'* hiring of former *Variety* TV editor Les Brown, "the most knowledgeable and influential person on the TV beat in the American consumer press," as a sign that the situation was improving for popular criticism. The attitude of newspaper management was slowly changing and for Deeb, Brown was an example of the dynamic, curious and astute journalists that TV criticism so desperately needed.

The response of Deeb, Kreiling and others to styles of criticism that were more about promotion than public service, would become a catalyst for a formalization of the profession. By the mid–1970s, the calls for change were answered with the establishment of the Television Critics Association (TCA), an organization that would spearhead the drive to replace junkets with less industry dominated events. In an environment where second generation critics, trained as journalists and accustomed to TV, began to reject the soft news approach of their predecessors, the TCA offered credibility. The eventual press tours the Association would organize afforded critics opportunities rarely given to those who wrote about other entertainment forms. Yet the idea of critics as adjunct promotional agents was never too far from the minds of industry leaders and television's creative personnel.

CHAPTER THREE

Movin' on Up: The 1970s

THE BACKLASH FROM GARY DEEB and others over what they felt were the professions' compromised journalistic standards was characteristic of a post–Watergate climate that inspired the press to value the power of their work. In the 1970s, television became a news beat with consideration given to how it operated as a business and a technology as well as how its programs communicated artistically and aesthetically. The ethical questions being asked after Watergate also lead to general changes in the field of journalism and more thought was given to reporters' relationships with their sources and those who they covered. The atmosphere of introspection extended to the practices of press based TV criticism. Critics took a hard look at the appearance of impropriety surrounding network junkets and the various ways they developed their relationships with industry executives. By the mid–1970s, close to one-third of newspapers started to pay for their TV critic's travel and hotel expenses.[1] Not long after, a group of critics decided to take a bigger step toward reform.

Critics who wanted to transform the compromised atmosphere of network junkets into a more professional press environment formed the Television Critics Association (TCA) in January 1978. Tired of rehashing press releases, they demanded less network control and more freedom to report critically on television. Their collective action was a call for a more formalized view of their profession as well as a show of strength, particularly among critics who were employed by smaller circulation papers and therefore had less influence and less access to industry players. In an effort to persuade the networks to take critics more seriously as journalists rather than extensions of their publicity departments, the TCA took control and replaced the problematic junkets with more credible twice-yearly press tours. The semi-annual tours were held in one hotel in Los Angeles, a practice that continues today. In January, the shorter winter tour focused on mid-season replacements and shows broadcasting their final episodes while in July, the longer summer tour featured new and returning shows. In the new structure, critics covered their travel and accommodation expenses and networks paid for meals and other costs associated with their presentations. Membership to the TCA was also vetted so that tour attendees were no longer a select group of specially invited critics. This allowed critics to ask harder questions and publish unfavorable reviews of programs without fear that the networks would retaliate by cutting off their access to information.[2]

Early in its development, the organization planned interview sessions with members of the industry's creative community, published a bimonthly newsletter that featured interviews with creative staff and network executives and offered a directory of members who were available as speakers for broadcast events, all in addition to the semi-annual press tours. As the TCA became more established over the next several decades, it produced less of this material but maintained the twice-yearly events. The press tour's format consisted of panel sessions that were held throughout the day followed by network planned evening parties. The daytime press conferences ended with formal question and answer sessions.

In recent years, there is also what is known as "the scrum," which is the name given to the group of critics who swarm around the panelists for a chance to ask questions they are either too uncomfortable or too slow to ask during the Q&A. Television critic Alan Sepinwall, who writes for online site *HitFix*, suggested that while the scrum used to serve the needs of critics from smaller papers with more insular questions they did not want to ask in front of the entire group, in its current form, it is a miniature version of the press conference minus the comforts of personal space: "Everyone is pressed together in a circle, holding out their phone or voice recorder and trying to get the attention of actors and executives who don't have eyes in the back of their heads."[3] Despite the chaos of the scrum, the press tours are tightly orchestrated events where twelve-hour days are not unusual. The after-hours parties are designed to give critics more informal access to their shows' stars, producers and executives but as Sepinwall noted, some networks go out of their way to entertain. One was known for staging concerts featuring famous musicians while another routinely held their party at a carnival, a good venue to win prizes but not an ideal setting for interviews.[4] For the *A.V. Club* television critic Todd VanDerWerff the tour is a mixed bag. Writing in 2012, he said that the experience was "somewhere between absolutely vital to doing my job and the most pointless thing I do all year."[5] While he acknowledged that the potential for network influence on critics was hard to ignore, VanDerWerff noted that the tour also provided important insights and taught critics how to wade through the hype and "better calibrate for the differences between people who really know what they're doing, and those who are just good at faking it."[6]

The TCA tours also afforded critics opportunities rarely given to those who write about other entertainment forms. Unlike the events film critics attend where no formal structure exists for access to studio executives, each network on the TCA tour holds an executive panel session. There are also opportunities for one-on-one interviews with network executives outside of that session and for more informal conversations throughout the day and at the nightly parties. For critics, there are several advantages to this unique arrangement including the ability to ask tough questions and gain information that would otherwise not be available regarding the creative direction of a show. *Washington Post* journalist Sharon Waxman, who attended a TCA tour in 1998, pointed out the benefits, including the fact that attendees participated in forums that were open to discussion and debate and offered many opportunities for questions. While this format meant that some critics would simply report the networks' spin to their readers, it also allowed critics to force industry executives to address specific issues.[7] Sepinwall's 2014 summary of the tour made it clear that the opportunities to speak to industry leaders were indeed unique and remain a vital part of the TCA's mission: "We're here for weeks on end, coming face to face with everyone from former presidents to puppeteers.... Not many other businesses force their top executives to regularly stand in front of a room full of hostile reporters and explain their every blunder.... Some love the scrutiny, some despise it."[8] According to Sepinwall, one who loved it was CBS's Les Moonves whose press conferences would be similar to a performance but other executives did not respond as favorably. In 1981, NBC's executive vice-president of corporate communications, Bud Rukeyser, refused to allow the network to participate in the July press tour because he objected to an incident that occurred during the previous January tour. Rukeyser was angry that critics repeatedly demanded an answer to a question about a lead character's sexuality in the show *Love, Sydney*.[9] His attempt at punishment failed when other networks simply filled the time NBC would have taken on the tour. Critics reported that with little to cover regarding NBC, they wrote about the other networks. NBC was back the following tour. During the 2012 winter tour, an anonymous executive wrote a harsh assessment of tour attendees in an article for the *Hollywood Reporter*[10] prompting one critic to angrily take both the author and the magazine to task. Adam Wright slammed the piece for its "bitter, cold and cowardly" tone, reminding the anonymous author that without TV critics, programs would not receive much needed publicity. He then blamed the magazine for shamefully giving the executive a soapbox when it should instead have lead by example.[11]

While the executive accessibility provided by the TCA panels demonstrated the networks' understanding of critics' cultural authority as well as the critics' achievement in getting the industry to recognize them as serious journalists, the idea of critics as adjunct promotional agents was never too far from the minds of industry leaders and television's creative personnel. Journalist Sharon Waxman argued in "Spoon-Fed News" that the tour was a chance for writers to speak with their sources but more often it was an opportunity for those contacts to curry favor with writers.[12] Waxman was concerned with the gifts that journalists received from networks during the tour but more problematic was the continuous promotional race "mounted, sponsored and run" by networks. The effect, she argued was dangerous because it added to an "atmosphere of collusion rather than one of skepticism" and impacted the credibility of journalists who were meant to be there to observe the television industry critically rather than to be guests of the networks.[13] Waxman's article made an impact. She noted that before it was published the TCA met with members who voted unanimously to "limit outside material to informational uses only." The objectivity and separation that Waxman urged the TCA to achieve, however, was still a challenge several years later when communications scholar Amanda Lotz described her experience attending the 2003 summer tour. While the organization's new rules reduced the extravagance of network gifts, they did not prevent networks from excessive giving of the items that were allowed. The problem was not that the permitted books and t-shirts unduly influenced critics' work. Rather, it was the indecorum they suggested. Lotz explained: "I returned home with no fewer than thirteen books, three tote bags, various CDs, DVDs, T-shirts, and the *Queer Eye for the Straight Guy* soap-on-a-rope. Again, the influence of a tube of sunscreen from the Travel Channel or a logo-emblazoned pen, T-shirt, bag, mug, or notepad is debatable, but the appearance of impropriety remains."[14] In addition to concerns over the volume of free gifts handed out by the networks, there were other problematic issues including scheduling of network sessions and the needs of a membership that had expanded beyond traditional print publications.

On the tour Lotz attended, networks lobbied for positions on the schedule that ensured them the largest attendance. Typically, this meant they wanted a spot that was not at the start or end of the schedule since these were the times that press critics with smaller budgets usually chose to skip.[15] The networks' efforts to secure the most well attended slots served their needs and created a clear hierarchy among cable, commercial and public broadcasters. In addition, the panel sessions that critics chose to attend offered some insight into which aspects of broadcasting they considered to be most significant but as Lotz argued this is often related to their readers' interests more than their personal preferences.[16]

The evolving membership of the TCA also raised challenges as the needs of critics who wrote daily columns for newspapers in major markets (the more traditional critics) conflicted with the priorities of those who wrote weekly or quarterly columns and those who wrote for internet-based publications. Of most concern to some of the more traditional critics, as noted by Lotz in 2003, was the emphasis of those who focused on celebrity culture, the majority of whom were based in Los Angeles. Their year-round proximity to industry players caused tension over access, which was heightened when they took up time in question and answer sessions with trivial, celebrity or even fan-based queries.[17] Some critics expressed concern that those types of questions caused the industry not to take the TCA seriously. The organization responded by implementing an additional yearly vetting practice where all existing members must submit multiple clips of their published work representing several months. The process made certain that all TCA members and thus all tour attendees were using up to date credentials and were primarily writing about television. While non-serious questions are still a regular feature of current tour press conferences—Alan Sepinwall notes that the questions range from smart to dumb to inexplicable: "Your sons, they're both boys?"—the strain between traditional critics and other tour constituencies is largely absent because most of the reporters who now attend publish their work for online outlets.[18]

The TCA's takeover of network junkets had an immediate effect on the relationship between critics and industry leaders. Writing about a press tour in 1978, critic Richard Levine noted the change in tone from the early days: "In heated exchanges the minority of younger, more vocal critics attempted to hold television executives responsible for the shows they put on the air."[19] Television editor for the *Dallas Morning News*, Rena Pederson, also commented on the changes in criticism taking place in the 1970s as junkets gave way to more formalized opportunities. Speaking to the Broadcast Education Association in 1979, she described the early years of the profession when junkets were prevalent noting that "there were a lot of cocktail parties and a lot of free time, and a lot of free tickets to plays."[20] A few years later, David Williams, critic for the *Arizona Daily Star* and TCA president in 1985, pointed out in a panel discussion that the atmosphere Pederson described was what prompted the organization's formation: "You cannot do interviews standing up at a cocktail party. You can't write and hold a drink. We were always on buses and we were always being given gifts and presentations and so forth. All we wanted was to get the hoopla out of it."[21] Both Williams and Pederson suggested that an important shift was taking place. For Williams, it was the perception that if critics as a group looked similar to a profession there was a greater chance they would get treated as one.[22] Pederson believed the change was either an evolution or a revolution where both critics and the newspapers that employed them recognized that TV was not merely "the electronic hearth, your friend, your glowing warm companion" but also "news."[23] As a result, she suggested, there was a more unmanageable, assertive and combative group of critics who were creating a lively, dynamic climate that was better for readers, viewers and the industry.[24] The collective action of the TCA was a reflection of this shift in attitude toward both the field of criticism and television itself.

The formation of the TCA reflected the critics' desire for formal legitimacy at a time when they were highly valued for their promotional influence but did not want to be defined by that role. Unlike the first generation of critics working in television's infancy, the critics who began their careers in the late 1960s and early 1970s had grown up with television. This second generation approached criticism from the point of view of reporters assigned to the television beat. Trained in journalism rather than the arts, many TV critics working in the post–Watergate era embraced the idea that the journalist was able to bring about important social change.[25] As a result, many of those critics expanded their purview beyond aesthetic critique of programs to include coverage of the technological, industrial and policy aspects that shape television's meaning.

Television in the 1970s

In the 1970s, television programming started to look and sound different as network executives pushed for relevancy. Their new attitude may have reflected a desire to accurately represent the social and cultural upheaval that was taking place off-screen but it also suggested that their views towards ratings practices were changing. In the 1970s, market research showed that young, urban adults aged 18–49 (particularly females) were the primary consumers of the types of products promoted on television. The networks' desire to capture that profitable demographic led to significant changes in program direction. Hoping to attract young adults, the networks announced a new group of shows that would represent the realities of modern life. The goal of the new "relevancy" shows was to depict contemporary themes through young, idealistic characters that served the downtrodden. Series including *Storefront Lawyers* and *The Interns* on CBS, *The Psychiatrist* on NBC and *Young Lawyers* on ABC, all featured young professionals helping people deal with real problems.

Programming was not only topical. It also looked different. More ethnic diversity appeared in dramas, comedies, commercials and newscasts. A man on television with long hair no longer immediately signaled hippie or protestor. Instead, he might be a respected professional or if he was on *Mod Squad* or *The Rookies*, even a member of law enforcement. Yet the TV relevancy movement was not as radical as it appeared. Advertisements for the new shows may have promised pro-radical positions but the programs generally steered clear of controversy. Social problems were "simply churned into standard television format drama wrapped in love beads" while issues were set up to be easily defeated so that the establishment, with the assistance of clear-thinking moderates, won.[26] The strategy was a ratings failure. Heavy-handed issues combined with a split focus (networks did not completely abandon the older demographic) meant that neither the younger nor older segment of the audience was interested in the new crop of programs. An unmarried career woman and a bigoted old man changed things.

Despite the audience's initial unenthusiastic response to the relevancy movement, the output of two production companies made an impact by addressing what was considered relevant to the "quality" audience, now defined by their youth and their spending habits. Norman Lear's Tandem Productions, producer of *All in the Family*, and Mary Tyler Moore Enterprises (MTM), the producers of *The Mary Tyler Moore Show* re-invented relevancy television with programming that took a new approach. Wary of the earlier failure of too much relevance, the shows produced by MTM and Tandem dealt with contemporary issues but relocated them to the workplace and to situations that arose from relationships. The flagship program of MTM, *The Mary Tyler Moore Show*, was the story of Mary Richards (played by Moore), a single woman who left her small town to work as a reporter in Minneapolis. Mary, her co-workers, her boss and her friends (some more realistic than others) were depicted as people who had contemporary attitudes and problems while Mary herself was a departure from traditional situation comedy depictions of women. Building a career on her own terms, she represented women as being capable of interests beyond the domestic concerns of housework, marriage and wacky situation comedy schemes.[27] Gary Deeb wrote that Moore's Mary Richard's character proved that viewers would accept a female heroine who was not a housewife, a widow, or a harebrained Lucille Ball type.[28] Looking back on the program's seven-year run, Deeb recognized it as an outstanding comedy that raised the quality of television.[29]

Around the same time that Mary and her colleagues were navigating the challenges of life and work, Archie Bunker (Carol O'Connor) was stirring up controversy and solid ratings on *All in the Family*. The comedy focused on the gruff and racist Bunker, his lovable, long-suffering wife Edith (Jean Stapleton), his newly married daughter Gloria (Sally Struthers) and his live-in son-in-law Michael (Rob Reiner). The weekly verbal battles between blue-collar, loading dock worker Archie and long haired, liberal, college educated Michael were the core of the show and sounded like nothing viewers had heard on network television up to this point. As one critic suggested, the show "violated all the polite rules of the game."[30] Archie used racial epithets previously considered taboo on network television. During his heated disagreements with Michael, who he usually called "Meathead," Archie routinely launched into a stream of ethnic and racial slurs. Puerto Ricans were "spics," Jews were "hebes," and African Americans were "jungle-bunnies." Yet he was not completely unlovable, a fact novelist Laura Hobson used to denounce the show for making bigotry enjoyable. Weighing in on the debate, *New York Times* critic John O'Connor, who called the show one of the "funniest" on TV, argued that of the most concerning facts about bigotry was that not all bigots were repulsive and may in fact be somewhat loveable. If Archie Bunker was this type of endearing but intolerant person, his character represented a familiar type of "loudmouth clod" who also happens to be a bigot.[31] For his part, Lear responded to the controversy by explaining that his goal was to enable black and white, Jew and Gentile to "laugh together."[32] Lear realized that goal but not immediately. The show attracted little viewer attention after its January 1971 premiere but not long after, it hit number one in the ratings and stayed there for five seasons. At least one critic predicted the show's success after previewing the pilot episode. Clarence Petersen of the *Chicago Tribune* gave his strong, early support suggesting the show would be the main topic of conversation the morning after its broadcast barring "a third world war, a double ax murder in a convent or one heck of a storm in the next 24 hours" and his readers should not miss it.[33] Looking back on the show, Petersen's fellow critic at the paper called it a milestone series that demonstrated a situation comedy could explore compelling issues.[34] Laurent labeled the show a "hostility situation comedy" and suggested that it allowed viewers "to rid themselves of the meanness and frustration that urban living" was sometimes too good at providing.[35]

The success of *All in the Family*, along with *The Mary Tyler Moore Show*, motivated Tandem, MTM and other production companies to try and repeat the winning formula. Media historian Erik Barnouw explained the strategy of *All in the Family* as one that introduced tension into comedy. The result was that taboos disappeared: "Interracial marriage, a young man's siege of impotence, an older woman's pregnancy and indecision about abortion, were suddenly topics of warm comedy, presented as casually as such old-time crises as: Will Dad notice the dent in the rear fender?"[36] Presenting contemporary issues in a comedic context delivered social and political relevance that felt authentic rather than alienating. The audience connected with characters in psychologically meaningful ways and still found something to make them laugh. It was a successful strategy that launched a new approach to programming. Because the show was the first continuing series to be popular while confronting racism, homosexuality, menopause, rape and alcoholism among other relevant topics, it paved the way for subsequent prime-time series to add controversial themes to their storylines.[37]

The popularity of the relevancy programming continued CBS' ratings dominance until a nostalgic sitcom starring a leather-clad hoodlum named Fonzie stole the number one spot for ABC. *Happy Days*, a show about a middle class family with teenage children living in 1950s-era America, started off slow, earning marginal ratings when it premiered in 1974. ABC executive Fred Silverman retooled the show in its third season by promoting the minor character of Arthur "Fonzie" Fonzarelli (Henry Winkler) to a major player. Fonzie was an over the top caricature but his cool, in-control problem-solving skills made him the show's and the audience's hero. The elevation of Fonzie helped to transform the nostalgic hook of *Happy Days* from a bland imitation of the world of 1950s sitcoms to the past as viewers wanted to remember it.[38] The show began as a top-30 program, moved to number 10 in 1975-1976 and hit number one a season later. For the first time in twenty years, CBS did not hold the number one spot.

Relevancy and nostalgia shared the 1970s programming schedule with the television special, usually an entertainment or variety show and the miniseries. An original film divided into parts and broadcast over several nights, the miniseries owed its style and structure to the British Broadcasting Corporation (BBC) and its innovative novels-to-television programs and original productions.[39] In 1971, PBS, an early adopter of the British format, imported the miniseries on a permanent basis with the broadcast of the network's flagship series *Masterpiece Theater*. American commercial television took notice and adapted the miniseries format. Not every series was successful but some exceeded expectations. In 1975, ABC broadcasted *Rich Man, Poor Man*, six two-hour original films broadcast over seven weeks. It was the first American production that came closest to matching the style and scope of the British miniseries and it averaged forty-one million viewers.[40] Two years later, ABC turned the Alex Haley novel *Roots*, about slaves and their descendants, into a twelve-hour miniseries broadcast for eight consecutive nights. Seven of the eight episodes made it into the top ten list of most-watched television programs of all time up to that point. It took an average 66 share or 130 million people, prompting *Broadcasting* to declare, "Television may never be the same again."[41] *Roots* was a cultural phenomenon but the success of the program and others like it (NBC's miniseries *Holocaust* earned record ratings second only to *Roots*) was only a temporary solution to the networks' growing problem of declining viewership.

Critics of the 1970s

While the TCA was a large part of the shift in critical thinking that took place in the 1970s, it started with writing that began to examine television beyond its programs. The work of Michael Arlen, John O'Connor, Les Brown and Tom Shales in particular, reflected the growing disillusionment of the late 1960s and continued to engage with 1970s television on a similar level. These critics went beyond evaluating a program's artistic quality to exploring television's larger cultural impact.

Michael Arlen started writing about television for *The New Yorker* in 1966 at the request of then editor William Shawn. He would go on to publish three books on television as well as several autobiographical narratives. An experienced journalist before he accepted the TV critic job, Arlen recalled in the introduction to *Living Room War*, a collection of his 1960s columns, that he had at the time no particular interest in television outside normal viewing: "I had no special feeling or fondness for television, beyond watching it in an ordinary way, and no prefigured theories or notions of how to proceed."[42] How he proceeded was to write about what interested him but only after realizing that television criticism was perhaps not what he initially thought it was: "For my first column, I produced the kind of thing I thought was expected of a television critic then: a strenuously urbane and mildly acerbic put-down of a standard piece of network dramatic waffle."[43] Looking for the next target, he rethought his approach. "I realized that, if I pursued this conventional approach to television much longer, I was likely to do myself out of a job. For if the burden of what I had to say about television was that it was silly, culturally inferior, and not worth the trouble, why then should anyone bother to read what I had to say about it?"[44] He decided that his interest was in the news, particularly the coverage of the Vietnam War.

Arlen's work on television was perhaps best known for his critical essays on TV's coverage of the Vietnam War but he also discussed other aspects of TV in equally thoughtful ways. His criticism explored how the images viewers see on-screen related to how they see themselves. He believed that television had a transformative effect on both the events it covered and the public who watched those events but it was difficult to figure out what that effect was.[45] Arlen may not have know exactly how to describe the ways that television transformed viewers but his writing challenged them to question its depiction of cultural life. Writing about documentaries, children's programs, Vietnam or political campaigns, he was interested in television's treatment of reality. He argued that commercial television's claim that it was a disinterested servant of the public and therefore depicted a worldview that was realistic, was problematic because it ignored the idea that there were many different lenses through which to view the same reality.[46] For Arlen, television was just one lens and the view it presented of reality was often distorted.

Arlen's contemporary, John O'Connor, took over for Jack Gould at the *New York Times* and was the paper's TV critic for more than two decades. Starting in 1971, he wrote a daily column that focused on reviewing individual shows, as well as longer essays for the Sunday Arts and Leisure section that often covered institutional issues in-depth. His columns appeared in a large number of daily newspapers via the *New York Times* Service, making his audience nationwide. Due to tighter deadlines and smaller word counts, his work was less theoretical and less personal than Arlen's. In an interview with communications scholar Hal Himmelstein, O'Connor explained that while Arlen was able to "lean back and look at something and do a long take on a program," he must function as more of a consumer guide because his readers expected it.[47] O'Connor guided readers by reviewing shows pre-broadcast, a choice that changed the nature of the *Time*'s TV column. Unlike Gould who preferred not to pre-review a show, O'Connor saw it as a necessary part of his critical role, particularly for a readership that he characterized as selective viewers, wanting to know current and future recommendations.[48] The choice made an impact on both O'Connor's fellow critics and NBC, the last network to allow reviews prior to broadcast. He told Himmelstein that when he started previewing, his influence as the *Times*' critic prompted newspaper editors to pressure their critics to review prior to broadcast and eventually, NBC reluctantly agreed to lift their ban on the practice.[49] While O'Connor was not the first critic to preview a show, his emphasis on the approach, backed by the power of his professional affiliation with the *Times*, shaped the direction of 1970s TV criticism.

Writing for the *Times* allowed O'Connor a level of institutional authority that he appreciated but it was not something he took lightly. The paper's influence on television's direction informed how he approached his work. He explained to Himmelstein that he chose not to be excessively cruel because his opinions, as a *Times* reviewer, could significantly impact programs: "I've got that kind of exposure that I'm not going to be flip, I try not to be overly flip about what I'm writing about…. Some people have the idea that if they're not mentioned in the *Times* they don't exist…. It's a strange thing."[50] O'Connor was well aware that his daily program assessments were valuable to industry leaders and television's creative community, even when he discouraged his readers from tuning in. Yet, unlike some members of the second-generation critics, he did not see himself as a journalist covering the television beat. In the interview with Himmelstein he said that he accepted the position at the *Times* on the condition that he would not combine the role of journalist and critic because he felt there could potentially be a conflict of interest between the two jobs.[51] Valuing his independence, he expressed little enthusiasm for the pop culture side of television, telling Himmelstein: "I don't want to interview, do celebrity interviews. I don't want to know about it."[52] What O'Connor did want to know about were the aesthetics of television programs. Many of his columns examined actor performances, production techniques and the narrative complexities of series. A 1979 review of a made for TV movie starring Bette Davis and Gena Rowlands on CBS offered one example. In the column he noted Bette Davis' iconic status in popular culture before judging her recognizable mannerisms to be a detriment to her performance, reaching the point of self-parody. Rowlands' performance was better but still over-worked.[53] While O'Connor's writing was strong on aesthetic evaluations of shows, he also situated his reviews within broader institutional contexts. In a piece on *Live from Lincoln Center*'s production of *Swan Lake*, he noted the smart direction of the performance but ended with a warning that if television gave in to the temptation to focus its arts programming on the more popular shows it would be ignoring its obligation to all the artistic offerings at Lincoln Center. The point of the broadcasts should be quality and not the size of the audience for a single production.[54] Generally, his style was to assess a program's complexity but not to ignore wider issues, particularly the institutional demands on television production.

Early in his reviewing career, O'Connor began a column by declaring that the majority of people, inside or outside the industry, will agree that television "conservatively speaking, is at least 90 per cent trash."[55] It was a bold and rather disheartening statement from a critic of the medium but this unimpressive statistic, he argued, was not unique to TV—theater, film, music and publishing also lacked the same percentage of quality product. The difference was that television offered a larger and practically universal target due to the sheer volume of programming it screened daily on multiple channels.[56] His opinion on the large amount of trash that made up the schedule was not reserved for one program type. Rather, it cut across all genres: "the inane situation comedies, the insane game shows, the insipid interviews, the overblown specials, the commercials bordering on downright fraudulence."[57] Within all these categories, however, a few programs rose to the top that proved the medium was capable of producing treasure within the pile of trash.[58]

O'Connor's qualified praise of commercial television was a theme that ran throughout his career as a TV critic. At the start of the 1975 television season, he again pronounced the majority of the new programs "trash, piled on mounds of the grossest cynicism" but suggested that quality could occasionally be found on commercial television.[59] He did find some examples in several 1970's situation comedies, even admitting that sometimes, reviewers treated the genre unfairly.[60] He named *M*A*S*H* an exceptional series, called *Barney Miller* a "clever commentary on urban vagaries" and suggested that *Taxi*, with its above average scripts and highly skilled group of actors, was an exceptional example of the genre.[61] *Mary Hartman, Mary Hartman* had a decent amount of very funny elements but *One Day at a Time*, despite its promising storyline was ordinary.[62] *Three's Company* fared worse. While it was simple with okay performances, an empty television screen was more preferable.[63]

For O'Connor, the blame for television's tendency to produce more trash than treasure lay with the networks' commercial interests. In a 1972 piece on the antitrust lawsuits filed by the Justice Department against ABC, NBC, CBS and Viacom, then a subsidiary of CBS, he outlined the basics of the suit (to prevent networks from gaining a monopoly over program production) and offered a brief historical perspective on the economic structure of broadcasting. His main argument, however, was that the networks' assertions that they were the best chance for quality programs to be produced was disingenuous and they were in fact ignoring both the selective viewer and the public, which they treated with disdain. The networks would consistently counter arguments for obligations to quality programming with appeals for accountability to shareholders.[64] The detrimental impact of the networks' commercial mandate was a topic he returned to several years later in a column that addressed the economic reality of television. This reality, he wrote, was firmly embedded in a bottom line that displayed growing profits while many critics and much of the public found TV to be a discouraging landscape filled with bland shows.[65] He attributed the lack of quality programming to a fundamental misunderstanding among network executives. Namely, their definition of quality was too narrow because they only associated it with the arts and culture series found on public broadcasting channels that in turn got low ratings when in fact, the boundaries of quality were wide and not exclusive of high ratings. The evidence could be found in shows like *All in the Family*, *The Waltons* or *Kojak*.[66] Commercial television was capable of broadcasting quality work that had solid viewer numbers but without a fundamental shift in perspective, network executives would continue to devote themselves to profit above all else. While he acknowledged the industry's commercial mandate, making it the primary consideration was to the detriment of the public interest because what mattered most was that market forces be prevented from becoming the "only governing criterion for a medium of such awesome pervasiveness."[67] A few years later, the commercial mandate of the networks had changed little, prompting him to write "the system of broadcasting has gone berserk in its quest for ever increasing profits."[68]

O'Connor's concerns over the institutional constraints on program production for both commercial networks and public broadcasting was a common theme. In a 1972 piece on the FCC's review of the Fairness Doctrine, a principle designed two decades earlier that required broadcasters to provide audiences with both sides of an issue, he again suggested that the idea of profits dictating programming choices was a disservice to the public.[69] Other columns discussed the funding challenges faced by the non-commercial system. One suggested that the reason American public television relied so heavily on productions from the British Broadcasting System was the lack of financial support while another outlined the difficulties in creating a distribution structure for the limited funding public broadcasting did receive.[70] In a longer essay, he raised questions about the level of content control that corporations should have over the programs they sponsored on public television.[71]

Along with discussing issues regarding sources of funding, O'Connor devoted time to how those funds were distributed. Of particular concern was the ability of independent producers to gain access to public television production and the broadcaster's tendency toward a conservative programming approach. The play-it-safe attitude of public broadcasting was shutting out independent producers and preventing diversified programming. O'Connor feared that public television executives were becoming too much like their commercial counterparts in their desire to attract larger audiences with lowest common denominator programming. Yet he recognized that broadcasting the work of independent producers, much of which was aimed at special interest groups, was not going to lead to public television's financial solvency. Finding a balance was an ongoing issue that informed much of O'Connor's critical dialogue on public TV.

For much of his career with the *Times* and throughout the 1970s, O'Connor consistently maintained that most of the programs on commercial television were of low quality. He generally rejected situation comedies, action-adventure and various specials as unworthy of serious evaluation. It was a stance that caused industry leaders and others to claim he was a cultural elitist. ABC president Fred Silverman, had O'Connor in mind when he claimed that many in the profession have a snobbish attitude toward network programs. In a late 1970s speech, Silverman remarked that "the public's opinion speaks infinitely louder to us than the wishes of a few people who apparently see a different role for television in our society than providing entertainment to millions of people."[72] O'Connor believed his readers were selective viewers but he dismissed Silverman's remarks that he was out of touch with the mass audience and responded, "no television critic could afford for a moment to despise popular entertainment and, at the same time, no television critic can be expected to sacrifice qualitative judgments to the quantity of audience ratings."[73] For O'Connor, critical integrity was a balance between recognizing the role that ratings played in expressing audience preferences and not allowing this understanding to overly influence judgments about those preferences. He may not have thought that the majority of genre series on commercial networks were due his thoughtful consideration but he was realistic about the programming landscape. He noted that even demanding critics would agree that there was value in good entertainment and television did not need to exclusively devote its broadcasts to programs that were considered inspirational to society.[74] Despite his personal opinions on the majority of programs, O'Connor did not relegate television to a position of low culture. He understood the value of popular shows but cautioned against excluding other, more challenging programs, in favor of those that only appealed to the mass audience. In his evaluative reviews, he offered knowledgeable judgments on production techniques and actor performances. In his longer pieces, he explored more complex issues, often framing institutional demands within a television production context. In his articulate role as a consumer guide and in his advocacy for structures and policies that allowed for more diversity in programming, O'Connor was an influential voice.

Taking a different but equally significant approach, *New Yorker* TV critic Michael Arlen's participation in the critical dialogue of the 1970s focused on how TV failed to capture the truth of an event. He was a witness to the violence between anti-war protestors and police during the Democratic National Convention in Chicago in 1968 and in a column on television's coverage of the unrest, reprinted in his book *Living Room War*, he suggested that what the audience saw did not give them the full picture because what was left out mattered. Sitting in their homes, in front of their TV screens, it was difficult, he argued, for viewers to understand how their knowledge of the events could be lessened, changed or restricted by those in power.[75] The disconnection between screen life and real life appeared throughout his work. He returned to it in an essay on public television. Sharing his views on the debates surrounding the formation of public broadcasting, he argued that it would only be valuable if it tried to faithfully represent reality. As it stood, television provided viewers facts without context but the most problematic component was that it gave audiences a fantasy world that said little about actual life and culture. For Arlen, public television had an opportunity to fix this problem and differentiate itself from the commercial system but only if it was willing to fracture the fantasy and screen an honest account of life.[76]

While he was often critical of television's failure to reflect the actualities of life, Arlen did recognize that in times of national sorrow it had the power to communicate a deeply felt truth. On television's coverage of the assassination of Martin Luther King, he wrote about viewers as members of the global village who listened to the voices of newscasters earnestly and sincerely speak to them so that the country could heal, connect and move forward through the tragedy. In fluid prose, he described his feelings as mediated through television: "One could almost hear the weeping out there, of real people in real villages, and the anger, this time, of abandonment."[77] The piece was a thoughtful and personal take on how the medium could communicate the sorrow of a nation and offer it some comfort.

Characteristic of the Martin Luther King commentary was Arlen's choice to recall a personal experience and connect it to a wider analysis. He did the same in a mid–1970s piece on TV's depiction of death. His uncle passed away and he shared his feelings with his readers then wondered what television communicated to its audience about death. To find out, he watched TV for ten to twelve hours each day for one week, noting references to death or dying and concluded that for the most part, television ignores the reality of death except to state it in terms of numbers or abstractions: "We do not die, apparently, except in numbers, or in Rangoon, or with blank faces in a gunfight."[78] While TV claimed to be a mirror reflecting society, it was only a partial reflection.

Writing a weekly column for *The New Yorker* gave Arlen the opportunity to have a more specialized, personal style than other critics who wrote daily reviews. Much of his work had a storytelling quality. Occasionally, he wrote an entire story, as he did in "The Holiday Dinner: A Fable," his version of what men are like when they watch a football game together at a family gathering. More often, however, he focused on assessment and analysis. In the mid–1970s, his columns included reviews of NBC's new sketch comedy program *Saturday Night* which he described as straightforward and funny,[79] several children's shows that he suggested were generally stuck in mediocrity[80] and *I Will Fight No More Forever*, a docudrama on one of the last Native American wars featuring the Nez Perce Indians which stood out as one of a very few ambitious broadcasts.[81] The program's initiative, however, did not prevent Arlen from outlining its historical inaccuracies.[82]

In 1974-1975, Arlen revisited the issues facing public TV. In an essay that began as a review of PBS's *Upstairs, Downstairs*, a British import, he outlined the limitations of a proposed funding bill for public television before demanding a strong public broadcaster that was unimpeded by political agendas. He started with a few thoughts on the series, describing it as notable entertainment that expertly recreated the atmosphere of its historical period. Its episodic structure had as much in common with soap opera conventions as it did with those of serious drama.[83] He continued with a deeper aesthetic critique of the show before posing what he called a political question, wondering how it obtained such a prominent position on the schedule and why the finest series on U.S. public TV was basically a British import. He then named the government, both lawmakers and several administrations, as the primary obstacles to a healthy public television system before laying out the failures of recent funding policies and explaining the consequences should the proposed Public Broadcasting Financing Act pass. He ended the essay with a forceful call for reform and announced that there was no real reason that American viewers were not being offered a strong national television system that was "honestly informative, creative, unfettered by the imperatives of hucksterism, and unhampered by the self-serving theories of transient politicians."[84] The piece was both an assessment of a program and a report on the issues surrounding public television. The combination represented the new approach that many critics were taking in the 1970s, covering television content but also engaging with the politics of the industry.

Regarding commercial television's output, Arlen was unimpressed with the superficial and inferior entertainment programming of the 1970s, citing it as one of the main problems in writing about the medium.[85] Perhaps because of this, the focus of much of his work during that time was television news. He was a passionate critic of the failures of broadcast newscasts in covering the Vietnam War. Looking back on the impact, he wrote that with few exceptions, the networks failed to use their financial resources to try and truthfully explore the actual situation in Vietnam during America's involvement in the country.[86] The insufficiencies of how television news treated the war in Vietnam, while a central preoccupation of Arlen's work, was not his only concern about broadcast journalism. He condemned network news for ignoring the public and focusing on newsmakers and rejected the elitist approach. While he had issues with the politics, point of view and entertainment quality of the news, his main concern was that it had become administrative, high-level and a product of the establishment. That authority was absent of party affiliation and was not liberal or conservative but rather an establishment of *newsmakers*.[87] For Arlen, television had a responsibility to rise above its commercial mandate and speak to the public in ways that represented their interests rather than those of bureaucratic elites.

Arlen was not only a television critic for *The New Yorker*. He also wrote several well-regarded non-fiction books including *Passage to Ararat* which won the 1976 National Book Award for contemporary affairs. His work as a TV critic, however, established him as a significant voice in the field. His commentaries on television news, particularly its coverage of the Vietnam War, represented the shifting nature of 1970s criticism toward investigating television as a powerful and flawed communicator. Rather than simply commenting on how it did or did not entertain its viewers, Arlen explored the self-serving agendas of politicians and industry leaders whose decisions impacted TV as an industry and as a communications medium. In terms of content, he challenged his readers to question television's representations and argued that it be accountable for its failures to depict those representations realistically. From the perspectives of documentaries to the casual depiction of war on the situation comedy *Hogan's Heroes* to the status quo approach of presidential press conferences, Arlen was concerned with the truth of the programs he watched. Stylistically, he was a storyteller, often sharing personal experiences as a way to structure his thoughts on the medium but he was also a journalist who investigated the industry and its politics. Of the 1970s critics, he was perhaps the most theoretical and was interested in speaking about television "as if it mattered."[88] Ultimately, what mattered was how it told viewers who they are and for him, this was more often a fantasy than a reality.

For Tom Shales, television was a life-long preoccupation. In the foreword to *On the Air!* a collection of his columns from the 1970s, he wrote that his first encounter with the family's TV set was "love at first sight."[89] Shales began his 39-year career with the *Washington Post* in 1971 writing for the Style section. In 1977, he was appointed the paper's chief TV critic and TV editor, a position he held until 2009.[90] His reviewing style was funny and witty but he was also known for caustic remarks that later in his career would stir controversy. Like Arlen and O'Connor, Shales saw too much mediocrity in television. His biting commentary was quick to point out a program's missteps and the industry's failures. Yet his work also maintained a consistent sense of joy for television and a respect for its ability to create powerful moments. Not all of TV was worth celebrating but there was much to admire:

> It's not a matter of learning how to stop worrying and love TV, because the worrying will never stop, ever.... But now and then I feel grateful not only that I'm alive in the age of television but that, unlike a lot of people I know, I can still find it, on occasion, marvelous. I can be delighted and astonished and exhilarated by it, and appalled.... The mere fact that hardly anybody works magic with it doesn't mean it isn't a magical instrument.[91]

From his program reviews to his insights on TV news to his opinions on the subtle but alarming impact of commercials, he found a balance between pointed evaluation and entertainment that made him a popular and powerful critical voice. In 1988, he earned the Pulitzer Prize for television criticism and appeared on TV and radio throughout his career. He wrote three books including a well-received history of *Saturday Night Live*.

Shales' work was a combination of traditional program reviews and interviews. Unlike O'Connor, he was interested in celebrity and many of his conversations with actors revealed his enthusiasm for both them and their work. He shared a drink with "The Great One," Jackie Gleason, who he called a "legend that shouldn't be fought,"[92] chatted with Johnny Carson in his home office about the changing landscape of late-night television[93] and interviewed Carol Burnett about her role in a made for television movie in which she played a mother whose son is killed in Vietnam. Shales called the movie "the most straightforward and heartbreaking dramatic work on the Vietnam war made available to a mass audience" and Burnett's performance was the highlight of her career.[94] He also described her as intelligent, peaceful and attractive. In an interview with actor James Garner, star of *The Rockford Files*, he called him a "man's man, a woman's man, an actor's actor and nobody's fool."[95] His admiration for Garner extended to what he believed the actor brought to the show, which had much in common with who he believed Garner was in real life. Like his character, Shales wrote, Garner would surely fight for justice and stand against bureaucrats. The actor, he told readers, had a personal stake in the show's success and he used his protective instincts as he fought against it becoming just another typical example of its genre.

Shales' writing style, he was as much a fan of television's celebrities as he was of the medium itself, created very little distance between him and the television audience. Where other critics referred to discerning viewers, Shales was inclusive, both a fellow viewer offering his thoughts on programs and a fellow fan, sharing his admiration for popular TV stars. In an interview with *Charlie's Angels* actor Farrah Fawcett, he began with a description of what she was perhaps best remembered for: "The hair! So fluffy, so billowy, so ultra-tawny. It cascades and tumbles to her shoulders like a waterfall straight out of Bambi. Farrah Fawcett-Majors, 29, is told her hair looks great."[96] Shales' reference to Fawcett's appearance reads like fandom rather than critique but it demonstrated that he understood the relationship between popular culture, celebrity, television and its audience. Stylistically, he rarely used the first person in his interviews. In the Fawcett piece for example, he wrote: "She is asked if she knows she is a sex symbol." The grammatical choice prevented his tone from becoming too personal and allowed him to slip in assessments that were not always complimentary. Later in the Fawcett interview, he referred to *Charlie's Angels* as one of the most "vacuous" and "insipid" hit shows in the history of TV. In this piece and others, he walked the line between fan and critic. His shared enthusiasm made him relatable to readers but he was careful to maintain enough distance to assert his critical authority.

Shales' authority also came from being the TV critic for the *Washington Post*, a position that opened doors to the industry and its players that were closed to other critics working for smaller, less influential newspapers. Shales spoke to television's producers, directors and program creators and sometimes went behind the scenes of a show. A piece on *Family Feud* included an interview with host Richard Dawson but also the game show's creator and its producer[97] while an interview with Robin Williams, who, in the 1970s, was the rising star of *Mork and Mindy*, described a conversation between Williams and the director that takes place during rehearsal.[98] In an interview with William Paley, then chairman of the board at CBS, on the release of his autobiography, he noted Paley's lofty position in the television hierarchy: "William S. Paley is someone on whom one does not drop in. We're talking megamillionaire here, we're talking American media monarchy."[99] He continues with a list of Paley's friends who include Nelson Rockefeller, Dwight Eisenhower, Randolph Churchill, David O. Selznick and Jack Benny. Naming Paley's famous friends allowed Shales to become a likeminded reader who was admiring Paley's social and cultural influence but it also primed his readers to place him among the privileged men who were granted access to television's elite. At a network party, watching a show rehearsal or talking to hard to reach power players, Shales used his status as a television insider to strengthen his credibility as a critic.

While Shales often used his privileged position within the industry to increase his cultural and critical authority, not all his columns relied on interviews with those in power or with the stars of hit series. He also evaluated shows for their narrative and performance qualities. Praising *Lou Grant* as one of the top shows of the season, he called actor Edward Asner's performance full of "bluster" and "sensitivity." He continued the review with a narrative analysis, arguing that the series, unlike most that season, did not cater to the viewer, deceive them or even flirtatiously arouse their interest. Noting a scene that represented the show's signature style where Grant is seated on a park bench silently mulling over a tough decision as church bells ring in the distance, he tells the reader that it's not an ostentatious or fanciful moment but was still striking as a wonderful and solemnly believable scene.[100] In the review, Shales demonstrated a more traditional approach to program assessment. He did the same in his critique of an episode of *Archie Bunker* that focused on the attempted rape of Archie's wife Edith. He called Jean Stapleton's portrayal of Edith a "particular triumph, an eloquent portrayal of fear, vulnerability, dignity and, finally, victorious resolve." Predicting that the episode's writers would be publicly criticized for injecting humor into a serious subject, he defended their choice, suggesting that the lighter approach was needed to avoid the episode becoming simply another show that focused on a social problem. The laughs made it more impactful and prevented it from seeming too controversial. He continued with an examination of the character of Edith, noting that her energetic silliness contributed to validating her as a believable character. She was also relatable. Similar to the character of Archie, the "magnificent, pathetic specimen to whom she is married and devoted" she was a reminder for many viewers of someone they knew.[101] He also connected his critique of the episode to his thoughts on television's larger cultural and emotional impact. Comparing a scene where Archie and son-in-law Mike return home and start frantically bumping into each other as they look for the rapist to similar slapstick moments on *I Love Lucy*, he gave the episode a historic context and noted how TV allowed viewers new ways to measure the passage of time in their lives. At its best, he argued, television disregarded aesthetic considerations and connected with its audience on an "intimate, personal and emotional level" that no other medium could replicate.

While television had the ability to impact viewers in meaningful ways, that power was not always used for good, particularly when it came to commercials. Shales took a humorous approach to criticizing television advertisements in several of his 1970s columns. In one, he made fun of the National Association of Broadcasters (NAB) code for regulating the content of personal product ads. Among other guidelines, the code mandated an acceptable approach to advertising feminine hygiene products, underpants and laxatives. Shales offered his own suggestions to cover all commercials including rules on food where sausages were not allowed to sing and dance and marriage, as a sacred institution, was not allowed to be undermined by scenes in which a husband and wife attempted to fool one another into believing that dandruff shampoo was baby shampoo.[102] While he made fun of commercial content, he also argued that the technology used in TV ads was a counterpoint to the banal themes and boring scenes used in many programs.[103] The special effects increasingly used in the commercials aired during the late 1970s, he suggested, were "oases of spectacle in an arid medium."

Shales was also interested in television news and his columns criticized some stations' move away from hard news in favor of a softer approach to presenting stories. In a piece on a local Los Angeles newscast, he argued that it and many other local news presentations were filled with frivolity and presented by a new breed of popular TV journalists he labeled the newsonality.[104] He explained that the function of this category of news-readers was that of "picker-upper" who "spread the gospel of everything's-going-to-be-all-right" because as an audience we had to have laughs. Underneath Shales' sarcasm was a call to his readers and the wider TV audience to accept their part in preferring image to substance.

Image was also on Shales' mind in an April 7, 1980, column called "Gunga Dan," where he described news anchor Dan Rather's report from behind enemy lines during the war in Afghanistan. Accusing Rather of making the coverage about himself, he suggested that after watching it, the viewer knew how the war was affecting Dan but little else: "Was it all a story about the war in Afghanistan or a story about the courage and gallantry of someone out of *Foreign Correspondent*—Danny Do-Right, ace reporter?" Rather's story, with its emphasis on his hardship climbing mountains and walking to remote villages over several days as well as his ill-considered decision to wear a blanket and an Afghan hat in order to dress like a local, Shales said, was nothing more than flashy gamesmanship and theatrics. Comparing Rather to an extra from the movie *Gunga Din*, the piece was cleverly titled "Gunga Dan" by copy editor Reid Beddow and remains one of Shales' most recognizable columns.

In a less sarcastic critique of broadcast news, Shales accused it of sanitizing its coverage of Chinese vice premier Teng Hsiaoping's visit to the United States in 1979 in order to please the American government. Shales criticized the reports as cautiously reverential and implicit and suggested that the deferential attitude of the journalists toward Teng's visit mostly likely pleased the federal government but achieved little else.[105] The news broadcasts focused on positive images, a choice Shales argued was exactly the type of symbolism that the White House wanted. This troubling alliance between the television news media and the state extended to public TV, which aired a live variety special from the Kennedy Center in honor of Teng's visit, a broadcast that Shales called "distressingly propagandistic." In his criticism of the news, Shales relied on his characteristic wit to entertain his readers but the pieces were also thoughtful commentaries designed to educate viewers about the relationship between TV news, politics and profit as well as their role in the trend toward less complex reporting.

Contemplating 1970s television, Shales ended his decade's worth of columns with an observation on the medium's social and cultural influence. Viewers, he suggested, should heed its growing pervasiveness as a warning that its role in their lives was becoming more intimate with the passage of time.[106] He used the example of a public TV play called *Home* to make a prediction. In the play, a future society was organized into human beehives with television as the link between hives and what was left of the outside world. Shales mused that as the 1980s began, and fuel shortages threatened to keep more Americans trapped in their homes than at any other time, the fantasy portrayed in *Home* seemed less science fiction and more a quietly realistic foretelling. For Shales, the idea that TV would link society in increasingly more complicated ways as a new decade began was a prognosis to be thoughtfully considered. His work throughout the 1970s and over his career celebrated television's ability to connect people through striking images—the wedding of Prince Charles and Diana Spencer, the Iran hostages returning home, the handshake between President Jimmy Carter, Omar Sadat and Menachim Begin—as much as it critiqued those images for sometimes failing to give people the complete picture. Beneath the characteristic sarcasm: "Television may have deteriorated in many ways over the years but it has triumphed in eliminating the unexpected," was criticism that urged viewers to recognize where TV let them down as well as where it surprised and delighted them.

In a piece for the *Journal of Broadcasting*, Lawrence Laurent wrote that non-review columns "may be the most important work a critic does."[107] In the 1970s, no one represented this viewpoint more than critic Les Brown. In 1971, Brown was an editor at the show business magazine *Variety* when he published *Televi$ion: The Business Behind the Box*. In the book, he discussed the financial motivations that drove the networks' broadcast schedules. What seems like common sense today was a startling idea to 1970s viewers who thought about the programs they watched as products rather than enticements to buy products. Brown's work became an important guide for many of the decade's critics who were starting to move beyond daily reviews and ask harder questions about television's cultural impact and social responsibilities. Several years later he published the first of several editions of *Encyclopedia of Television*, a reference guide that included entries on the industry's central players, short histories of the networks and brief explanations of technical terms. Still considered essential reading by many critics and industry personnel today, it cemented Brown's status as a pioneering television scholar who took the medium seriously and urged his colleagues to do the same. In 1981, he launched

Channels of Communication, later called *Channels*, a magazine that offered an analytic approach to the technological, artistic and business sides of television. Covering the regulatory environment, programming strategies, deals and markets of the industry, early essay topics included the rise of cable TV, living in a "ratings republic," video and telecommunications advances and the impact of technology on broadcast news.[108]

In 1972, Brown left *Variety* for the *New York Times* where he continued his authoritative coverage of television. His examinations of television's influence within the broader context of social trends along with his interest in educating his readers on the business side of the medium, earned him respect among his peers including prominent academic television scholar Horace Newcomb who called Brown "a giant among television commentators in the formative years of the medium as well as a fierce critic who was "always concerned with what television meant for the society at large."[109] His approach to television criticism influenced generations of his colleagues, creating a lasting legacy.

Brown's *Variety* articles challenged the television establishment and his fellow critics to take a hard look at their practices. In a August 4, 1965, piece entitled "Medium Needs Respected Jury," he gave several reasons for what he felt was the dire state of TV criticism. He laid some blame on critics who he categorized into types. There was the columnist who focused on celebrities and all the perks that came along with interviewing them, the one who was in it for acclaim and promoted himself by taking advantage of the community's moral hysterics and leading campaigns that resembled PTA-type agendas and the writer who served his newspaper's commercial goals by expertly denouncing its broadcast competitor. However, he also implicated both the newspaper industry and the television networks for their role in creating a substandard critical environment. Journalists, he argued, were uninterested in accepting the TV assignment because it offered no career advancement, had low status among the journalistic hierarchy and a small salary. As for the networks, they had little interest in facilitating respected critical work because they considered the TV column little more than a publicity outlet where a positive review from a tough critic was a "laurel to send to the head of the station group to show how well things are going, or an advertisement to accompany an awards presentation." It's not until the end of the piece that Brown touched upon the familiar argument that to be taken more seriously by the press, to enlist the heavyweight jury he referred to in the column's title, television would have to earn it through better programming, which did not include "a three-a-week *Peyton Place*, another imitation of *Beverly Hillbillies* and a raft of western melodramas." While Brown's argument concluded with a judgment on programming quality, the piece offered more than a rant against the networks' fondness for repeating show formulas. It was a deeper look at a common complaint.[110]

Going beyond the surface of an issue was a hallmark of Brown's work. In one column for *Variety* he discussed what was behind his colleagues' complaints about the predictability of shows. Discussing the reasons for poorly written scripts, he suggested that a program's dialogue should not be at the expense of its production values considering that the quality of production mattered little with viewers at home unless it was offensively bad.[111] Demanding a high standard for set design, cinematography and lighting while neglecting script quality, he argued, had a significant economic impact. Focusing on rich production details over complex and layered storylines only resulted in formulaic shows with second-rate content, which failed. In making those choices, the networks were ultimately responsible for the high cost of programming. In the piece Brown offered a new perspective on a common critical complaint by seeking to understand what was behind the negative reaction to homogenous programming. He agreed with his fellow critics that shows did lack originality but in demonstrating the part that the networks played in the problem, he made it more difficult for the industry to dismiss the critics' judgments.

In terms of reviewing programs within the pages of *Variety*, Brown had a confident, authoritative style. Discussing the debut of Public Broadcasting Laboratory's *PBL* program, he praised its "sense of vigor" and "journalistic brashness" and applauded its courage in tackling a controversial subject matter (racial tension) with no fear of alienating certain viewing publics or advertisers. But the program had its negative qualities. The documentary scenes did not all flow and the TV screen, he noted, "abounded in talking heads."[112] In a review of *Sesame Street*, Brown called the series "sweet," "forceful," "captivating" and the "most naturally integrated show in television" before expanding the discussion to include a comprehensive analysis of its ratings performance and the implications this had for the show's future.[113] Both pieces showcased his strengths, combining assessment and analysis.

Brown's work at *Variety* also reflected the fact that the magazine is primarily a trade publication so it is unsurprising that his columns had an analytic focus. Yet his move to the *New York Times*, while including more traditional program reviews, maintained his signature approach. In one piece he used a CBS News special broadcast on the Watergate tapes to explain why networks were not willing to sacrifice primetime hours for news programs and how air time was allotted to network news divisions. He pointed out that "the story of the Presidency is least available on commercial television when the audience is most available."[114] Brown took a column on a primetime news special and skillfully used it to inform his readers about how the economic considerations that occupy the commercial networks impact their access to information.

Business interests were again a topic for Brown in a column on the decision by CBS to put *60 Minutes* on hiatus for several months in order to broadcast football games in the news magazine's usual timeslot.[115] In an accessible style, he answered what many of his readers were probably asking: Why not move the show to another timeslot? The reason, he wrote, was business constraints. The series lost money for the network when it was aired in primetime on Tuesdays but on Sundays it made a profit despite the fact that television use was much higher on a weekday at 10 p.m. than on a weekend at 6 p.m. Brown explained that the show was not competitive for prime time TV and unsuitable for the early Saturday evening timeslot but had found its place in the one time period of the week that it was required to give up to football for a third of the year. Basically, the show's success on Sundays was also its failure. Emphasizing the point that television's primary role was to serve its stakeholders rather than its viewers, he nevertheless saw the economic reality as a limitation worth noting.

Brown's highly regarded 1971 book: *Televi$ion: The Business Behind the Box* laid out the differences between the three major networks, explained the ratings system, the complicated strategies used to plan the broadcast schedule and the role fear played in programming decisions. Fear on the part of network executives, he suggested, was related to the idea that they would personally make a bad decision that would effect job advancement and embroil the network in unwanted controversy that could catch the attention of politicians. As a result, shows were chosen that had the least chance of failure rather than the most chance of success. For some critics, including John O'Connor, who highly recommended Brown's book for its "hilariously chilling details," the executive attitude he described was the reason that programming suffered and viewers were left with "making the best of a bad lot."[116]

What viewers saw on their TV sets, Brown argued, was designed as a sales system above everything else. Commerce before communication may not have been the industry's initial goal but it had become its lasting one because the impact of advertising was immediately recognizable: "Product salesmen, who would be turned away at the door, were admitted into every household through the small electronic screen; and the world of business came to know that nothing could sell as well as television."[117] A network would have been foolish to ignore the economic implications because a quality program schedule was not what the critics said it was but what a salesman deemed it to be, one that would quickly sell at top prices.[118] Profit growth demanded that networks reject shows that viewers did not quickly embrace. He explained that the advertiser's power, while not as great as it was in the past when a company sponsored, selected and paid for a program with the accompanying right to exercise creative and editorial control over it, was still influential. In the television climate of the 1970s, advertisers continued to create a positive or negative environment for certain types of shows and played a decisive role in the kinds of audiences that the networks chose to court.[119] The system left viewers with little influence beyond the role they played in ratings because television was between the network and the advertiser who was more interested in watching numbers and charts than a show. The public was merely part of a transaction. Within television's daily commerce, it was not actually interested in the business of communications. It was in the business of delivering viewers to advertisers: "People are the merchandise, not the shows. The shows are merely the bait. The consumer, whom the custodians of the medium are pledged to serve, is in fact served up."[120]

Brown's arguments were groundbreaking at a time when television viewers believed that the medium was meant to cater to their interests. For critics, the book offered validation for a complaint they had been voicing for years—homogenous programming was lowering standards of quality. By exposing how and why the networks purposely chose program formats that were known to succeed and rejected new or experimental forms that were potentially slower to gain viewer acceptance, Brown made the networks' long held defense that they gave the people what they wanted less convincing.

While the situation was not easily changed, he saw promise in consumer advocacy. Industry leaders and network executives were tied to the system, but the public was not. At the end of the book, he suggested that hope for television survived in the public's ability to exercise their freedom and that freedom was the medium's "time bomb."[121] A few years later, the time bomb Brown predicted while not yet exploded, was in play. In a *New York Times* column, he reported on the opening session of the National Association of Broadcasters annual convention. At the meeting, broadcasters complained that citizen activist groups were adversely effecting their business by challenging their licenses, calling for more minority-interest programs and demanding reforms in children's shows and advertising practices.[122] Perhaps taking that as inspiration, Brown published a book in 1979 that offered suggestions for citizen action to improve programming and to demand that the industry develop a better response to viewer concerns. *Keeping Your Eye on Television* urged the public to believe they could make a difference. With empowering language and examples of how individuals had caused meaningful change, he praised existing efforts and pushed for more public involvement. Fundamental to the movement was the idea that television's impact was universal: "Whether or not we watch television, we are all, one way or another, in the medium's thrall and subject to its commercial imperatives. Television is not a mechanical appliance; it is not a toaster or a Waring blender with a picture. It is an environment. What happens on television is as real, in its implications and its influences on everyday life, as weather, the quality of air, or a plague of the gypsy moth."[123] Television was everyone's responsibility and its airwaves belonged to the public. Citizen action groups were the real critics and their work, when targeted to disrupt the marketplace, could create lasting outcomes.

For Brown, television had the privilege of being the most powerful, social, political, and cultural force in society but the daily press would never offer the necessary support for truly important TV criticism.[124] He believed that the popular press was more concerned with stories on ratings, celebrities and network strategies when it should be performing the kind of criticism that made television meaningful and relatable to the viewer's life and times.[125] His work was based in the belief that the public could not understand modern society without understanding where television fit in and understanding television was being knowledgeable about the business behind it.

As the 1970s came to a close, the structure of television was undergoing radical change. The 1980s marked the beginning of the end for the traditional big three networks. A growing public broadcasting system, the rise of independent stations and the arrival of the cable television industry all put pressure on ABC, NBC and CBS. More challenges to the broadcast networks' dominance came from cable and satellite technologies that allowed for distribution based on a subscription model while new consumer video devices threatened to further weaken the networks' monopoly on the distribution of entertainment to the home. The increased competition once again made critics vital to the networks as promotional agents who could guide the fragmented audience to find programs.

Cable television, pay television, satellite transmission, portable video cameras, home video recorders and video games altered methods of production and distribution, changing the business of television. Politicians were quick to recognize the shift and responded by holding a meeting of the House Subcommittee on Communications to revise the 1934 Communications Act. The purpose of the revision was to create a more open, competitive market for the new technologies that would serve the public interest. The networks, unsurprisingly, did not welcome the proposed amendments, having little desire to weaken their competitive advantage. One executive went even further, declaring that the new technologies posed very little danger to his network's business model. Gene Jankowski, president of the CBS Broadcast Group, suggested that the new industries were intriguing and an aspect of communications that CBS may even want to enter into but he also considered them small businesses and therefore not a serious threat to the network.[6] While some network executives downplayed the effect on their business, other commentators who studied the industry sounded alarm bells. Technological advances, they predicted, would result in less expensive and more efficient program distribution systems across the nation and increase the number of viewing channels available to audiences. The unavoidable outcome of more channels was more choice and this would erode the traditional networks' share of the audience.

For the cable industry, the challenges to the traditional system were nothing short of a cultural revolution. Viewers, they argued, would learn to use television in different ways and to expect different results from it.[7] If a 1979 survey on viewer attitudes toward cable television commissioned by the National Cable Television Association was anything to go by, one of the things they expected was program diversity. The survey found that 80 percent of the respondents saw at least one major advantage of cable TV and it was related to a broader choice of shows.[8] The call for a less homogenous approach to programming was a refrain that had followed the networks since the early days of television, mostly voiced by critics. A potential multi-channel environment meant that viewers who felt the same would now have options. Les Brown suggested, "the growth of new satellite distributed networks on cable television and the emerging markets for videocassettes and over-the-air pay television are opening new worlds of programing diversity."[9] In his view, market forces would compel the networks to change or at the very least start playing the game differently.

By 1985, the competition from cable television had intensified and the three-network oligopoly was stagnating. Takeover rumors spread. When Capital Cities Communication, Inc. bought ABC in March, the deal was the largest buyout in corporate history outside the oil industry.[10] A month later, Ted Turner, the Atlanta-based businessman and owner of the Cable News Network (CNN), CNN Headline News and satellite distributed superstation WTBS pursued a hostile takeover of CBS. Turner failed but the television industry was officially put on notice. After Turner's attempt, CBS successfully fought off other takeovers under the leadership of CEO Laurence Tisch but debt, cutbacks and the decline of the network's news and entertainment divisions marked his tenure.[11] NBC was not spared but like ABC, it was the target of a friendly merger. At the end of 1985, General Electric bought the network's parent company RCA.

Another blow to the networks' hold on the industry was the influence and eventual success of Home Box Office (HBO). When HBO's subscription model proved that catering to target audiences rather than advertisers worked and the network chose satellite distribution for programs rather than terrestrial microwave delivery, other cable networks followed its example and entered the market. The result was an explosion of niche channels. From 1976 to 1983, networks including ESPN, USA, Showtime, Nickelodeon, C-SPAN, BET, TLC, MTV and the Weather Channel, among others, ushered in a new era of specialized stations. Alongside this expansion was another challenge to the networks that history said would not work. The idea of a fourth network to rival ABC, NBC and CBS had failed for decades but with the leadership of Barry Diller and the money and media holdings of Rupert Murdoch, the Fox Broadcasting Company broke the curse. Launched in 1986, Fox's success at targeting the urban eighteen to thirty-four-year-old demographic with riskier programs put even more pressure on the traditional commercial networks.

As much pressure as the specialized cable networks and Fox were exerting on ABC, NBC and CBS, it was not on their ratings, at least not in the early 1980s. During this time, the traditional networks were comfortably ahead of their rivals on cable but the model of targeting a prized demographic with edgier or specialized programs breathed new life into an old idea. The quality television traditions of the 1970s, the hallmark of MTM, seeped into the 1980s as the concept of accepting a lower rank in the ratings table for a higher rank among a highly sought after demographic gained traction. The driving force behind this push was former head of MTM Grant Tinker who was appointed to run NBC in 1981. Tinker's programming agenda recognized the pull of the multichannel environment and his solution was to keep viewers tuned to NBC by redefining what ratings success meant among the commercial networks. The result was a collection of shows that captured both the zeitgeist of the 1980s and the attention of the critics who played an important role in promoting Tinker's quality agenda.

Television in the 1980s

As the shift toward narrowcasting shook the increasingly fragile foundations of network television, the idea of appealing to the lowest common denominator became a less attractive programming strategy. Technology added even more pressure. Along with the VCR, which by early 1988 was in more than half of U.S. households, the remote control changed viewing habits. Viewers could jump between channels, avoid commercials and watch more than one show at the same time. By 1991, 37 percent of all domestic viewers said they preferred channel surfing to watching one specific program.[12] The audience was in control of its viewing choices like never before and among those choices were programs that in style and content reflected the lifestyles of the sought after eighteen to thirty-four-year-old demographic. Labeled yuppies or young urban professionals, they were a representation of the decade's concentration on corporate upward mobility and a cultural category that effected demographics. With the introduction of the people meter to ratings technology which added a remote control keypad to the existing system and for the first time recorded key characteristics of individual household members, they became a quantifiable demographic. It was now possible to know who was watching which programs and when. Critics of the technology argued that the people meter favored young, urban professional viewers because they were more comfortable adopting and using the advanced remotes. It was not a problem for the TV industry, however, since the demographic was the primary target of most advertisers.

For the creative community of television, the lifestyle elements of the constructed category of yuppie were a rich resource. The yuppie way of living included an obsessive focus on career, materialism expressed in home decoration and food culture and women who were equal to men who were in turn, in touch with their sensitivity.[13] Many of these elements were incorporated into a collection of the decade's shows. Some came from writers who worked for MTM Enterprises. Steven Bochco, James L. Brooks, Dick Wolf and Glenn Gordon Caron were a few who found a likeminded colleague in former head of MTM, Tinker, as well as Brandon Tartikoff, who was appointed NBC's president of entertainment in early 1980. During the 1981-1982 season, Tartikoff's request to renew a mid-season show that ranked eighty-third out of ninety-seven in the prime time series line-up was granted by outgoing NBC president and CEO Fred Silverman. *Hill Street Blues* was one of the lowest rated series ever to be given a second season. It also became one of the most celebrated television shows of the decade.

The narrative that followed *Hill Street Blues* in the press was that Tartikoff (and by extension NBC) believed in the show and was willing to go against the ethos of commercial television and overlook the first season's dismal ratings. John O'Connor noted that the series had an unusual amount of support from corporations and suggested that it was teaching the television business an old lesson: sometimes an advantageous series needed time to develop an audience.[14] While Tartikoff had a reputation as a champion of quality series, the decision had a practical side as well. NBC had been in last place for several years, had nothing to lose and the show was a critical hit. O'Connor called it a "substantial asset" for the network with an outstanding cast and a unique point of view that was widening the borders of the standard format police series.[15] A fellow *New York Times* journalist said it was the top series on primetime and "one of the most inventive and consistently absorbing."[16] Howard Rosenberg, critic for the *Los Angeles Times*, noted that several narrative characteristics including its refusal "to rely on easy answers to tough questions" put the series beyond traditional police show mediocrity.[17] For *Boston Globe* critic William Henry III, the pilot episode was the season's best. Its courageous storytelling was graphic and authentic with fast edits from scene to scene, loud background noise and dialogue that overlapped.[18]

The critics' positive reactions often included quotes from the show's producers that stressed NBC's willingness to allow them the creative freedom they wanted. A piece by Tony Schwartz in the *New York Times* offered an example with this quote from Bochco: "If NBC's primary concern was to protect its corporate image against pressures from minorities, the F.C.C. and special-interest groups, then we felt we couldn't do the series." Bochco went on to emphasize that the series had to be gritty, dark and blunt if it was going to realistically depict the mentality of police with no promise of success made to the network.[19] Using the interview with Bochco, Schwartz constructed NBC as the network that was willing to broadcast edgier shows with little regard for financial rewards. It was an idea often repeated in reviews of the show and one that depicted the network in a way that followed another familiar narrative. Quality was synonymous with the shows that came from production company MTM and in this case, the network that recognized that an MTM program should succeed on its merits in spite of bad ratings was NBC. It was a status the network happily embraced. Yet NBC's willingness to break the mold of industry thinking on ratings had as much to do with its executives' beliefs in the merits of *Hill Street Blues* as it did with their recognition that the show's valuable demographic was its own reward.

For many critics and some cultural commentators, *Hill Street Blues* was a creative triumph more than anything else. If the business logic behind keeping the show on the air was mentioned, it was often overshadowed by the idea that the series was stylistically distinctive from the rest of television. Tom Shales' comments were typical of the discourse: "Is there room on television for a program that is truly in a league by itself?"[20] The answer to Shales' question was a resounding yes, at least in the living rooms of those who were highly selective about their TV viewing. In a cover story for *TV Guide*, novelist Joyce Carol Oates said the show was one of a very limited number of series that many of her Princeton colleagues watched because it was one of the few programs on TV that was "as intellectually and emotionally provocative as a good book."[21] Looking back on the show's first season, O'Connor wrote that it "was being talked about by people who normally don't watch very much television. It was scoring with the opinion makers."[22] The idea that the show had found favor among a discriminating audience confirmed its quality status. After the series received twenty-one Emmy nominations and won in eight of its twelve categories, the wider public took notice but it was its initial popularity among the "opinion makers" that proved that targeting niche audiences was a sound financial strategy and demonstrated the complicated equation between quality programs and quality demographics.

The idea that *Hill Street Blues* raised the programming bar by demonstrating that television was capable of producing art contributed to legitimizing the medium.[23] As critics helped spread the word about the show, the cultural conversation about TV changed and watching it became a respectable past time. The critics' praise for *Hill Street Blues* and for the programs that followed its blueprint promoted the idea that not only did TV have redeeming artistic and social value but it was also experiencing a second golden age. Television scholar Robert Thompson explained the show's impact twenty-five years after its debut. At the time of its premiere, TV shows were considered amusing distractions but not usually thought of as art. The series was a "high-brow show in a mostly low-brow medium ... [that] started a run of quality television that continues today."[24] The run of quality programming that began with *Hill Street Blues* continued with *St. Elsewhere*, *thirtysomething* and *L.A. Law*, among others. Doctors, yuppies and lawyers were captivating viewers and so was a Texan named J.R. Ewing.

Dallas began with little fanfare in the spring of 1978. From the same production company responsible for The Waltons, the new entry to prime-time was a far cry from the homespun family stories of John Boy and company. Dallas was a glossy soap opera that celebrated the wealthy world of the Ewing family, oil-rich Texans who ran a powerful energy empire. J.R. and Bobby, the sons of patriarch Jock Ewing and his wife Miss Ellie, lead a cast of characters in a saga of power and greed. In J.R. (Larry Hagman), the show had created a villain audiences loved to hate. Scandal and sexual intrigue propelled it to the top of the ratings where it remained in either the number one or number two spot from 1980 to 1985. When J.R. was shot, the November 21, 1980, cliffhanger episode set a record, reaching ninety million viewers. "Who Shot J.R.?" became a cultural catchphrase and Dallas went on to become an international phenomenon, broadcast in over ninety countries.

As popular as Dallas was, its serial melodrama did not rise to the level of storytelling found in the new generation of quality dramas. Yet its emphasis on a continuing narrative, intertwined plots and large cast was reflected in series including St. Elsewhere, thirtysomething and L.A. Law.[25] These shows reached new levels of emotional depth. Writing for the Boston Globe, critic Gail Caldwell named thirtysomething one of the smartest programs of the past ten years and praised its truthful depiction of reality. For Caldwell, its power and innovation came from its refusal to deal in cliché. It aimed and succeeded in giving its viewers an authentic depiction of the pain everyone felt in life, both ordinary and extraordinary but in a way that made the hurt bearable. It was, she wrote, significant for television.[26] Los Angeles Times critic Howard Rosenberg noted that it was the characters' sensitivity that gave the show a strong sense of dramatic realism as well as stories that had "rare scope, dimension, intelligence and creative vitality." It played, he wrote "like a fascinating extension of life."[27] Newsday's Marvin Kitman declared thirtysomething the best drama of its season[28] and praised its authenticity: "Everybody can relate to this slice of reality.... You see yourself right before your eyes."[29]

The reaction to St. Elsewhere and L.A. Law was similarly effusive. Boston Globe critic Ed Siegel called St. Elsewhere, a series that focused on the doctors of a chaotic hospital in a deteriorating section of Boston, "the best-written series on television" that drew viewers to its "mixture of social, human and political issues."[30] Writing about the producers' decision to end the series in 1988, Kitman said he felt " a personal sense of loss and betrayal" and pointed to the combination of tragedy and comedy in each character as the reason it was one of the best television shows of the decade.[31] For Howard Rosenberg, it was *L.A. Law* that set the bar high: "There should be a law requiring more series like ... *L.A. Law*." The show, a mixture of soap opera, sit-com and legal genres, was co-created by Steven Bochco and focused on the professional and private lives of attorneys working in a Century City law firm. Describing a scene from the premiere episode, Rosenberg called it "high-pitched, unforgettable, knockout, electrifying TV." His review also repeated the idea that a show from Bochco was quality and NBC was once again, the network that raised the bar in primetime. The series was more evidence of the producer's talent and energy for smart, stimulating and relevant television but also NBC's commitment to a primetime line-up that met high standards.[32] Collectively, these shows disrupted typical formulas, mixed genres and tackled contemporary issues in ways that suggested TV series could challenge and surprise audiences while also relating to their experiences with moments that felt honest and authentic.

While television's content was changing so was the gender balance of the creative community who made it. Women, previously underrepresented among the industry's creative personnel, were increasing their numbers behind the scenes. One of these women was Terry Louise Fisher who, prior to co-creating *L.A. Law* with Bochco, was a head writer and producer on *Cagney & Lacey*. Premiering in 1982, the Emmy–award-winning CBS series lasted for six seasons and featured two female undercover police officers who succeeded in their male dominated profession. The show was the first primetime series to have mostly women filling personnel roles behind the camera. Created by Barbara Corday and Barbara Avedon, women were producers on all of the show's 125 episodes, writers or co-writers on seventy-five of those episodes and directors on twenty-one.[33] The trend of women producers continued with Marcy Carsey and partner Tom Werner's *The Cosby Show* (1984), and *Roseanne* (1988), Susan Harris' *The Golden Girls* (1985), Linda Bloodworth-Thomason's *Designing Women* (1986) and Diane English's *Murphy Brown* (1988). All of these series made their mark on 1980's television but one conquered the decade, drawing in both sought-after niche viewers and the older segment of the mass audience.

The Cosby Show debuted in 1984 in the 8 p.m. timeslot against the popular CBS series *Magnum, P.I.* The Hawaii-based private detective was no match for the Huxtables, an upper-middle class black family—the father is a gynecologist/obstetrician and the mother an attorney—and their five children. It was a ratings phenomenon. From 1985 to 1988, *The Cosby Show* was number one in the Nielsen rankings.[34] At its height, the series averaged between fifty-eight and sixty-three million viewers per week. Cliff and Clair Huxtable were the ideal affluent couple whose conservative family values were represented in their five happy, well-adjusted children. It became part of several shows regarded as appointment television, a popular phrase referring to series that viewers purposely took time out of their schedule to watch rather than mindlessly watching whatever was on. For NBC, *The Cosby Show*'s success not only propelled the network past ABC to takeover second place behind CBS but also raised viewer awareness about its well-regarded but underperforming Thursday night comedy line-up. *Family Ties, Cheers* and *Night Court* all benefited from the show's extraordinary popularity with *Family Ties* (then in its third season) profiting the most, following its *Cosby* lead-in straight into a top ten spot.

Critics enjoyed *The Cosby Show* as much as its millions of viewers. John O'Connor called it a "rare commodity" that works so effortlessly, "it would be easy to underestimate the talent and sheer hard work involved."[35] Fellow *New York Times'* writer Sally Bedell Smith praised the show for its relatable moments and its absence of contrived storylines and clipped one-liners. She felt the show tried to echo reality and succeeded because it was filled with small moments that could elicit knowing laughs of recognition. The family was a loving one but not without an edge. The kids fought and the parents got frustrated.[36] Even *Newday*'s Marvin Kitman, who found little to like about television, enjoyed the show: "It's true *Cosby* doesn't have much bite.... It can gum you to death. But it's ... filled with human touches people can relate to regardless of race, creed, religion or size of mortgage."[37] The show was also notable for being socially progressive in its representation of race on television. Bedell Smith noted in her article that the series broke through the stereotypes "to portray another view of the black family: intact, successful, sensible and funny without the self-deprecation of such series as *The Jeffersons*."[38] The fact that the series was so popular during a period when racial tensions were making headlines made it important beyond television and much of the press coverage on the show reflected this. Critics and commentators discussed the show's social and political significance, interviewing black academics on the subject as well as Bill Cosby himself. Not everyone agreed the show was a model for all black families, primarily because its storylines failed to deal with racial prejudice. John O'Connor tapped into the frustration felt by this minority when he reviewed the show again in 1988 suggesting that racial tensions were non-existent due in part to Cosby's desire to uphold his "reputation as this decade's *Father Knows Best*" as well as his strategy of appealing to a wide audience in order to offend as few viewers or groups as he could.[39] Yet O'Connor as well as many of those who criticized the series for all but ignoring issues of prejudice, was also quick to recognize Cosby's profound impact on television. His lasting accomplishment, O'Connor wrote, was profoundly changing television's attitude toward race by bringing "black upscale role models to a medium that too often tended to use blacks, when they were employed at all, as diverting clowns."[40] *The Cosby Show* added popularity to NBC's quality reputation, as did the success of *L.A. Law*. By 1986-1987, the network was number one where it would remain through the 1991-1992 season.

Earning the number one spot came with a price and NBC was already worrying about how to pay it almost as soon as it reached its goal, knowing that even a hit like *The Cosby Show* would eventually run out of steam. The network understood, as did its rivals, that successful shows often resulted in a corporate mandate to continue the winning formula. If audiences rebelled and wanted variety, they had options. One of these was Rupert Murdoch's Fox network. Fox may have slowly entered the market in the spring of 1986 but from the beginning, it was determined to distinguish itself from the competition in both its scheduling practices and its programs. Of these, *Married ... with Children* had the longest run and the most buzz. An irreverent look at marriage and family life, the show featured Al and Peg Bundy (Ed O'Neill and Katey Sagal) and their two children Kelly and Bud (Christina Applegate and David Faustino). Al and Peg were frustrated by their lives and resented their children. As a family they were the opposite of the contented, harmonious representations usually found on television. The humor was brazen and bawdy and established Fox as the network that was not afraid to be edgy. Its programs that first season were not hits and it was not considered serious competition. Yet the fact that it was on air as a fourth network was a significant victory and one that would influence the television landscape.

By 1988, cable's steady penetration of American households had passed 50 percent and by 1991, the three-network oligopoly faced competition from seventy-four new cable channels, almost 300 independent stations and fourth network Fox. The mass-market and mass-culture business models of commercial television were declining as the niche-marketing approach of appealing to a small, targeted demographic shifted the industry strategy from broadcasting to narrowcasting. Cable's syndication rights to off-network series emerged as a savvy counterprogramming measure.

New delivery and distribution technologies were supplanting traditional systems. Television's second age was well underway.

Television in the 1990s: I Want My Specialty TV

In the multi-channel universe of the 1990s, choice was expected. Viewers could demand their Music Television (MTV), watch the past on the History Channel, laugh it up over at the Comedy Channel, get lifestyle advice from Home and Garden Television (HGTV), improve their cooking techniques with the Food Network and wander the globe with the Travel Channel. News, sports and children's programming had devoted channels, as did specific demographic groups (Lifetime, BET, Univision for Spanish-speakers). The ideas behind formulating network brands were linked to genre in new ways and so were the industry, business and creative sides of the medium as they navigated their way through the processes of program development. With the passage of the 1996 Telecommunications Act, the move toward greater competition was put in motion with the goal of providing more choice for media consumers. Slow implementation, however, allowed for mergers and a consolidation of ownership.

The 1996 Act was one signpost on the road from the Cable Era to the Digital Era. Another was the quick up-take of the Internet that allowed tens of millions of Americans access to what was previously the domain of computer scientists and other technology professionals. Audiences became even more fragmented. The response from broadcasting, cable and satellite TV was to implement business models that focused on how viewers personally used television. Synergy was the new corporate mandate as television channels spread their content across numerous platforms. Adapting content for video, the Internet, audio and print expanded areas of revenue for a channel's parent corporation and allowed network operators to meet their viewers' demands any time of day or night, all year long. Another consequence of the increase in audience fragmentation was that program genres grew from production strategies into sophisticated marketing tools, essential to a channel's branding. TV genres became central to the creation of a network's identity. Unlike previous types of branding, this more sophisticated type was designed to tap into the interests of a target audience and create an emotional bond.[41] In the Digital Era, networks capitalized on a deeper connection between themselves and their target viewers by trying to build an experience that fostered loyalty.

For loyal fans of 1980s phenomenon *The Cosby Show*, an animated troublemaker named Bart Simpson, was not going to convince them to abandon the Huxtables in the 1990s. Yet Fox's choice to move *The Simpsons* into the Thursday night timeslot opposite *Cosby* during the 1991 season was a strategic victory for the network, if not a ratings win. Fox executives knew that the bold move was about increasing network exposure and visibility. *Cosby* easily won the timeslot but positioning the edgier animated series against the more mature show was in-line with Fox's overall strategy of branding itself as the network for younger viewers. *The Simpsons* was part of Fox's plan to schedule five nights of primetime, up from three the previous season, but the effort had little impact on its distant fourth place among the networks. Yet *The Simpsons* and other shows on Fox including *In Living Color* and *Beverly Hills 90210* were well-received among the network's younger demographic which was also a prime target for advertisers.

While Fox was carving out more time on the broadcast schedule with its distinctive programming strategy, the big three networks were finding some ratings success with more familiar offerings. On NBC, the men and women of the New York City Police Department and its district attorney's office were telling their stories on the fictional *Law & Order*. The show's procedural formula, following a crime from arrest to trial through the state's point of view, captured viewers' attention for two decades and resulted in several spin-offs. On ABC, audiences were spending time with stand-up comic Tim Allen who played family man Tim Taylor in the comfortably familiar situation comedy *Home Improvement*. The show was a top ten ratings hit for the network and ran until 1999. Two other stand-up comics appeared on primetime alongside Allen. Paul Reiser explored married life in *Mad About You* and comedian Jerry Seinfeld was a fictionalized version of himself in *Seinfeld*.[42] Focusing on everyday activities in the lives of Jerry and his friends, the show about nothing, as it came to be called, was actually an intricate combination of several plots per episode. The premiere episode in 1989 drew a disappointing sixteen million viewers but the series went on to average thirty million viewers each week. When it ended in May 1998, seventy-six million people watched the finale. At the time of airing, it ranked as the sixth most watched television event in history (excluding Super Bowl games).[43]

With Seinfeld driving the success of NBC's Thursday night comedy line-up, the network introduced a group of six single Manhattan based twenty-somethings in the 1994-1995 season. Slotted between *Mad About You* and *Seinfeld*, the hit ensemble comedy *Friends* drew viewers with funny banter and engaging characters. Closing out Thursday nights was _ER_, a medical drama where the personal and professional lives of doctors intersected in fast paced, emotionally layered stories. The show ended the season in the number two spot, the highest debut ever for a new drama, ensuring NBC's dominance of Thursday nights.

A few TV seasons into the 1990s, more cops and detectives joined stand-up comics on the schedule with mixed results. Steven Bochco and David Milch's _NYPD Blue_ brought edgy police drama back to television and ABC reaped the benefits as viewers and many critics embraced the show. The series pushed network television's boundaries of sex, violence and language, prompting a viewer advisory warning to be posted at the beginning of each episode. John O'Connor named it the top series of the 1993 season, noting that it had brought together a cast, which perfectly captured the excitement and fear of city living in the 90s and that even the show's theme music, "a driving beat overlaid on a dirgelike melody, distill[ed] the inherent ambiguities."[44] Marvin Kitman said the captivating stories had made him a weekly fan and it was a series that ABC should take pride in broadcasting.[45] Ed Siegel, however, was not as impressed, calling the show "minor league David Mamet." It was "full of naughty sounds and violent furies" that were a "regression to adolescence on the part of the producers."[46] Howard Rosenberg thought that while the show did not rise to the level of excellence found in Bochco's earlier work on _Hill Street Blues_, "it benefit[ed] from a superior cast, fine production values and lots of visual texture."[47] Equally gritty but less impressive in the ratings race was _Homicide: Life on the Street_, a critically acclaimed show that followed Baltimore homicide detectives and a series Kitman named the best police show on commercial television since the debut of _Hill Street Blues_.[48] The CBS network's contribution to the line-up of police shows was _Burke's Law_ about a millionaire cop and _Diagnosis Murder_, featuring Dick Van Dyke as a curious coroner. The coroner outlasted the millionaire to become a fixture on the network's schedule. On Fox, the detective show took a different approach by featuring two FBI agents who investigated strange occurrences. _The X-Files_ used the popularity of unexplained phenomenon and the idea that shadowy forces in the government knew more than they revealed to weave a conspiracy story. With one agent a believer and one a skeptic, partners Fox Mulder (David Duchovny) and Dana Scully's (Gillian Anderson) interactions kept the storylines balanced and intriguing.

The debut of _The X-Files_ happened at the same time that the Internet was expanding so fans of the show could take advantage of digital connections. Online interactions made the show accessible in new ways and also allowed the Fox network to use the promotional potential those online connections offered. For some media scholars, the show marked the beginning of cult television's association with quality. In this conception, cult status was about discovering a quality show outside the mainstream and assigning it value.[49] Shows that were given cult status were another way that television was made to be more legitimate in the 1990s. Fans of *The X-Files* created a discourse of quality around the show that suggested that watching (some) television was a valuable way to spend time.

The type of fan investment seen with *The X-Files* began a few years prior with the series *Twin Peaks*, a show hailed by *Time* critic Richard Zoglin as "the most hauntingly original work ever done for American TV."[50] Kitman called it "stunning for a TV mystery" with a "slow, hypnotic movement ... like being in a dream that couldn't be forgotten upon waking."[51] The show debuted on Sunday, April 8, 1990, capturing an average of 33 percent of the audience before moving to Thursdays opposite the highly successful situation comedy *Cheers*. Holding its own against *Cheers*, the show earned thirteen Emmy nominations, two Golden Globe wins and an online fan community that was often described as cultish. The Internet fandom was unsettling to co-creator Mark Frost who, looking back in 2010, remembered it this way: "Honestly, the most annoying and troublesome aspect of making the show was dealing with that entire segment of response to it, because it was so unrelated to the actual work itself. The Internet was in its infancy and I remember someone coming in and plopping down like 500 pages of transcripts from Internet chat rooms and being absolutely stunned."[52] Frost may have been annoyed by the intense online fan response to his show but it gave the series a status that suggested it was the exception in an otherwise underwhelming TV landscape.

In the popular press, *Twin Peaks* was often touted as being unlike anything ever broadcast on television. Joyce Millman, a finalist for the Pulitzer Prize in criticism in 1989 and 1991, noted in her 1990 review that there had never been a series on primetime "as rich in hidden meanings." She argued that the series was the first created to be recorded and made to be viewed using freeze frames and the instant replay button. It changed TV by creating a new genre based on the technology of the time.[53] The show's singularity was also tied to the outsider status of its creator David Lynch, a filmmaker known for pushing the boundaries of sex and violence in his work. The fact that Lynch could get a show made on television was used as a way to distinguish *Twin Peaks* from the rest of TV. Richard Zoglin, writing for *Time*, noted that the show was a rarity because Lynch was the opposite of the corporate establishment in charge of network TV. He summarized the situation for his readers: An offbeat film director persuaded a network to let him make a primetime show that they agreed would confuse many of their viewers but decided to broadcast anyway. It was a scenario, he quipped, that was "enough to restore one's faith in television."[54] *Entertainment Weekly's* coverage of the show had a similar tone: "Prime-time network TV would seem off-limits to a purist like Lynch, what with the hang-ups of standards-and-practices departments and commercials cutting minute by minute into his filmic vision."[55] Gail Caldwell said Lynch was "so guileless and subversive at once that he's the perfect double agent for popular culture." It was the filmmaker's exceptionally artful vision and detailed combination of light and darkness that made *Twin Peaks* such a profound departure for television.[56] When television critics discussed Lynch as a TV outsider while simultaneously praising the show, they helped to legitimize the medium. Here was a show that was different from and more valuable than most television, which in turn elevated it as a whole.

The critical hype surrounding the uniqueness of *Twin Peaks* also recognized the show's relationship to traditional genres. Caldwell's review noted that the series played off some standard conventions of smart television drama. Yet, it was still unique enough to earn the distinction postmodern Gothic, despite its obvious relationship to mystery and soap opera conventions.[57] It was the show's relationship to typical TV genres that Lynch and Frost discussed in interviews. In Zoglin's review of the series, Frost, a former *Hill Street Blues* writer, stated that he hoped the show would appeal to "a coalition of people who may have been fans of *Hill Street, St. Elsewhere* and *Moonlighting*, along with people who enjoyed the nighttime soaps."[58] Lynch was quoted in the *Boston Globe* saying *Twin Peaks* was "a regular television show."[59]

A regular television show or a singular triumph, the effusive praise for *Twin Peaks* was tempered as it settled into its lower rated second season but even at the height of the critics' love affair with the series, some pointed out the economic logic behind the show's existence. *Entertainment Weekly* critic Mark Harris noted that the network's interest in *Twin Peaks* was a business decision to stem the flow of viewers turning to cable and pay channels. After outlining declining audience numbers across all networks, the piece suggested that ABC's choice to take a chance on a show outside the mainstream may be a future reality for network television: "But ABC's gamble on *Twin Peaks* represents more than an attempt to lure disaffected viewers by replacing the schlock of the old with the shock of the new. It could foretell a decade in which network television programmers will have to face many more excursions into the unknown."[60] The viewpoint stressed that riskier programming choices were about more than bringing back a segment of the viewership. It was a financial reality for a network's commercial survival.

While he stressed *Twin Peak's* impact on the economic interests of the medium, Harris' comments on the series were also part of a larger critics' conversation that suggested television might be headed in a new and improved direction aesthetically.[61] In one article, the series was grouped with other programs and cable channels as a sign that TV was no longer a wasteland. *The Village Voice* wrote about *Twin Peaks,* the Fox network and MTV in a 1990 piece on "Rad TV" and asked: "How can it be that TV—so recently reviled as the boob tube—is suddenly hip?"[62] In another, *Twin Peaks* was singled out at as a teachable moment for television executives. Critic Ed Siegel noted that a lesson could be learned from the series' performance against *Cheers* that even a network executive would be capable of understanding. He argued that in a time of multiple choices, cable and home video, the way to be distinct was to be bold and offer the public unique shows: "If you give them something different, if you build it creatively, they will come."[63] Analyzing the show twenty years after its debut, critic Michael Giltz wrote that the show was the forerunner of many trends including film directors working in television, complex storylines that last several seasons, intense online fandom and "the creative risk taking that everyone from major networks to tiny cable channels must dare in order to survive."[64] For some critics, the innovation behind *Twin Peaks* was not only capable of expanding all of television's creative possibilities but was also necessary for the commercial networks' economic viability.

In the 1990s, critics helped to legitimize television by promoting the idea that the quality of certain shows rendered them unlike anything else offered on the program schedule. The idea was that specific series elevated television because they did not resemble it. Cult fandom added to this process of legitimization as did technological advances that blurred the boundaries between media. Content moved across platforms and television became harder to distinguish from film, the Internet and other digital forms. In this way, TV could more easily share or even upset the cultural status of those media.[65] It was not too long before the industry began to use the growing legitimization of television as a promotional tool. Cable channels, interested in distinguishing themselves from their broadcast rivals, played on the idea of quality by boasting that their programming was better than TV. Bravo ran *Twin Peaks* in 1993 with the slogan: TV too good for TV.[66] In 1996, HBO's tagline, "It's not TV. It's HBO," used an anti-television pitch to promote its original programming and to take advantage of the elevation of the medium that was occurring in the popular press at the time. Stressing the idea that its content was different from standard network products, the slogan positioned HBO as a higher art form than the rest of television; a brand that gave viewers content they could not find elsewhere. The marketing had a financial component—if the channel wanted subscribers to pay for content every month, it had to convince them that what they received was worth their money—but it also played on the idea of quality TV that was circulating in the press. By promoting itself as the channel that gave viewers an exclusive television experience with original programs that took risks and pushed boundaries (unlike broadcast TV), HBO successfully associated itself with recognizable features of quality.

HBO promoted its not TV message in aggressive marketing campaigns and the popular press followed. TV critic Mike Duffy, writing for the *Boston Globe* in 1997, told his readers that HBO had "firmly established itself as an imaginative provider of some of television's best and most adventurous original programming" before adding that the channel's original movies and series were provocative and high quality.[67] The piece included comments from then president of HBO original programming Chris Albrecht, who made sure the channel's exclusivity message was heard: "The networks make movies to get ratings. We make our movies to get awards and critical acclaim and please our audience. We can keep our eye on the quality.... We only have to make our subscribers happy. And we're doing that."[68] Albrecht tied the idea of subscriber satisfaction to the channel's quality programming, reasserting the message that HBO was the place where viewers came to experience television as a form of art.[69] The series that came to be closely associated with the channel's anti-television version of quality TV was *The Sopranos*.

The Sopranos premiered on HBO in 1999 with a thirteen-episode season. The ratings for its first season finale translated to roughly nine million viewers, the largest number of viewers for an original series in the history of HBO at that time. A hit with the channel's subscribers, the show was also a favorite of the critics who praised the story of a New Jersey Mafia boss experiencing an emotional crisis. Howard Rosenberg called it "the best reason to own a TV set"[70] while Caryn James at the *New York Times* wrote that it had accomplished an almost impossible victory by being "an ambitious artistic success, the best show of this year and many others" and that rare series that audiences not only discussed but got excited about watching.[71] Marvin Kitman wrote about his love for the show, noting that it was *everything* he looked for in a drama.[72] *New York Daily News* critic David Bianculli called it the "first gotta-love, gotta-watch" TV show of 1999.[73]

Critics praised the show for the many ways it was beyond TV, feeding the idea that HBO was the home to quality programming that existed outside the boundaries of broadcast TV. Rosenberg wrote that the show elevated pulp fiction to art and compared the choices of series creator David Chase to those of filmmaker Francis Ford Coppola, suggesting that Chase balanced the multiple views of a criminal subculture similar to the way Coppola approached the characters in the *Godfather* movies.[74] The idea that the series was similar to other art forms was repeated in a *New York Times* review that called the characters and events "of Dickensian dimension and color." In the review, the show was not television. It was a megamovie and comparable to "such seminal works as 'Berlin Alexanderplatz' (1980), Rainer Werner Fassbinder's 15½ hour adaptation of Alfred Doblin's epic 1929 German novel."[75] Pondering the reasons for the show's magic, *Boston Globe* critic Matthew Gilbert, noted that each episode felt like a short film, with no artificial highs to lead into commercial breaks.[76] It was, he concluded, "a show for viewers who want an alternative to TV dramas that too often ask us to accept oversimplification and feel-good-ism." In this case, the alternative could only be found on HBO. Caryn James argued that on network television, the series would be lessened and could only appear on cable TV.[77] In an earlier review, Gilbert suggested that the scripts were "the sort of writing you'll find only on cable channels like HBO, not simply because the language is authentic but because the themes are as unsettling as they are intelligent.... The show has cemented HBO's reputation as the home of groundbreaking series."[78] In a piece on *The Sopranos* and other HBO series including *Sex and the City* and *Oz*, *Newsweek* declared that the channel's shows were fundamentally different from most broadcast television because they were "smarter, edgier, better written and better acted" and went "boldly into places the networks fear[ed] to tread."[79]

For creator David Chase, the only home for the show was HBO, an idea he repeated often in the press. In the introduction to *The Sopranos Scriptbook*, Chase said that the show's complexity and unique pace were only possible on HBO.[80] In an interview with the *New York Times*, he commented that a commercial network would not have permitted the level of violence necessary to achieve his vision for the show or Tony Soprano, its main character: "I just know they would never sit still for Tony being this ruthless guy. I know they would have tried to make it that, on the side, he's helping the F.B.I. find the guys who blew up the World Trade Center. That claptrap. That would have been horrible."[81] In the same piece, Brad Grey, the head of the studio that owned the rights to the show admitted that he made a mistake when he initially offered the series to the Fox network which rejected it: "The truth is I was wrong. You could never have made this at Fox or any other network." The executives at HBO were happy to add to the rhetoric. Pointing out various risky decisions the channel made that the networks were not willing to consider, including shooting the series in New Jersey, allowing Chase to direct the pilot and casting James Gandolfini as Tony, head of programming Chris Albrecht noted in a separate *New York Times* article that HBO's business model was important because the other networks would have included commercials and fundamentally altered the show's dynamic.[82]

Within a few years, some of the networks and basic cable stations were taking cues from HBO, promoting series as equally edgy and complex to those on the subscription service. The president of FX told *Advertising Age* that his network did not feel that "the HBOs and Showtimes have a monopoly on compelling, quality adult programming."[83] When FX debuted *The Shield* in 2002, a series about a cop who often sought justice outside the law, *TV Guide* critic Matt Roush wrote that the show was "a breakthrough in commercially supported television—it really looks like pay cable. It's the closest show yet to come in the wake of *The Sopranos*."[84] Roush's comparison follows the network's lead in appropriating the HBO brand of quality television. It also distinguishes the show from commercial TV while at the same time applauding an advertiser-supported network for airing it.

When critics praised *Twin Peaks*, *The Sopranos* and other series during the 1980s and 1990s as quality, their judgment fed into a larger legitimization process that validated television. Instead of certain programs being an exception to the general dismal state of the medium, shows including *The Sopranos* were proof that television was capable of being an art form in its own right.[85] Critics still maintained familiar hierarchies within their evaluations of programs (soap operas, for example, were low on the hierarchy) but the shows that were judged to be *not* TV elevated the medium. Artier or edgier series on narrowcast networks like Fox and niche market subscriber supported networks like HBO and Showtime also heightened interest in the criticism that recognized and assessed them as quality. When critics discussed the complexity of storylines and characters on these shows, they took on the role of connoisseur as television became more respectable.

Critics of the 1980s and 1990s

In the opening essay to *The Camera Age*, Michael Arlen's 1981 collection of *New Yorker* pieces written between 1976 and 1980, he lays out the impact of television's images: "For some time, we have been surrounded by camera images, and in the past decade we have started to actually live by them: to revere what the camera reveres, to see what the camera sees, to be guided by what the camera shows us."[86] Arlen was writing at the beginning of the cable era when the power of the camera's images was growing across multiple channels. Like the advent of previewing, the emphasis on investigative journalism after Watergate, the formation of the TCA and other technological and industrial factors, the post-network television landscape once again shifted the role of critics. The increased number of programs across cable channels and subscriber networks, as well as the changes in how viewers watched shows meant that critics had to rethink how they chose which series to cover. As a result, the work of critics was more diverse than during the three-network era when they were likely to review the same shows. More content choice for critics and viewers meant more competition for the networks. Responding to the pressure, networks looked to critics as extensions of their promotions departments but unlike in the past when they needed critics to first, promote the medium for the purposes of social uptake and later, to draw viewers away from the shows of only two competitors, the networks now depended on them for something more basic: to help audiences find their programs among the multichannel TV universe. Advertising a show during a commercial break on their own airwaves was no longer an effective strategy for the networks because the potential audience could be watching many other channels. Critics' columns, capable of drawing attention to a show and possibly creating buzz around it, were more valuable than ever. Their work was free promotion that carried with it a perception of authority.

Not all critics agreed with the network's idea of their role. For *Boston Globe* TV critic William Henry III, people looked to him to make sense of their viewing experience because programs were not of great literary value but rather more significant as political or sociological representations.[87] He believed that television shows were a mirror that metaphorically reflected social and cultural realities. He did not view his work as a way to influence viewers to demand higher quality programs. Rather, he wanted his criticism to help his readers more fully understand and deal with the television that they were going to watch.[88] His style was thoughtful and engaging, informative and often entertaining. He was not afraid to poke fun at the networks or write a negative assessment of a show, even when it starred a television icon like Lucille Ball. His work could be very personal, one column described his childhood memories of TV, and it could be political, one piece chastised a documentary for its depiction of the relationship between the United States and Mexico. Whether it was fondly reflective or sternly critical, Henry's criticism made broader connections between television and culture so that his readers could understand how each shapes the other. His efforts earned him the 1980 Pulitzer Prize in the criticism category.

Henry started his journalism career in 1971 reporting on education for the *Boston Globe.* He went on to serve as an art critic for the paper from 1972 to 1974. He also covered the state house as a political reporter and worked as an editorial writer. In 1977, he was made the *Globe's* television critic and the Field News Service syndicated his columns. He was a founding member of the TCA and earned journalism prizes from the Associated Press and United Press International. He wrote several books including *The Great One*, a biography of Jackie Gleason and *Visions of America*, a widely praised look at the 1984 election campaign. His TV documentary on director Bob Fosse was awarded an Emmy in 1990. At the time of his death in 1994, he was the drama critic at *Time* magazine and had just completed the book *Visions of Elitism.*

In columns for the *Boston Globe*, Henry covered a variety of topics from reviewing shows to analyzing network strategies to discussing FCC rulings. Often, a review of a series began with how it fit into a broader cultural picture. In the case of a CBS TV movie called *White Mama* starring Bette Davis as a widow who takes in a troubled black teenager, the cultural picture revealed the network underestimated its viewers and assumed they would use their instincts rather than their logic to analyze the show.[89] After outlining the movie's failure to depict believable situations, Henry criticized CBS for imagining the audience would be too blinded by Davis' celebrity to notice or care how bad the production was. Admitting that it was frequently difficult to believe television's take on situations, he ended the piece asking his readers to consider why the network thought the fictional material would be appealing. Maybe in addition to telling an audience what it wanted to hear, he suggested, the movie's storyline should have made them think about why they wanted to hear it.

In a column on television advertising, he employed a similar technique when he asked his readers to think more critically about the commercial side of the medium. In the piece, he pointed out that the majority of TV advertisements were from companies whose products were sold in supermarkets, while the rest of television ads were designed to sell a good public image. Using the example of the company ITT, who ran ads during the children's program *Big Blue Marble*, he noted that before the program, half the American public had a negative impression of ITT. After two years of airing the spots, that number dropped to less than a quarter despite the fact that the corporation had never apologized for various unscrupulous activities, including its involvement in an attempted coup in Chile.[90]

Offering cultural and social insights into viewers' experiences of the shows they watched was a hallmark of Henry's work but he also looked at those experiences from the industry's perspective. In an interview with several producers and Brandon Tartikoff, then president of NBC entertainment, he explained why the industry would cancel a show for low ratings but renew others that had rated marginally higher. It came down to the tone of the storyline and the network's attitude toward a one-off TV drama versus episodic series. A one-time drama was allowed to be downbeat but a full season show needed to celebrate human nature and depict hope through happy endings so the public would embrace its message. Only in this way would the program sell and the networks make an effort to persuade viewers to watch.[91] The commercial considerations behind show cancellations may not have been new information to Henry's readers in 1980 but what may have made them think differently was that he asked them to consider how networks conceptualized the public as a TV audience. In this case, they were a viewing public who only responded to happy endings.

How television shows did and did not resonate with cultural and social reality was a common theme throughout Henry's columns for the *Boston Globe*. In a negative review of *Lucy Moves to NBC*, he criticized the comedienne's slow timing and the show's storytelling choices for being stuck in the early 1950s, which discounted the decade's more sophisticated audience.[92] In the same piece, he condemned NBC's choice to broadcast Bob Hope's entertainment special to the troops in Afghanistan as nothing more than a way to benefit from the public's fear and take advantage of its desire for an unobservant sense of patriotism. It was a criticism that again stressed how television reflected the cultural mood, this time, for the worse.

In discussions where he argued that television failed to resonate with contemporary life, Henry often began by laying out facts before demonstrating how a program distorted or ignored them. Reviewing an NBC news documentary on relations between the United States and Mexico, he started with demographic statistics before assessing the program's weaknesses. He argued that it failed to discuss the morality or the common sense of welcoming to the country all who wanted to enter, except for a few experts and advocates who offered opinions on the impact of illegal immigration without using details or statistics.[93] In a review of *Skag*, a show about a steelworker, he again offered statistics on the high number of working class viewers then suggested that representations of them on television were generally inauthentic when it should in fact be one of the most distinguished on TV. While television often extolled white collar workers, blue collar ones were not the heroes of dramas but rather comedies and even then they were usually figures of amusement.[94] A piece on a show called *The Gangster Chronicles* used a similar format, citing the immigrant backgrounds of many who ran the industry before arguing, with a few exceptions, that television had largely ignored the stories of immigrants, including their economic conditions, difficulties in learning and speaking English, rejection from business and civil service communities, mishandling by politicians and their fight to be considered equal Americans.[95] The review then suggested that choosing a series focused on three gangsters who were all born in ethnic ghettos, no matter how broad the sociological context, was not and should not be a replacement for addressing those parts of our shared heritage that were honorable.

While Henry often criticized television for not mirroring society's trends, he did not ignore the times it succeeded. Discussing the news show *Universe*, he suggested that it had the potential to make viewers aware of how technology is the foundation for much of society and the economy.[96] In a column on reruns, he argued that they were more than symbols of times past. They were a type of social artifact and offered viewers the opportunity to remember their origins and to understand the feeling of perhaps wanting to return to a different age.[97] America, he wrote in the same piece, offered various messages and so too should television.

Throughout his Pulitzer Prize winning TV criticism, Henry was concerned with helping his readers see their viewing experience in new ways. Whether that was by revealing how news producers chose which issues to cover during political convention broadcasts[98] or how dramas represented race relations,[99] he sought to enrich his readers' understanding of television's impact on social and cultural life. Writing his last column for the *Boston Globe*, he contemplated his career as a TV critic and noted that if he had one goal beyond earning a living it was to seriously and thoughtfully communicate the impact of television as both a teacher of values, and a medium that connects a varied and turbulent America.[100] For Henry, television did not always succeed as an instructor but it was one worth paying attention to because it spoke to everyone.

Howard Rosenberg, like William Henry III, was a critic who raised questions about television's meaning and influence. Now retired from his job as TV critic for the *Los Angeles Times*, a position he held for twenty-five years, Rosenberg is an adjunct professor at the University of Southern California where he teaches courses on television criticism and news ethics. He won numerous awards and honors while at the *Times* and in 1985 joined Henry as a Pulitzer Prize winner in the category of television criticism. He is a co-author of *No Time to Think: The Menace of Media Speed and the 24-Hour News Cycle*, a look at the impact of the twenty-four hour news cycle on journalism as well as *Not So Prime Time: Chasing the Trivial on American Television*, a collection of his *Times* columns from 1986 to 2003, with a strong emphasis on essays that covered the news. The message of *Not So Prime Time*, he wrote, was to foster critical awareness. Viewers should resist the temptation to approach what they watch mindlessly or as Rosenberg descriptively put it: "Resist the lobotomy. Don't become a zombie. Don't be swept up in a TV programming strategy like a tuna in a net."[101] He believed that while television was capable of charm, brilliance and amusement, its more mundane offerings combined with its wide reach was increasing the chances that audiences would lose their sensitivity to it and letting it beguile them, eventually allow programming standards to drop.[102] A critic's job, for Rosenberg, was to give viewers the tools to challenge television when it fell short. With an engaging style that used sarcasm and humor to communicate serious points about television's meanings, his work ranged from traditional program reviews to insightful commentary on how TV shaped public perception.[103]

In an early 1980s column, he offered one example of television's power to frame reality. In the piece, Rosenberg used a letter from an angry reader to make a point about TV's influence. The reader claimed that comedian Andy Kaufman's behavior on an episode of the show *Fridays* was in fact real while Rosenberg claimed it was an act (Kaufman behaved erratically at the end of a live show and shoved a producer). Rosenberg's response to the reader's accusation that he was cynical was to quote the show's executive producer John Moffitt, who confirmed that the stunt was a planned improvisation. He then made a larger point: "As TV's capacity to serve and occupy us in infinite ways increases manifold, TV becomes the all-enveloping, all-providing world we swim in. Piped through the same screen, fantasy and reality ultimately become interchangeable and indistinguishable."[104] Rosenberg argued that the audience had become so comfortable with TV's predictability that it equated that familiarity with reality making it hard to believe that Kaufman's unorthodox stunt was fake.[105]

The column was a call to viewers to realize how television's ability to create a comforting reality may affect them.

A 1985 column that gave examples of how network executives were taking the humor out of situation comedies by infusing them with social relevance, employed a similar style to the piece on *Fridays* as Rosenberg used the foundation of programming to build a broader commentary. In the piece, he listed the subjects of recent episodes of situation comedies— child molestation, drug abuse, alcoholism, dyslexia—then quipped: "Thank goodness *The Dukes of Hazzard* was canceled before it gave us an episode on starving Ethiopians" before reviewing an episode of *Benson*, a show about a former butler who makes his way through the ranks of the governor's mansion. The *Benson* episode dealt with a simulated nuclear holocaust and Rosenberg declared that not only was it unfunny but its handling of the subject was so abbreviated, moralizing and severe that it made the danger it wanted to stress appear trivial.[106] Using the episode review as a lead-in, he suggested that television's depiction of life's harsher side supported an academic study by the University of Pennsylvania which coined the phrase mean-world syndrome to explain how those images may convince viewers that the real world was as hostile as the world often depicted on screen.[107] Informing his readers about the study, Rosenberg brought academic television criticism into the popular press while also using it to lend authority to his argument that programs had the power to frame the TV audience's worldview.

In his program reviews, Rosenberg was descriptive and detailed, often taking time to discuss plot points and give insights into the main characters' personalities. In a review of an HBO drama series on inmates that he found compelling, he noted the main characters' defining traits. One used sarcasm to hide his inner struggles while another character was a dreary tough guy loner.[108] In another review, he applauded a British made PBS documentary on the disabled for its creativity and matter of fact but still imaginative, use of real-life segments and film clips to depict severely disabled persons' need for kindness and love.[109] The broadcast, he suggested, demonstrated another power of television—as a means through which society can learn to be more empathetic. While social norms defined what was considered to be deformities or ugliness, television, more than any other visual medium, could bring awareness to individual differences.

Rosenberg's work was often funniest when he was discussing shows he disliked. In a review of a slow paced and predictable CBS melodrama called *Stone Pillow* starring Lucille Ball, as Flora, a New York bag lady, he described Ball's character as "impersonating an unmade bed while shuffling through lower Manhattan."[110] He continued with a scene in the story featuring a naïve junior social worker and Flora where Flora schools the social worker on the finer points of living on the street, including where to go to the bathroom. It was an in-depth discussion, he quipped. He ended with some thoughts on the movie's soundtrack noting that it yanked rather than tugged at the viewers' heartstrings and jokingly asked for an antacid to dull the pain. A drama about two documentarians who make a film on child abuse did not impress Rosenberg either. Describing the character John Ryan, one of the documentary filmmakers, he explained that the TV movie's weakness was that it was too focused on the characters of Ryan and his wife Claudia and not the victims. While various scenes depicted Ryan losing it playing basketball and pool with his friends and in one, Claudia rejecting him romantically, the action culminated in a scene where Claudia asked her daughter if she would like more cereal.[111] He grew more sarcastic in a review of a lifestyle and variety talk show called *America* that starred Stuart Damon, Sarah Purcell and McLean Stevenson as hosts. After declaring that the three "go together like bacon and eels," he saw some hope in Purcell, but only because her forced level of excitement suggested that she "could have fun sitting alone in a raft in the Pacific Ocean."[112]

Not a fan of commercials, Rosenberg expressed his thoughts on them in various columns. In a review of a TV movie he enjoyed, he noted that "while commercials were the economic foundation of television, the ones attached to this particular movie frequently disrupted its tone similar to the way a sledgehammer would deliver a love tap."[113] In another column, he got more personal describing the mishaps of having a floor installed at his home and then imagining how his family would have handled their frustration if it had been part of a commercial. He muses that they all would have enjoyed multiple beers on the patio with a beautiful sunset behind them as they engaged in witty debate and pondered the meaning of life and hops.[114]

Not off limits to Rosenberg were network executives, whose decisions and comments were occasionally a column topic and the target of his sarcasm. In one, he shared his thoughts on CBS's decision to hire then fire news anchor Phyllis George who was paid her multimillion dollar contract despite being terminated. Rosenberg pointed out that while George was being paid handsomely for a position she no longer had, the network had fired over 70 deserving news employees and blamed the decision on the legal bills they had incurred in the fight against Ted Turner's hostile takeover bid. He then suggested that if the network needed a loan, they could ask George.[115] In another piece he talked about ABC network president James Duffy's three-year plan to promote television through a series of commercials that stressed the contributions the industry makes to cultural life. Rosenberg had other ideas, noting that there was no time like the present and he could contribute a few ideas with the assistance of Anthony D. Thomopoulos, president of ABC Broadcast Group.[116] He went on to quote excerpts from Thomopoulos' speech to Georgetown University that he then supplemented with examples from ABC's publicity releases. The long list began with a quote from Thomopoulos who told the Georgetown audience "network TV is a theater without parallel." Rosenberg suggested an example, which was Zsa Zsa Gabor and Morris the Cat as in-studio guests on _Foul-Ups, Bleeps & Blunders_. His sarcastic wit occasionally took a more serious tone, as it did in a column on the refusal of the networks to air a public service message on contraception. Comparing the networks to moral militants he noted the hypocritical stance of using sex for commercial reasons but not using it when it came to the public interest.[117] Sometimes, Rosenberg focused his sharp eye on fellow critics. In a column on the controversy surrounding a docudrama where the boundaries between fact and fiction were unclear, he quoted fellow Pulitzer Prize winning critic William Henry III on the subject, taking exception to his comments. Henry, he wrote, seemed to suggest that if viewers were confused by the docudrama, which took place in Atlanta, they were at fault for being too uncaring to investigate the crimes. Rosenberg's sarcastic response was that maybe Henry was right and viewers should have taken a flight to Atlanta to explore the facts.[118]

While Rosenberg seemingly enjoyed poking fun at network executives and the occasional colleague, he was not afraid to turn a critical eye on his work, in the form of letters he received from disgruntled readers. In a December 16, 1985, column called "Cutting a Critic Down to Size," he devoted the entire piece to quotes from angry viewers. Pamela K. Walters from Las Vegas told him that his review of _Perry Mason_ was badly written and mean because he was a nasty, overconfident person who would surely feel foolish knowing that the show would always be popular with the people who mattered. He was happy to make fun of himself again when he wrote a column on winning the Pulitzer Prize joking that the prestigious award was not supposed to be given to a man whose friends call him Howie and that one interviewer was so impressed with his work that she wanted to know what position he held at the newspaper.[119]

Rosenberg saved his harshest assessments for television news, a frequent topic of his work from 1986 to 2003 and a theme of _Not So Prime_

Time. He believed that news was increasingly favoring a tabloid approach that featured celebrities, trivia and promotion. His columns on the subject often used examples to demonstrate how the news was failing in its role as the third estate. In one piece, he noted that NBC's *Today* show featured an interview with NBC news personality Maria Shriver about a documentary she had produced that was going to be shown on NBC. He argued that the idea that a news program had presented self-promotion as news and was not publicly criticized for it was surprising because it was ethically questionable and an autocratic interruption of news standards. More than that, the choice revealed how the network's entertainment division could exercise its will on the news division.[120] The piece was in line with his philosophy of raising his readers' critical awareness.

Part of Rosenberg's push for critical thinking was for his readers to understand how television frames events. In several pieces on the coverage of the deaths of public figures, he argued that television's coverage turned into manipulative spectacle. On the death of Princess Diana he wrote that television itself felt like it was mourning as footage from the funeral was chosen for maximum emotional impact.[121] The networks use of images, including slow motion footage of Diana cut with scenes of Elton John signing a reworked version of his song "Candle in the Wind," was meant to elicit viewers' tears. It was a choice, Rosenberg argued, that reflected a worrisome trend where newscasters presented the most somber events as a type of entertainment.[122] He continued with a point about the relationship between news story coverage and the market forces that determined them, noting that while some Los Angeles stations would not spend money to send reporters to Sacramento to cover state government, they would pay for news and camera crews to fly to Paris and London to cover Diana's death.[123] Rosenberg's point about commercial considerations guiding news coverage also subtlety implicated viewers who were complicit in the tabloidization of the news.

Unafraid to raise tough questions about sensitive subjects, he made a similar argument about the coverage of John F. Kennedy Jr.'s death calling it slightly "crazy and hysterical ... to say nothing of manipulative."[124] The coverage was not all bad. He noted that an interview with CNN reporter Christiane Amanpour about her friendship with JFK Jr., contained intimate insights and avoided the florid language of many of the other newscasters who reported the story.[125] Yet, it was also an example of a worrying trend where television had created the phenomenon of the wealthy celebrity journalist who covered those within their same economic class and with whom they socialized. Noting the high ratings that the coverage received, he again suggested that viewers played a role in how the news presented it. For Rosenberg, these events and others like them, including the memorializing of the space shuttle Challenger disaster, demonstrated how television provided a universal voice when tragedy bound society together.[126] He wanted audiences to recognize that television was both the nation's "whoopee cushion and its security blanket."[127] Only by becoming critical viewers would they see the medium's strengths and weaknesses. Throughout his career, Rosenberg's analysis of television repeated this idea with wit and insight.

For Marvin Kitman, who was New York *Newsday*'s TV critic for thirty-five years, the medium had more weaknesses than strengths, a point he liked to make with humor that was described by one journalist as "sarcasm dried to a delicate crisp."[128] His criticism, which at times read like a comedy routine with a joke inserted into every other line, took the position that television was worthy of contempt and occasional fascination, a contradictory viewpoint he was skillful enough to maneuver. Kitman began his career in 1967 writing about TV for *The New Leader* before moving on to *Newsday* in 1969 where his column, *The Marvin Kitman Show* ran more than 5,500 times and was also distributed by the *Los Angeles Times* Syndicate. A prolific writer, he is the author of nine books, including one on TV host Bill O'Reilly and two best sellers on George Washington's election in 1789. He wrote a short-lived TV series called *Ball Four* in 1976 and a regular column for *The Huffington Post* in 2008. In 2011, he wrote columns on business, media and politics for the *Investor Uprising*, a now defunct business information website and in 2013 started posting columns on television and politics to his website, marvinkitman.com. One of the longer lasting critics, his TV columns for *Newsday* were conversational rather than authoritative, drawing his readers in with chatty, accessible language that created a sense of fun and collective viewership.

While Kitman admired some of what television had to offer, he more often mocked its creative products with sarcasm. In a scathing review of the eleventh season of *Saturday Night Live*, where he declared both the cast and the writing awful, he renamed the show "Saturday Night Land of the Living Dead" and suggested that the lack of laughter from the live audience was because they probably left within the first hour.[129] Despite being hosted by Madonna, who was a winner, it could not be saved from Lorne Michaels' disastrous production. Kitman's recommendation to Michaels was that he not stray too far from the Manhattan party circuit. Even when he liked a show, it did not escape his wisecracking style. Reviewing the series *Morningstar/Eveningstar*, a drama about orphans who live with seniors in a retirement home, he suggested that it brought together two groups that no one was interested in watching, the homeless and the elderly, in adventures that would induce sleep. He declared that the contrived storyline was like "*The Waltons* meets *The Waltons*."[130] The clichéd script, he argued, was a product of an industry that failed to give viewers the credit they deserved for wanting to watch wholesome TV that was more than simple narratives designed for old people who had one foot in the grave. While he declared the show was not going to make his top ten, he credited CBS for broadcasting it and noted that it was a welcome contribution to the schedule particularly since the second episode was a vast improvement over the premiere.

Kitman was often more inclined to write about what he disliked about television but he sometimes focused on what he liked, including the unpretentious TV movie, which despite having no redeeming social value, was still a fun escape from the real world.[131] He also noted the impressive work that the network news did when it broke the story of the space shuttle Challenger's explosion in 1986.[132] The column pointed out the power of TV to make viewers feel like the shuttle's crew was part of their families but also like characters on a show. Television, he remarked, so often created a numbing effect to violence and tragedy that when it depicted images of an actual tragedy, it was tempting to imagine it was not real. Yet, despite becoming desensitized, the astronauts' deaths were a reminder that reality was often a stunningly sad experience and one that he could personally live without.[133] In a rare somber moment, Kitman made a strong point about the power of television to shape reality.

Kitman's work predominately focused on show reviews but he occasionally addressed industry issues, though not without his typical sarcastic banter. In a column on the lack of creativity among the industry's programming executives, he first blamed the weather in Los Angeles (too much sun) before suggesting that living in the city in general was the reason for mediocre shows and viewers should have low expectations. It was hard, he noted, for those residing in L.A. to be creative when they shared a similar life to that of citrus fruit. The solution to the problem for the New York based critic? Living in New York, of course. It was after all, the home of the golden age of TV.[134] In a more serious piece on the introduction of people meter ratings technology, he criticized the press for its too cozy relationship with the TV industry, although the earnest argument did not stop him from beginning with this line: "After 36 years of not understanding what the Nielsens are ... we will have the people meters to not understand, either. Some people today still think all the Nielsen families are named

Nielsen."[135] Suggesting that people meters might be the largest non-story in years, he argued that the technology would have value for advertisers but mean little to viewers. Going further, he took an unusually serious tone by criticizing his peers in the press for publishing ratings numbers without context and pandering to the powerful Nielsen system. The practice, he argued, was unfair to those critics who were using their work to encourage network executives to think independently rather than have a slavish dependence on statistics that were often misused.[136] The change in tone demonstrated that Kitman took his critical role seriously, as he made a strong argument about the press' responsibility when reporting on the industry.

In his last column for *Newsday*, Kitman remained true to his signature style, starting the piece with "I want to thank television for being so bad. It gave me enough to write about for 35 years."[137] He continued with a list of all the things he found wrong with television and expressed little hope for the future, noting that the current state of programming was a golden age in light of what he predicted was coming. Kitman's mockery of a medium he also found fascinating was a way to engage his readers in a collective call for television to increase the quality of its programming. Underneath a writing style that often came across like a stand-up comedy routine with a string of one-liners was a serious point about the medium's power and reach as well as its responsibility to offer more than what Kitman liked to call drivel. In his columns, he created a sense of shared distaste for the medium. He was, like his readers, fed up with mediocrity, but his columns were more than weekly complaints about the poor state of television. The sarcasm was a way to persuade readers to demand more from their viewing experience. Lamenting the poor state of programming was nothing new in critical circles, but Kitman took it to a new level that for thirty-five years, spoke to viewers across the country.

While Kitman spent the 1980s and 1990s lambasting television shows, his fellow critic Dorothy Rabinowitz was focusing her sharp critical eye on television's place in politics and culture. A tough-minded commentator, her television columns for *The Wall Street Journal*, where she currently serves on the editorial board and has worked as a TV critic and editorial page writer since 1990, discuss topics including news coverage, narrative devices and character development. She is the author of several books including *New Lives*, *Home Life*, and *No Crueler Tyrannies*, an investigative study of cases of false accusations. In her TV work, her informative and perceptive style encourages an active relationship with television viewing. In 1998, the second year she was nominated for the Pulitzer Prize for criticism, her columns ranged from addressing the intersection of television news and politics to reviews of TV movies, documentaries and dramas.[138] Then and now, she lays out thoughtful arguments in accessible language that go beyond a program's storyline to suggest deeper social and cultural meanings. The overview of her work included here focuses on a selection of her 1998 television critiques.

In 1998, a scandal emerged over President Bill Clinton's relationship with intern Monica Lewinsky and television was on the front lines of the story, a misguided choice, as Rabinowitz argued in a February column. She wrote that in the past, the merit of a news story would not have been judged by the public's alleged poor response to it and that response would also not have been raised to the absurd status of major news, as it had been in the reporting of the president's scandal.[139] Critical of what she saw as journalists' desires to keep the story in the news at the expense of producing thoughtful reporting, she took them to task for depending on poll results and focus groups. A journalist she did find worthy of praise was David Frost whose interview skills, she suggested, would be welcome in the political climate of 1998, now that the outlet of the TV interview had become a final refuge for the ill-fated or the politically contentious.[140] She was less kind to Geraldo Rivera whose coverage of the players in the Clinton scandal left her unimpressed. His eagerness and urgency in announcing facts using language better left to novelists ("Ken Starr is squealing like a stuck pig!") was the fault of NBC's news management team who made it almost continuously accessible. She wondered: "Who could ask for anything more?"[141] Rabinowitz applied the same sharp observation and witticism to her program reviews. Discussing a Lifetime network movie about Pamela Harriman, the daughter-in-law of Winston Churchill starring Ann-Margret, she described the result as a coarsely fictional account of Harriman's life and offered a few thoughts on Ann-Margret's performance, noting that her over the top reliance on sex appeal would have stilled the heart and "other relevant organs" of any man.[142] She quipped that the actress's attempt at Harriman's British accent was even less successful and could lead viewers to determine that Margret had a terrible disease that disrupted her speech before they quickly discovered that her efforts to mimic a British accent were "some variant or other of lockjaw."

Rabinowitz was also quick to find the humor in the absurd, as she did in a review of the program *Alien Invasion Week* on The Learning Channel. Discussing Elise, one of the featured abductees, who she described as breathless with affection for the aliens who had materialized through walls to captivate her, an act, Rabinowitz remarks, that Elise was not inclined to blame them for, she ponders a question. Namely, why, if aliens are so intellectually superior and all-knowing, do they insist on choosing such simpleton breeding partners?[143] Her review of *The Practice* was equally dismissive, as it focused on a singular theme Rabinowitz found tiring, despite the show's ability to raise interesting legal questions.[144] The problem, she argued, was that every piece of dialogue came down to the same issue, if a viewer were to accept what the writers of *The Practice* suggest lawyers spend their time doing, which was engaging in fiery debates over right and wrong. There was, she quipped, "not much danger, of course, of running into lawyers like this in the real world."[145] Rabinowitz's television critiques then and now are sharp and amusing, a combination that continues to both inform and entertain her readers.

In a multichannel environment where audience fragmentation was the new order, the 1980s and 1990s were not a good time to be a network. Cable channels that siphoned ratings away and subscription based services that held out the promise of quality programming to viewers increasingly tired of settling for risk adverse stories shook the economic foundation of the big three. Helping to legitimize television through its cable offerings, critics played their part and the industry once again depended on them in a promotional capacity. Critics brought viewer awareness to the networks' schedules but some were successful in bringing more than publicity to what television had to offer. William Henry III, Howard Rosenberg, Marvin Kitman and Dorothy Rabinowitz were among the critics who helped their readers develop critical skills that could change how they understood television's messages and in turn, their overall experience of the medium.[146] Collectively, their analysis of the industry and its programs demanded that popular television criticism be taken seriously.

CHAPTER FIVE

Extreme Makeover, Television Edition: The New Millennium

IN 1995, VIEWERS WERE LAUGHING along with *Seinfeld*, *Murphy Brown* and *Frasier*, exploring space with *Star Trek: Voyager*, spending time with the doctors of *Chicago Hope* and *ER* and in October, more than 130 million of them were watching the live verdict in the O.J. Simpson trial, at the time the largest TV audience for a live news event. But 1995 was also notable for another reason. It was the year that the World Wide Web became broadly accessible and the Internet captured the attention of the general public, becoming the fastest growing form of communication in history. The Internet took four years to be adopted by fifty million U.S. households while TV took twenty years to achieve the same.[1] The spread of the Internet, along with the mergers and consolidations that were taking place at the time transformed television. Legislative deregulation opened pathways between telecommunication industries so that each sector was able to economically benefit from offering multiple services. Independent production companies were sold and networks produced more of their own programs, which they then broadcast and syndicated nationally and globally with little regulatory interference. From the network era to the cable era to the digital era, television survived each shift, reinventing itself.

By 2005, more people were watching television than ever before with viewers in the United States averaging a little over thirty hours of television a week, or watching more than four and a half hours a day.[2] Many of them have also embraced the time-shifting and place-shifting freedom that is

116

a hallmark of a connected society. Rather than signal the decline of television, the unprecedented expansion of the Internet has reinvigorated it. Programming is no longer confined to a television set. Networks have taken advantage of the Internet's reach through broadband services that mean their shows can be downloaded, streamed and subscribed to on any number of portable devices. Their websites are no longer just promotional pages but content providers. Netflix, Hulu and Vudu have joined broadcast, cable and satellite networks, offering viewers subscription based on-demand content, including original TV series, on any device with an Internet connection. The uptake has been swift. Netflix launched its streaming service in 2007 and in less than a decade, has more than seventy million subscribers in over 190 countries.[3] Television, like other Internet media content, is now consumed on the go in an instant gratification model that takes personal usage to new heights. With so much choice, viewers are in a powerful position to impact content creation. Online networks, in particular, understand that innovation and hit series are what maintain and increase the subscriber base.

A popular series also creates buzz and contributes to a network's brand identity. In the present multidimensional distribution structure, generating word of mouth excitement about a show is one key to keeping viewers interested and the critic is a central part of the process. In the saturated television environment, getting audiences to simply find a show is a challenge for the less regularly watched networks while all networks, regardless of size, recognize that even for routinely viewed programs standard publicity efforts are not as effective as they once were. In the new millennium, critics, perhaps more than at any time in their professional history, are important facilitators in the circulation of television's creative products.

Another consequence of the increase in programming is that print based critics must carefully consider their readership when choosing which shows make it into a column. With so many series to choose from and limited column space, many write about programs that their readership is likely to have access to and interest in rather than series that appear on more obscure channels their readers either do not watch or do not have because they are part of more expensive cable options. Premium digital packages and their readers' level of interest in more unconventional series are some of the factors that many newspaper critics now have to weigh against their own standards when assessing shows. The Internet has eased this pressure.

Online venues have significantly changed both the reach of critics and the level of engagement they have with their readers. Opportunities exist to publish blogs specifically for the web in addition to republishing online versions of print columns, which reach beyond their papers' geographical subscriber base and encounter less editorial restrictions. The Internet has freed critics from traditional print constraints on space, deadlines and readership specific considerations, enabling them to write about shows that may not appeal to their newspapers' subscribers, at a length and on a schedule of their choosing. Online criticism has opened an interactive dialogue where engaged viewers are able to instantly participate in ongoing discussions with critics who in turn receive feedback that among their off-line readers, would be limited to those who have the time and the interest in corresponding.

In the vast online world, television criticism has allowed critics to experiment with more casual and informal writing styles and to develop immediacy with their readers across a number of websites ranging from the creative commentary on *Pop Matters* (www.popmatters.com) to the more academic but still accessible work on *Flow* (www.flowtv.org) and Myles McNutt's site *Cultural Learnings* (www.cultural-learnings.com). *TV Worth Watching* (www.tvworthwatching.com), started by NPR's *Fresh Air* critic David Bianculli, is, as its name suggests, a review site that discusses the best of what television offers. The selection is determined by a variety of critics who each have their own columns on the site. *Television Without Pity* (www.tvwithoutpity.com) popularized the recap style of reviewing which is a detailed summary of every episode of a series published within a few hours of broadcast.[4] Other sites have continued the recap trend including *Vulture* (www.vulture.com), *AV Club* (www.av club.com) and *Hitfix* (www.hitfix.com). With the space for readers to post comments, all of these online venues allow for conversations that make critics more accessible. Some even give nonprofessional critics the opportunity to post reviews. On *Metacritic* (www.metacritic.com), users post their reviews next to a curated selection of critical responses, offering a democratic snapshot of a show's reception. Additionally, with new distribution models that offer every episode of a series on demand, online TV criticism offers the chance for both the critics and the audience to post immediately on a newly released season, expanding the opportunities to read and to engage with thoughtful discussions of television.

Television in the New Millennium

When a plane was deliberately flown into the North Tower of the World Trade Center on September 11, 2001, footage of the crash was available because a documentary filmmaker named Jules Naudet happened to turn his camera to the sky while he was filming members of a crew of a New York City firehouse on an unrelated call near the scene. Naudet's footage caught the impact and was the first visual of a tragedy that would change countless lives, reshape the geo-political landscape and become an unprecedented television event. A little more than fifteen minutes after Naudet captured the North Tower crash, network news cameras were filming the aftermath when a second plane hit the South Tower. By 10 a.m. the South Tower collapsed on live television. The North Tower would follow just before 10:30 a.m.

The televised images of the September 11 attacks were stark, real time depictions of terrorism that launched seventy-two hours of non-stop news coverage. The traditional networks cancelled all programming while most cable channels did the same, filling airtime with news feeds shared across channels owned by the same parent company. Setting aside competition and commercial losses, the industry worked together to deliver stories of heroism and loss. By September 15, TV started to return to its entertainment schedule and viewers began to filter back. New fall shows that had been delayed premiered, including spy dramas *Alias*, *24* and *The Agency*, whose subject matter was now more topical than ever. Aaron Sorkin, writer and creator of the presidential drama *The West Wing*, responded to the real life politics that were taking place with a special episode that featured the main characters in a security lockdown with high school students who were on a tour of the White House. In the episode they made general references to September 11 while discussing the international political climate. For viewers taking tentative steps back into their TV life, returning programs featuring first responders, police, firefighters and rescue personnel were popular while sitcoms offered some comfort. Comedies including *Everybody Loves Raymond*, *The Drew Carey Show*, *My Wife & Kids*, *Will & Grace* and *Friends*, with their focus on the funny side of personal relationships, were welcome distractions from harsh realities. Several months into the season, audiences seemed ready to welcome back reality programs that in the aftermath of the attacks felt silly or ill considered. Contestants were back challenging themselves to face their fears on NBC's *Fear Factor* while MTV had a hit with *The Osbournes* featuring warmhearted but dysfunctional family interactions between Ozzy Osbourne and his wife and children.

For ABC, however, the days of soaring reality TV ratings appeared to be over. At the end of the 1990s, Regis Philbin was asking the question *Who Wants to Be a Millionaire* and the answer seemed to be most of the

TV audience. The British quiz show made its American debut with popular talk show personality Philbin as host in August 1999. It was successful with every demographic and became the lynchpin to ABC's programming strategy for the 1999-2000 season leading the network to the number one spot. As the new decade got underway, however, the audience for the overexposed *Who Wants to Be a Millionaire* rapidly declined and ABC tried out a new concept. A group of women would compete for the heart of one man looking for love. The idea paid off. *The Bachelor* premiered in 2002 and the search for a spouse continues to captivate viewers twenty seasons later. On its debut, *The Bachelor* joined returning reality programs including *The Amazing Race* and guess the saboteur show *The Mole* but it was the outwit, outplay, outlast format of returning series *Survivor* that continued to be the talk of reality TV.

Premiering along with *Big Brother* in the summer of 2000, *Survivor* featured contestants who were dropped off on an island with little supplies, divided into tribes and tasked with making the stark environment livable for several weeks while competing in physical and mental reward and immunity challenges. The winning tribe or individual of an immunity challenge was exempt from the end of show tribal council where one person was voted off. In between the challenges and the vote, contestants had free time to fill and cameras recorded everything. To survive *Survivor*, tribe members had to make and break alliances so being opportunistic and deceptive was routine but to win the million-dollar prize at the end, the sole survivor had to be chosen by a jury made up of those who were voted out. With a premise that encouraged contestants to blindside one another and editing that maximized drama, *Survivor* was a hit. Its first season was the highest rated summer series in the history of TV.[5] Critic Gail Pennington of the *St. Louis Post-Dispatch* declared she was hooked, calling it charming and a shrewd blend of several other shows including MTV's *The Real World*.[6] Fellow critics Alan Sepinwall and David Bianculli were also fans with both noting that the series was addictive.[7] The love affair with *Survivor* was not just a summer fling. Viewers eagerly watched the next round of machinations in the January installment, catapulting the show to the top of the ratings and CBS into first place for the 2000-2001 season. Thirty-two seasons and counting, *Survivor* continues to be a ratings draw for the network.

As the decade progressed, other reality competitions made their mark. *American Idol* debuted in 2002 and quickly became a blockbuster hit. Women got their chance to choose a husband with the premiere of *The Bachelorette*. *Joe Millionaire* took the concept to a new and somewhat cruel level, featuring a millionaire looking for love who was actually a blue-collar worker. Only the audience, the millionaire and his butler knew the truth. While audiences were enjoying the romantic misadventures of real people, another reality was taking place on the all-news cable channels.

Operation Iraqi Freedom began in March 2003 with several hundred trained members of the press reporting from the soldiers' perspective. Embedded with various military units, journalists gave live reports from the field but also focused on the perspectives of those who were part of the action. As a result, viewers experienced the political and personal side of the operation along with the press. Television coverage of the operation in the Gulf gave viewers a new way to understand military campaigns but by the end of the 2002-2003 season, the event most were glued to was the series finales of *Friends* and *Sex and the City*. The last episode of *Friends* drew much higher ratings yet both finales were promoted as popular culture moments not to be missed.

For ABC, the end of ratings powerhouse *Friends* was welcome news as the network began Fall 2004 on the back of poorly performing series. The comic primetime soap opera *Desperate Housewives* and the dreamy doctors of *Grey's Anatomy* eventually raised the network's ratings. It was a group of plane crash survivors stranded on a mystery island, however, who really changed ABC's fortunes in the 2004 season. More than eighteen million people watched the pilot episode of *Lost*, a scripted series with a sophisticated narrative structure, compelling characters and complex themes. Philosophy, spirituality and mythology blended with science fiction and fantasy elements to create one of the most talked about shows of the decade. *USA Today* critic Robert Bianco called the premiere a "totally original, fabulously enjoyable lost-at-sea series ... with real characters and honest emotions."[8] Writing for *Entertainment Weekly*, Ken Tucker said the first episode was "one of only two new shows this season at the end of which I was yearning to see a second hour right away."[9] Some critics were unsure about the show's future. Phil Rosenthal of the *Chicago Sun-Times* said it might be a gem but it could just as quickly "go down in flames"[10] while *Variety* critic Brian Lowry said "it's suspect how well the show will hold up without a more concrete sense as to what's happening, barring Gilligan and the Skipper showing up to whisk them away."[11] By the end of its six season run, *Lost* had won eighty-five awards and been nominated more than 300 times across various industry bodies including the Primetime Emmy Awards, the Golden Globes and the Screen Actors Guild Awards.

While *Lost* helped ABC turn things around in 2004, it was CBS who held the number one spot in total audience ratings that year. The home of the procedural drama, CBS depended on a slate of crime shows and expanding franchises to keep its audience tuning in. *CSI: New York* joined *CSI* and *CSI: Miami*. Military crime fighters were tracking down bad guys in *JAG* and *NCIS* while *Cold Case* and *Without a Trace* were re-investigating closed cases and tracking down missing persons, respectively. In the comedy category, a bachelor and his brother were vying for laughs on *Two and a Half Men*. NBC had a less successful season despite three different *Law and Order* series. Its decision to do a trial run of a U.S. version of the British comedy *The Office*, however, would prove to be a good one. Nine seasons later, the series, styled as a mockumentary about office workers at a paper company, would receive a total of 150 award nominations and win thirty-eight times, including a Golden Globe and several Primetime Emmy awards. Rounding out the noncable networks, Fox continued having success that year with *American Idol* and new addition *House, M.D.*, a medical drama featuring a brilliant but prickly Sherlock Holmes type doctor who solved unsolvable cases.

When traditional networks began to adopt the cable concept of screening multiple seasons of a program in the same year (shows included *Survivor* and *American Idol*), it was a sign that free to air broadcasters knew they had little control over the audience's viewing habits. Digital video recorders (DVR) gave viewers power over when and how they watched their television content, forcing broadcasters to change their programming strategies. Live results shows were promoted as event TV but the must-see angle was a limited one. Still, it did not stop the traditional networks from trying to create buzz around specific shows. *Prison Break*, *Heroes* and *Ugly Betty* were all heavily promoted. With the flexibility to start a new series at any time, cable channels looked for a few signature shows to elevate their brand. AMC proved a tough competitor. The home of critical and fan favorites *Mad Men*, *Breaking Bad* and *The Walking Dead*, the network built a reputation for innovative and gritty programming. In the second decade of the new millennium, television also became more diverse. African American men and women are the leads in primetime shows *Scandal*, *How to Get Away with Murder* and *Rosewood*. Comedies *Fresh Off the Boat*, *Blackish* and *Jane the Virgin* focus on family life in Asian, African American and Latino households, respectively. Gay and transgender characters and storylines are featured throughout network and cable programs.

The changing face of programming is one story of TV in the new millennium. The other is technology. Free to air networks, unable to benefit from the commercial model of their cable competitors, had to find ways to make their advertisers happy in a world where viewers could use their DVR to conveniently skip commercials. Using Video on Demand services, they made re-runs of current series and eventually, both free and paid downloads available, along with streaming of shows on network websites. Some series would produce special webisodes or self-contained episodes outside their normal storyline. Original shows would be created for and could only be viewed online. Outside the cable and network arena, new ventures including online subscription based streaming services Hulu, Vudu and Netflix would launch, giving viewers both original content and on demand, instant access to television shows and movies. With the start of YouTube, users rather than networks could decide what programs were buzz worthy by editing and posting clips that in turn could become viral hits. Apple, Google and Amazon expanded into television content through a mixture of acquiring, selling and creating. Revenue, distribution models and traditional metrics used to judge the profitability of a series transformed the TV landscape. In the current ratings environment, numbers that would have meant cancellation for a series on network television are reconsidered when combined with the ratings across delayed viewing and other platforms such as Hulu. Multiplatform viewer numbers are not as profitable for a network as those that represent viewers watching on a TV set but with hundreds of scripted shows on the air, it's good business to think outside of the box.

In the brave new world where streaming, choosing and controlling television content on multiple platforms has now become routine, talking about TV online is one more way viewers exercise their power. For TV critics, this means greater opportunities to engage their readers and a chance to rethink what it means to review a program.

Too Much Good TV

For some critics, talking about twenty-first century television in what one journalist called its *Third Golden Age* was an opportunity to publicly celebrate the medium.[12] In a *New York Times* piece, Lisa Schwarzbaum argued that the new century represented a compelling time in the creative cycle of popular culture. The best TV, she argued, was "embracing complexity, subtlety and innovation in storytelling with an exciting maturity." The moment, she continued, was one where detailed structure and character development in long-form dramas could withstand comparison with the best literary texts.[13] Another critic who suggested that television had become one of the most engaging topics that could be covered in American media shared the sentiment. It could be "as exciting as movies and even more when you consider the long forms TV work in and the number of eyes trained weekly upon it."[14] All this good TV, however, also lead critics to question how much was too much and what the vast numbers of shows meant for their selection criteria. In the past, critics had to justify why their job was important. In the past few years, they have had to explain why they might not be doing that great of a job. The increase in original scripted programming has not only changed the amount of time a show is given to evolve into possible success, it has also created programming tiers that effect critics' work. Alan Sepinwall explained that while exceptional series were variable, there was a manageable number of them to review and they generally remained at the top of his viewing priority list much longer. The levels right below the top, however, were growing increasingly populated, making those series more difficult to manage.[15] The increase and the ensuing lack of time to watch it all meant that he often did not pay attention to or have enough patience to stick with good second tier shows that may have only needed a few weeks to develop into great top tier shows. The viewing and reviewing priority list, for Sepinwall, was filled with shows that fit his particular style of episodic review, demonstrating how television's growth had impacted his work.

A few years later, Sepinwall revisited the expansion of scripted programming noting that the amount of shows at the end of 2015 would rise above 400, nearly doubling the number made in 2009. While the problem of selecting what to watch and review remained the same (a problem, he admitted, that was hard to complain about too much), the idea of *peak TV* had the benefit of increasing diversity in both the types of quality series and the types of people whose stories were being depicted.[16] National Public Radio television critic Linda Holmes expressed a similar idea arguing that one of the benefits of the increase in programming was the wider variety of points of view that originated with newcomers who were "cultivating ground that has been allowed to lie fallow by the holders of all that old money."[17] For Holmes, one solution to the complexity of the too much TV argument was that instead of bringing every program they had to air, networks should only bring their best shows to viewers.

Technology had a part to play in the impact of television's expansive offerings. The ability to create a lineup of shows on a DVR gave viewers control over when, how and what they watched. It also, as *Los Angeles Times* critic Mary McNamara argued, gave viewers ownership. In a November 21, 2014, column called "How TV's Age of Exploration Put Viewers in Control," she argued that the portability and permanence of television shifted the experience of the medium from something most people did to something many people possessed. Television could be catalogued and collected like other forms of art. McNamara noted that a program "no longer fades into the ether or migrates into reruns; it accrues, it accumulates."[18] The result was that many of the conversations about TV had begun to focus on quantity and the difficulties critics had keeping up. In her view, despite the pressure to catch up with hours of recorded shows, the possibilities that technology offered benefited the audience because television felt like it belonged more to the audience than the networks. The audience's sense of ownership through technology may have changed the culture of television and elevated the medium but it also changed the nature of the critique.

The Recap Debate

Television's third golden age may have been an exciting return to quality programming for most critics but covering it was also more challenging. While the volume of content required critics to think about the criteria they used to decide what to cover, social media's immediacy, in particular, impacted the nature of their work. With platforms including *Twitter* and *Facebook*, instant online communities grew around a program and hashtags encouraged an interactive viewing experience. How viewers watched, shared and interacted with television became more social than solitary.[19] When some of those viewers started summarizing single episodes, they disrupted traditional models and launched a style that would influence professional practice. It would also raise questions about what constituted legitimate forms of critique.

The origin of the recap style of critique, where each episode of a series is summarized in detail, dates to 1994 and Daniel Drennan who wrote popular wrap-ups of *Beverly Hills 90210* for an online bulletin board system in New York City. Drennan offered his take on the show's writing (bad), the actors' performances (awful) and the characters' problems (silly) and eventually moved the commentary to his own website. Sarah D. Bunting and Tara Ariano met through Drennan's forums and started contributing wrap-ups of *Dawson's Creek* to it before creating Dawsons Wrap.com. The site expanded and became MightyBigTV.com in 1999 and

Bunting and Ariano changed wrap-ups to recaps. A few years and a new website name later, TelevisionWithoutPity.com (TWoP), made it onto *Time*'s list of the fifty best websites of 2002. Other outlets took TWoP's lead including the *A.V. Club, The Huffington Post, HitFix, TVLine, TV Guide, New York, E! Online, Gawker, Vulture* and *Entertainment Weekly*, and began publishing recaps.

More than summaries, recaps are descriptions with commentary. While some of this commentary is more snarky than insightful, the best recaps make the reader feel like they are discussing the show with both a good friend and a smart insider who understands an episode's strengths and weaknesses. Casual, personal and perceptive, the intimate nature of recapping makes it a natural fit for involved viewers. Recaps capitalize on the changing nature of the twenty-first century TV audience, who, aided by the speed and reach of blogs, online magazines and *Twitter* feeds, are able to easily comment on episodes of their favorite show and just as easily find likeminded individuals to join the conversation. As a fixed space of discussion for those who take advantage of delayed viewing options, recaps have even more appeal.

For Internet outlets, recaps have one purpose: to drive web traffic. Gilbert Cruz, Deputy Editor of *New York* magazine's *Vulture*, noted that all websites had to "play the traffic game" and if he were to remove recaps from the site, the financial consequences would be severe.[20] The economics of engaged viewers suggests that recapping is here to stay but not everyone is happy about it. Alex Gansa, an executive producer of *Homeland*, said he refused to read recaps and voiced his displeasure with the style in a 2013 interview: "This insane scrutiny and dissection of each episode as if it has a beginning, middle and end is kind of maddening to those of us doing the show."[21] A year earlier, in an interview with the *New York Times*, *The Wire* creator David Simon offered his opinion of episode recaps: "The number of people blogging television online—it's ridiculous. They don't know what we're building. And by the way, that's true for the people who say we're great. They don't know. It doesn't matter whether they love it or they hate it."[22] While in the same interview Simon noted that he found *Twitter* useful because the feedback helped writers and creators understand if they had failed to give viewers the clues they needed or if viewers were focusing on the wrong idea within a scene, his controversial comments about episodic reviews caused an online uproar to which critic Alan Sepinwall, among others, responded.[23] Sepinwall commented that while he greatly admired Simon's work, he was very disappointed that Simon felt episode reviews were flawed because they lacked perspective on how a part fits into the whole. Simon's preference for television to be a novelistic medium that should not be reviewed "chapter by chapter" but rather carefully considered in its entirety, missed the idea that a viewer could still express opinions of a chapter or characters or a plot twist before completing it.[24] The weekly review, Sepinwall noted, was not intended to decide the meaning of a series before it ended but rather to offer a reaction to how the reviewer was responding to an episode as it was broadcast.

For critic Noel Murray, the Simon controversy reflected the changing nature of TV, criticism and entertainment reporting. The speed and impact of social media encouraged an environment of more personal communication between artists and those who had an opinion on their work (with not all of this opinion being happily embraced) but the shift toward weekly reviews of TV shows was also about starting a conversation. Rather than harsh judgments, episode-by-episode reviews were "another version of sitting around the living room with (ideally) smart, informed friends, and talking about what we just saw."[25] The success of these online conversational spaces were obvious in the number of comments weekly reviews received on the many sites that posted them.[26] This attention, however, did not mean that all recaps were created equal. Murray commented that the majority of online writing about TV was terrible and lacked the elements that made TV criticism a form of art including considerations of themes, historical context and aesthetics.[27] *New Yorker* critic Emily Nussbaum shared a similar viewpoint, noting that the emphasis on speed over quality was troubling: "I don't think the entire environment should consist of people's first drafts."[28] Cultural critic Ken Tucker, who has written about TV, books and movies for the *New York Times*, *New York* magazine and *Entertainment Weekly*, called it a "mug's game" and argued that there was little chance of consistently producing recaps "without becoming either burned out or a hack."[29] The challenge, he argued, was to create varied aesthetic propositions that went beyond the Internet's narrow range of responses, which he said "ran the gamut from this-is-awesome! blog posts to fitfully edited twelve-thousand-word essays about this or that show's elaborate mythology." Matt Zoller Seitz took a more sympathetic approach and argued that the intensity and pressure of producing a review overnight meant that it was more difficult for writers to self-censor which often resulted in something like a diary that charted the writer's changing feelings toward a series.[30]

Lousy or insightful in content, the recap as a form, had become a template that not all critics welcomed. In a 2011 essay, critic Ryan McGee urged a radical reconsideration of the style. The model started by sites like

TWoP and refined by Alan Sepinwall, while successful, had become so reproduced that it was hard for critics to consider new approaches. Saturating the market with even more weekly reviews did nothing but stifle television criticism. To advance it, McGee suggested that critics lead the way by widening the rotation of the shows they covered, creating podcasts and vodcasts and writing collaboratively.[31] These ideas were not about doing away with existing critical models in favor of new ones. Rather they offered ways to explore options that could shake professional practice out of what, for McGee, had become a tired routine.

Another pitfall of the week-to-week reviewing model was that critics were often likely to get things wrong. Critic Scott Tobias explained that the problem was losing sight of the big picture as any complaints made early on could be shortsighted. A payoff could come several episodes into the season, making observations or predictions obsolete.[32] Limited perception aside, Tobias saw "tremendous analytical possibilities" in the notion of "crowd-sourcing as criticism." For Matt Zoller Seitz, these possibilities were beyond analytical. Comment sections started conversations about television culture because people talked about more than the show. They discussed what may have inspired it, what other critics said about it and what ethical, philosophical, sexual, political and economic topics might be related to the series. For Zoller Seitz, the reviews and comments told people about more than what happened on an episode, they told them about "what life was like on that particular night."[33] The comments section, agreed critic Noel Murray, was a significant component of episodic review and one that often went far beyond the critic's authority. He commented that to a degree, critics were merely giving a space to a show's fans and detractors, where both could make their voices heard and it often did not matter what critics had to say because there would always be a segment of people who clicked on a review only to scroll down to the comment section.[34] Rather than find the trend disheartening, Murray argued it was a reflection of TV's growing popularity with a byproduct that ultimately benefitted the profession in practical terms: "While our film-critic pals have been seeing their word-counts shrink and their jobs disappear, websites have been adding TV blogs left and right."

Job security was one benefit. Another was less pressure to meet the parameters of conventional criticism. Zoller Seitz noted that writing for the Internet meant he was free from the burden of having to justify the news value of every article he wrote to an editor and the old way of writing about TV—via newspaper or magazine columns published weeks or months apart—was "a poor match for the form."[35] The advantages that online spaces had over conventional reviews were clear whether critics were driving the conversation or merely providing a place for viewers to do the same. In the end, television as a whole reaped the rewards.

Part of the critical conversation about the rise of the recap was a discussion about the merits of episodic versus serialized television. Recapping an episodic series offered less opportunity than serialized shows to delve into narrative complexities so many critics chose to focus their recaps on long form series. Murray wondered if critics were paying too much attention to the serialized form of television to the exclusion of the type of TV that the majority of viewers actually watched and challenged the notion that shows having one long story to tell deserved more attention from critics than those with stories that started and finished in one episode.[36] For Tobias, serialization was a key indicator of quality that subsequently elevated the critical profession. He argued that achieving an exceptional level of storytelling in a dramatic show was impossible without a powerful and prevailing serialized component. This element, he argued, was what all significant shows of the last decade had in common and they succeeded because they were continuously moving forward and unveiling new ideas about characters and the cinematic world they inhabited.[37] These shows in turn, contributed to advancing television criticism because their sophistication demanded complex assessments. Murray agreed that serialized drama was responsible for a great majority of the finest pop culture in recent years but worried about the dangers of excluding other types of television. The solution was balance, on the part of both critics and viewers when choosing which programs to elevate and watch. He suggested that it was important to enjoy "the finer qualities of a three-camera-with-laugh-track sitcom and a case-of-the-week procedural in order to better appreciate the single-camera comedies and serialized dramas."[38] To do otherwise risked losing the ability to enjoy the basic pleasures of less complex programming.

The rich characters and plot developments of the growing number of serialized shows may have benefitted those critics who wrote detailed recaps but for Alan Sepinwall, their rise also had a downside, as the art of creating a satisfying standalone episode was being lost in the demand for long form storytelling. With the addition of streaming services like *Netflix* and *Hulu*, the aftermarket model shifted from selling syndicated repeats to selling long form shows. Sepinwall noted that once a dirty word in network TV, serialization suddenly became more appealing to cable and broadcast channels.[39] He argued that the industry was moving too far in an all-serialized direction which ignored the idea that most shows were watched weekly by audiences and even when series were viewed in one long session, the creative advantages of solidly crafted standalone episodes still had a lot of drawing power. Alyssa Rosenberg, blogging for the *Washington Post*'s Opinions section, had a similar view, arguing that the episode format was one of the most important factors in making television a truly unique medium and audiences "should insist that each hour or half-hour of television work well," even if it was contributing to a larger whole.[40] Critic Todd VanDerWerff took a different approach suggesting that while a great episode provided enormous viewing pleasure, the days of watching a series from week to week were finished.[41] Viewing patterns were changing and critics needed to change with them. Program reviews, he argued, should reflect how viewers experienced serialized shows. TV critics, himself included, needed to catch up with the behavior of the audience and begin to watch those series as they were meant to be viewed, in full seasons rather than separate pieces. For VanDerWerff, critics better served the needs of their readers when they evaluated episodes of serialized shows as parts of a larger whole. Weighing in on the debate, *New York Times* critic James Poniewozik took a broader view and argued that streaming had the potential "to create an entirely new genre of narrative: one with elements of television, film and the novel, yet different from all of those."[42] While Poniewozik's piece went on to look at the pros and cons of streaming shows, Sepinwall and VanDerWerff took a more decisive stand. Yet, in debating approaches to criticism, all recognized the role the industry played in determining content.

While the move from broader analysis to narrow weekly reviews raised questions about the advantages and disadvantages of a new style of critique, TV critics were doing more than highlighting occupational concerns. They were revealing how television was changing as an industry and a technology. Columns about the creative strategies of episodic versus serialized shows uncovered industry motivations and gave readers insight into why for example, they might suddenly find that their favorite series was becoming a chore to get through. The technological advancements that allowed viewers to control how and when they watched became as important a topic as what they chose and all these choices filtered into critical writing. Following a show week to week as it unfolded was a different experience from dropping into it midway through its season, which was again different from watching a season's worth of episodes in a few days on demand or on DVD. Writing affective criticism meant considering viewing habits and patterns as much as analyzing characters and plots. The explosion of weekly reviews significantly altered the practice of critics' work but the debates the style started and the engaged readership it created were equally meaningful as ways to understand television as culture.

In 2011, *Slate* published a piece exploring Alan Sepinwall's influence on the field. Generally acknowledged as the critic who brought recapping out of the shadows, Sepinwall is known for his incisive commentary, sense of humor and output—he regularly produces work on ten or more shows per week. The article wondered if the impressionistic nature of much of Sepinwall's work exposed a level of fandom that undermined thoughtful critique. It also suggested that the ephemeral nature of weekly TV criticism made it more suitable as a complement to broad based analysis rather than as a replacement.[43] The fact that critics had been discussing the issues raised in the *Slate* article for several years did not lessen its impact: TV criticism had hit the mainstream.

The *Slate* piece briefly turned popular culture's attention to television criticism as a discourse. Sepinwall commented on it and received 129 comments in return. James Poniewozik, responded on his then *Time* magazine blog, *Tuned In*, that the article touched on larger issues that impacted most people working in media. Namely, how to drive traffic to a blog or website and gain the public's attention without making that economic reality the only reason a piece is written and how to grow an online community without indulging it.[44] At issue in online television criticism, like all Internet communication, was navigating commercial concerns that impacted creative choices.

The economic realities of page views and advertising revenues for critics working online also meant dealing with the dynamics of audiences and commentators. Some saw their role in this interaction as leading the conversation within a like-minded community. Sepinwall suggested in his response to the *Slate* piece that he felt his blog *What's Alan Watching* was as valuable for what his readers had to say as what he did.[45] Others saw value in a community of readers who took an opposing view to their own. Myles McNutt noted in his response to the *Slate* piece that in his work for the *A.V. Club* he enjoyed "the idea of the tension between critic and reader turning into a sort of ethnography of comment culture."[46] Readers' expectations of what constitutes criticism often dictate the tone of their online reaction but whether they believe a TV critic should hold the same opinion as they do or not, their responses have become an integral part of twenty-first century TV criticism.[47] The level of moderation and participation on the part of critics to those responses varies but most recognize that the Internet's democratization of television criticism demands, at the very least, they pay attention.

Chapter Six

Critics of the Twenty-First Century

DEALING WITH THE REALITIES of television criticism in an online environment, the critics featured in this section approach their work with thoughtful considerations of television as a form of culture. Some write overnight reviews. Others focus on broad analysis. A few tackle large trends and big questions. Several blend impressions with commentary and wit. Where some focus on visual analysis and close-readings, others prefer discussing the more practical side to storytelling and character development. Conversational or academic, concerned with politics or representation or gender, all rise above the role of viewer guide. What follows is an overview rather than an exhaustive account of those whose work represents some of the best that twenty-first century television criticism has to offer.

Having made quite a few references to him already, it only seems fair to start a survey of modern day critics with a discussion of Alan Sepinwall whose career transformation from journalist/critic to recapper/blogger is itself a commentary on the changes that have taken place in television and its viewing and reception practices. Sepinwall credits *NYPD Blue* with launching his career, a show he wrote about for a fan site while a student at the University of Pennsylvania. After graduation, he worked as an intern at New Jersey newspaper the *Star-Ledger* where he was eventually made TV critic, a position he held for fourteen years. During that time, Sepinwall's coverage of *The Sopranos* made him the go-to source for post-episode analysis of the groundbreaking series. The success of those morning-after write-ups lead to a popular blog that he took with him when he left the newspaper to join entertainment website *HitFix* in 2010. The blog, *What's Alan Watching?*, went from an extension of his print journalism work to his fulltime job as he made the transition to exclusive online TV criticism. It includes episodic reviews, advanced reviews of shows, analysis of breaking news about TV and thoughts on series midway through the season, all with active comment sections. His 2013 book: *The Revolution Was Televised: The Cops, Crooks, Slingers, and Slayers Who Changed TV Drama Forever* features twelve influential series that together form a television canon. He also wrote an anthology-reference book on the most significant TV shows in history, *TV (The Book)*, with Matt Zoller Seitz.

Widely regarded as the critic who did the most to popularize the episode-by-episode review, he does not take credit for inventing the style, as some have suggested.[1] Still, Sepinwall is so closely connected with the form that it's hard to find a reference to recaps without his name being mentioned.[2] His work is conversational in tone and impressionistic, often telling readers how he feels about what he watched and always ends with the question: What did everybody else think? The invitation stresses the importance of the community his brand of criticism has created and the value he places on their participation. Sepinwall, perhaps more than any other critic working today, has democratized television criticism. He empowers his readers to analyze TV along with him. What he thinks about an episode is as important as what they think. They experience television together.

Sepinwall is a fan of TV, which is almost a requirement for the style of critique he has popularized. Posting morning after reviews on multiple series every week takes a level of commitment and endurance that would be much more difficult without liking most shows being screened. Sepinwall is often the TV critic as advocate, a role for which he has been criticized. In a campaign to save the series *Chuck*, he posted an open letter to NBC executives where he listed six reasons the show deserved to be renewed. In reason number two, which he labeled *recession escapism* he wrote that the show was "always the highlight—and greatest relief—of my day, week after week."[3] In a follow-up piece, he noted that co-chairman of NBC Entertainment Ben Silverman, told him that he was the reason *Chuck* was returning.[4] He also gave credit to other critics including Maureen Ryan, Daniel Fienberg and Joe Adalian who took up the cause and a strong social media campaign that urged viewers to save the series. While the success of the campaign was most likely due to the collective efforts of several critics as well as an organized action where fans made a purchase at Subway, one of the show's sponsors, on the night of the season finale,

Sepinwall's insider status meant that he became most associated with the story.

For Josh Levin, whose *Slate* piece questioned Sepinwall's ability to maintain authoritative distance in part, by reviving the controversy over his efforts to save *Chuck*, (as well as a guest cameo he did on *Community*), the popular critic had altered television criticism by sacrificing a necessary level of objectivity.[5] Sepinwall's perceived lack of objectivity goes back to debates about his style of critique. Because episodic reviews naturally appeal to a fan base that eagerly wait for and closely watch the shows in question, they privilege intimate readings of a show and for some detractors, this tone dulls the critical discourse. The negative reaction to Sepinwall as a fan of *Chuck* was, in turn, tied to the easy attachment those who write episodic reviews often develop for the shows they cover. Yet Sepinwall's authority is also tied to his readers' knowledge of what he likes and his episodic pieces respond to readers' viewing practices.

Sepinwall recognizes the hazards of writing for an audience of hardcore fans and has admitted that his blog readers want him to be "a cheerleader for what they're a cheerleader for."[6] In his response to Levin's accusations, he addressed his lack of objectivity saying that claiming a review was not impartial "seems to miss the whole point of the subjective art form of criticism."[7] He acknowledged that his passion for a show might cause some to feel that the line is too easily blurred between critic and supporter and noted that it has caused readers to react negatively if they feel he is not agreeing with them.[8] He claimed, however, that his style would not change and characteristically opened the discussion to his readers.

Sepinwall's posts, the longer ones can number close to 2000 words, are a mixture of detailed plot review, critical analysis and opinion. He uses first person to express his feelings on a scene, a character or a plot point, often writing phrases such as "I feel like," "What is still concerning me" and "I get the sense that." The tone brings the reader into his confidence, as if they were discussing an episode of their favorite show while having coffee with a friend. Expressing his joy or frustration over detailed narrative developments also speaks to his readers' fandom and his own personal stake in the programs he reviews. Talking about a particular scene in a 2010 review of a *Chuck* episode, he wrote: "I get the sense that she has no expectations of Morgan ever amounting to anything; she's just making Casey suffer.... And that's amusing to me."[9] Sepinwall might be a fan but he is also a critic and he infuses his work with analysis that goes beyond feelings even while he expresses them. In a review of *Friday Night*

Lights' season four finale, he connected his pleasure with an ending viewers *deserved* to a discussion of the show's key themes. In this case it was the healing power of sports which might not alleviate the problems a community faces but was capable of offering a "distraction, and a sense of common purpose, and a feeling of uplift in the worst of times."[10] The lengthy post continued with an overview of the highs and lows of the fourth season as they related to the finale as well as a thoughtful take on predictable storylines.

While his writing may occasionally include minutiae that only diehard fans would find interesting—reviews might list pop culture references or notes on the soundtrack—Sepinwall's work also communicates a sense of the personal and cultural importance of the subject. A review of episode two, season five of *The Wire* referred to a commonly held belief that David Simon used his former bosses as stand-ins for unflattering characters. Sepinwall pointed his readers to a piece written about the subject in the *Columbia Journalism Review* and argued that it was worth seeking out because it was "less about the he-said/he-said of what happened at the *Sun* a dozen years ago" and more about conflicting ideas over how to depict the difficulties of the urban poor, which in his view, was the main point of that particular season.[11] The review went on to connect narrative details to the real life debates that shaped the episode's storyline. In this way, Sepinwall gave his readers a behind-the-scenes look at the personality of David Simon but also broadened their knowledge of the episode's social significance.

There is a strong sense of community around Sepinwall. Reader responses are routinely thoughtful and often respond to him directly, as if writing to a friend: "Alan, you are far too kind," "Alan, I agree with you." It is a tone that he encourages with his end of column question but also one that he has cultivated through a passionate engagement with television. Sepinwall is open about the personal rather than professional investment he has in certain shows. He has said that his attachment to a series is sometimes "an ephemeral, hard-to-explain connection" that makes it "if not critic-proof, then critic-besides-the-point."[12] Yet his feelings do filter into his criticism: "I would say for instance, that 'Homicide' at its best was better than 'NYPD Blue' at its best, but I never felt quite the level of affection for those guys and therefore took a tougher eye when that show began to slip than when 'NYPD' did."[13] Being transparent about his preferences, however, is not the same as over attachment. Rather, Sepinwall is responsive, painstakingly detailed and deeply invested. It's an approach that fits the energy of television's online community and has made him one of the most popular and influential critics writing today.

Where Sepinwall is primarily concerned with the more detailed and practical side of characterization and storytelling, fellow critic Matt Zoller Seitz, who co-wrote the column *All TV* with Sepinwall while at the *Newark Star-Ledger*, is focused on visual and literary analysis of television. A film critic for more than twenty years, Zoller Seitz has been covering television and film simultaneously for more than fifteen years. He is the editor in chief of RogerEbert.com, author of the books *The Wes Anderson Collection, The Oliver Stone Experience* and *TV (The Book)*, an anthology co-written with Sepinwall. The TV critic for *New York Magazine* and Vulture.com and former TV critic of *Salon*, he has written, produced or edited hundreds of hours of video essays about film history and style and was a finalist for the 1994 Pulitzer Prize in film criticism. His television work covers current and classic series and is a combination of longer thought pieces and shorter reviews of single episodes. He demonstrates broad knowledge of not only television history but also visual styles and storytelling models that together form a collection of informative and intellectual criticism that is both accessible and engaging.

In many of his columns, Zoller Seitz discusses the ways that scripted TV and film intertwine. Discussing a special Christmas episode of *Glee* he noted: "The filmmaking was vintage 1963, letting action play out in waist-up medium shots and head-to-toe long shots with a minimum of cutting."[14] In a review of *Boardwalk Empire*, a show he labeled "a modern version of default old-movie storytelling," he provided the reader with a cinematic context for an actor's performance: "Pitt's acting ... seemed pitched somewhere between 1940s-era Joel McCrea or Dana Andrews and the kinds of performances that Montgomery Clift gave in the 1950s."[15] A column on *American Horror Story* made the connection between scripted TV and theatrical cinema even clearer as he listed films and earlier TV that the series borrowed from as well as its relationship with early 1960s movies. The result, he concluded, was singular: "If it were possible to take a classic early '60s camp horror movie, feed it massive amounts of cocaine, then turn it into a basic cable drama, the result might look like this."[16] While *American Horror Story* spoke to 1960s horror films, *Hannibal* combined cinematic and literary qualities that were not natural to the horror film but "to the most sophisticated third-person omniscient novels. It is literary and cinematic at the same time.... It represents a major step forward in scripted TV's artistic evolution."[17] Zoller Seitz's celebration of the literary and cinematic merits of series is one part of his critical voice. The other part is exploring how television reflects contemporary culture.

Many of Zoller Seitz's pieces are concerned with the relationship between television's images and today's social climate. In a column on the HBO series *Enlightened*, he noted that the show's tone "feels like a definitive statement on a troubled era."[18] He explained that the series' corporate intrigue was central to the nation's *moral crisis* and commented that it posed a tough dilemma: "Do we continue to accept business as usual out of a weary belief that change is just too hard? Or do we say something, and do something, even if it means enduring humiliation and abuse?" In a piece on *Homeland*, he tied the series' themes to America's preoccupation with surveillance and issues of twenty-first century security: "Our hunger for fresh images, fresh drama, is enabled not just by TV and Internet news but by the various sources of audio and video that feed TV and the Internet.... Life itself is dependent upon surveillance."[19] Zoller Seitz wants his readers to recognize television's connection to culture but also the part they play in the relationship. A column on reality television, prompted by the suicide of a cast member on *The Real Housewives* series, asked readers to consider the harmful effects that the show's environment might have on the mental health of the cast but also its effects on the audience. He urged his readers to "get real about reality TV" and question their role in what he called *blood sport*. He argued that whether they were a contestant or a spectator, people needed to accept what that environment did to those involved.[20] The piece suggested that two layers of psychological screening should be "a moral and legal imperative" for unscripted series that have the potential to damage cast member's psychological well-being. It was a passionate argument that spoke to the idea of active viewers. Watching intense reality TV was not a passive experience for Zoller Seitz and he urged those who enjoy series like *Real Housewives* to take a deeper look at the social and personal impact of their viewing experience.

Other work continues the theme of the intersection between culture and television including a review of the HBO mini-series *Show Me a Hero*. In the column, he explained the focus of the story in a way that again, made it personal to the viewer. The series was about the disconnection that takes place between well-intentioned government and the people it was meant to serve. What differentiates this statement from others in television, he pointed out, was how the series made it by carefully selecting and arranging the issues on the screen rather than through "monologues or pronouncements or slogans." He explained that viewers had "to make a decision to care equally about every character" in the series. While this was a small decision, the show deserved praise for urging or even requiring viewers to make it because the desire came from the "same impulse that moved a federal judge to order the construction of affordable housing in Yonkers."[21] The close reading Zoller Seitz gave to *Show Me a Hero* challenged viewers to consider the show on an equally thoughtful level.

If the review style of Sepinwall is like having a chat with an informed friend about the details of your favorite show, the critical style of Zoller Seitz is having a chat with that same friend who also makes you consider the broader cultural picture as it relates to your experience. It's an approach that matches his view of television shows as "organisms that coexist with us in time and space as we live our lives."[22] For Zoller Seitz, viewers enter into relationships with shows, with all the emotions they entail and hope that in the end, it was valuable: "Committing to a series … you experience pride and elation, tedium and heartbreak. And you hope that whatever frustrations that you experience ultimately seem worth it." Helping his readers understand those frustrations and connect their personal viewing experience to wider cultural concerns is a hallmark of his work.

Similarly, chief television critic for the *New York Times*, James Poniewozik, explores how media, pop culture, politics and society intersect. *Time* magazine's TV critic for sixteen years, Poniewozik launched the magazine's first blog, *Tuned In*, which was a combination of short reviews, longer cultural essays and recaps.[23] Prior to working at *Time*, he was the media critic for Salon.com where he covered a variety of subjects including television news and the advertising and magazine industry. While he speaks with authority and makes clear critical arguments, he does so in an entertaining style with sentences that often stand out for their creative descriptions. The second season of *True Detective*, "turned and spun, like a driver on one of its complex California highway interchanges, circling and circling and never finding the right exit."[24] Poniewozik also uses a conversational tone in much of his online work. A review of *Show Me a Hero* began: "I'm going to tell you about David Simon's new HBO miniseries … but first I need you to work with me."[25] Asking the reader to put aside their belief that a series about a fight over housing policy would be boring, he continued with a clever reference to television's representation of home: "As countless HGTV shows know, there are few things in the average life more fraught with stress, emotion and psychic investment than obtaining and keeping shelter. A home is not just four walls." He approaches his critical role as more than a guide to what is good or bad about a series. Instead, he is concerned with the ideas that exist within television's narratives and how they reflect the world.

Poniewozik draws connections between shows and society. In a review of *The People v. O.J. Simpson: American Crime Story*, a docufiction series about the trial of the legendary football player and the murder of his ex-wife and her friend, he discussed character, performance and tone but also broadened the analysis. The series examined "the power, and the competing claims, of identity politics. The marathon news stories packaged as entertainments ... the idea that black and white Americans can look at precisely the same scene and see entirely different realities."[26] In an essay on the long running animated series *South Park*, he suggested that the show's latest season was "sketching something like a grand—if messy—unified theory of anger, inequality and disillusionment in 2015 America" and outlined how it was achieving this with numerous examples that both informed the reader about the season's storylines and expertly connected them to the larger argument.[27] A review of the reality show *I Am Cait*, which follows the journey of Caitlyn Jenner's transition, took a similar approach by examining the details of the series and connecting them to a wider social issue, in this case, the documentary's "sense of mission beyond its star subject."[28]

Along with show specific reviews, Poniewozik writes longer pieces on broad television topics. The essays maintain his signature approach, exploring the interconnections between the medium and American culture. A piece on Donald Trump examined how the business mogul turned Republican presidential candidate confounded TV comedians who found it difficult to satirize him as they did all hopeful contenders during campaign season. Moving through various examples of late night comedy news and sketch shows that failed to out–Trump, Trump, he laid out an argument that demonstrated his broad knowledge of television and his keen understanding of the Trump brand. He wrote: "Election parodies traditionally exaggerate candidates. But Mr. Trump exaggerates himself—he's the frilled lizard of politics, inflating his self-presentation.... Satire exposes candidates' contradictions and absurdities. But Mr. Trump blows past those."[29] Other essays tackled television's diversity and the industry trend to pull episodes of shows in response to real life tragedies. The pieces offered carefully crafted arguments that demonstrated a sharp understanding of how television works culturally and economically. Explaining his viewpoint on cancelling ill timed episodes in the wake of violent acts, he shared a personal memory of experiencing September 11 from his home in New York City and offered this thought: "After a trauma, there's no clean line distinguishing what pop-culture content is unsettling and what isn't.... Maybe a better rule would be: Tell good, substantive stories about things that matter to people regardless of the timing."[30] Noting that even trivial, silly entertainment helped society confront its fears, he explained television and popular culture's larger purpose as a vehicle for "how we dream collectively" and "how we share nightmares—communal, cathartic nightmares that allow us to conceive awful things at a safe remove." To help readers gain a clearer understanding of what diverse television meant, he wrote a piece, with Wesley Morris, examining TV's representation of race and ethnicity. It was an informative look at the medium's current landscape, made stronger by Poniewozik's discussion of the issue's economic realities. Noting that broader representation was primarily due to smaller TV audiences, in other words, networks were no longer programming for "an imagined audience of tens of millions of white people," he pointed out that younger viewers expected to see racial, religious and sexual diversity. That audience, he commented, wanted reality and advertisers desire that audience.[31] His point was a rational example, but it was also an astute observation that stressed the commercial imperatives that often drive television's creative decisions.

In his drive to communicate the connections between the world of TV and what exists outside it, Poniewozik reaches an audience who are increasingly their own viewing specialists. He has a sharp understanding of the television landscape and sees his role as one beyond passing judgment on what is positive or negative about a program. Much more than viewing recommendations, his work offers readers insight into what makes them care about the shows they watch.

Poniewozik joined the *New York Times* as chief television critic after Alessandra Stanley left the role for a new beat covering the wealthy. The paper's head TV critic for twelve years, she was previously a foreign correspondent, working in the Moscow and Rome bureaus. In 1993, she was awarded the New York Women in Communications Matrix Award in the newspaper division. Stanley demonstrated a broad knowledge of television and popular culture. Her reviews often gave readers a way to relate to a series by suggesting its similarities to other television shows and films before offering her analysis, tying its themes to wider cultural preoccupations and ending with a final assessment. In a 2005 review of *Weeds*, she compared its premise (a widowed soccer mom starts selling weed to her affluent neighbors to maintain her lifestyle) to incidents of suburban crime in the real world before explaining its satirical take in relation to other TV and film: "*Weeds* is not a genre or period series like HBO's *Sopranos* or *Deadwood*. It is a darkly comic drama loosely wrapped in playful satire, a little bit like *American Beauty* and a little bit like *Desperate Housewives*."[32] The review continued with a brief discussion of the show's theme of suburban listlessness as it related to popular culture and ended with the opinion that *Weeds* was well written and absorbing with a "slick balance of satire and soap opera." She took a similar approach to a review of *Grey's Anatomy*. Starting with a reference to Mary Tyler Moor and Marlo Thomas as early examples of the unconventional but adorable career woman character, she then suggested that *Ally McBeal* marked a disappointing turning point in women's roles in TV comedy where "competent-but-flaky hardened into basket case," before assessing the themes of *Grey's Anatomy*: "it is troubling that even in escapist fantasies, today's heroines have to be weak, needy and oversexed to be liked by women and desired by men."[33] Her opinion on the overall value of the show ended with a suggestion that much like hip-hop's use of obscene lyrics and coarse music videos to degrade women, sometimes "even the most bourgeois women's television shows" do the same. The style of these reviews was an effective way to tie television series to larger social themes as well as their place in programming history, both recent and past.

Along with single show reviews, her work also grouped several shows together that shared a theme. One that began as a critique of *Locked Up Abroad*, covered a group of similar "cautionary tale" travel shows[34] while another used a reality series on A&E and a few situation comedies as a launching point for a discussion of television's representation of alcoholism.[35] In a column on how various television series and stars were changing the representation of female bodies, she framed the discussion with a brief social history and noted, with examples from both television and popular culture, how "society makes a show of supporting people who make peace with their extra pounds" but "we really celebrate those who declare war on their bodies."[36] It was an insightful analysis of how television's representations reflect shifting cultural norms.

Stanley's writing was often witty in its descriptions. In a review of *The Newsroom* she called the characters "fast-talking, preachy know-it-alls who told truth to power every time they ordered coffee" and described the show's sense of mischief as "tethered, like a chiffon cocktail dress with its security tag still attached."[37] In a piece on travel shows that emphasized the dangers of exotic destinations, she quipped: "there is nothing quite as hypnotic as a travel show that suggests it's better to stay home"[38] and in another column described cooking show host Paula Deen, who appeared on the *Today* show to apologize for using a racist epithet, as rising to fame "on her buttery, folksy way with words, as well as ribs."[39] Her way with words, however, was not always well received during her tenure as the paper's chief TV critic. In a column on Shonda Rhimes, creator of *Scandal* and *Grey's Anatomy*, Stanley began with the lead: "When Shonda Rhimes writes her autobiography, it should be called "How to Get Away with Being an Angry Black Woman."[40] The line, a play on the title of Rhimes' newest series at the time, *How to Get Away with Murder*,[41] and a reference to the show's star Viola Davis as "less classically beautiful" than lighter-skinned African American actresses, ignited a controversy on social media and in print where *New York Times'* subscribers and others who read the article, called the piece offensive. Several went further, describing it as racist. A piece on the scandal published in the opinion pages of the paper argued that readers and commentators were right to protest the column: "Intended to be in praise of Ms. Rhimes, it delivered that message in a condescending way that was—at best—astonishingly tone-deaf and out of touch."[42] Stanley responded that while she "referenced a painful and insidious stereotype," it was "solely in order to praise Ms. Rhimes and her shows for traveling so far from it." She noted that if making that connection offended readers, she did not feel good about it but argued: "a full reading allows for a different takeaway than the loudest critics took."[43] She also suggested that her style often included "arch, provocative ledes" and expressed surprise that the paper's readers would take the sentence at face value. The review, as others argued, was out of touch and the ensuing controversy spoke to both the destructive impact of stereotypes and the paper's editing procedures, particularly in stories about women and race.

In her twelve-year career as a TV critic, Stanley produced reviews that gave readers an insight into their viewing experience and the medium's history. Using series, often several at once, to explain how television is both a mirror and a window to the world, she demonstrated the medium's place in culture in ways that were both clever and as the Rhimes column showed, sometimes misguided.

For *Variety's* chief TV critic Maureen Ryan, being able to cover and review so many shows in her career has made her a *lucky human*.[44] The *Chicago Tribune's* TV critic until the fall of 2010, she published print and online columns under the title *The Watcher* before accepting the lead TV critic position at *AOL TV* from 2010 to 2011. The column she filed under the *AOL TV* banner, named *Stay Tuned*, moved to the *Huffington Post* under *HuffPost TV* in 2011. In 2015, she began covering television for *Variety*, which named her one of the six most influential critics in America in 2007. She has also produced a podcast, *Talking TV with Ryan and Ryan*, with fellow TV critic Ryan McGee for several years.[45]

Ryan's work is a mixture of straight program reviews and reporting on industry news. Her style is funny and conversational. She has a passion for television that comes through in all her columns and her analysis of fictional characters shows a sharp appreciation for them. Often, she returns to a show throughout its lifespan, updating readers on story developments, assessing season-to-season strengths and weaknesses, offering video preview clips and reporting on news issues, such as casting changes. For example, her coverage of *Damages*, an FX network series staring Glenn Close as a manipulative lawyer, totaled ten articles during the life of the show that ranged from traditional reviews, to reporting on actors to answering reader questions. In one of the *Damages'* pieces, her signature style was evident as she discussed her thoughts on the complexity of the series: "It could get pretty confusing at times ... and there were many times I was glad for the pause button on my DVR, because I needed to figure out where things stood in the plot and who knew what about whom."[46] In a friendly, chatty way, Ryan placed herself alongside the audience. When the review shifted into assessment, she maintained her unique tone: "Still, I'd rather a TV drama overestimate my mental abilities than treat me like a moron, and *Damages* was one enjoyable ride. Close gave a typically galvanizing, crafty performance." With a critical voice that is part expert, part fellow viewer, Ryan's particular strength is insightful analysis of characters and performances that builds rapport, as if she understands the fictional players in a way that makes them more authentic. In the *Damages'* piece, she described actor Ted Danson's performance of his character Arthur Frobisher as reaching something like an epiphany before giving a detailed scene analysis and commenting on why Danson excelled in the role: "Danson always gave Frobisher that edge of neediness and insecurity ... but the billionaire was also capable of gross self-indulgence and thoughtless brutality. Still, no matter what he did, you couldn't look away from him, and that's the definition of a great character." The scene critique demonstrated her appreciation for Danson's performance, a sharp understanding of the fictional man he played, and a clear judgment on the merits of the show's characterization.

Returning to the topic of the DVR, Ryan took the review into reportage and analysis with a discussion of how ratings are related to a series' survival. In the case of *Damages*, the series' live audience numbers were much lower than the number of people who delayed their viewing. While this suggested that audiences were responding to the show, it did not improve its chances for renewal because advertisers were not interested in paying for non-live viewing. Her coverage of the issue, including comments from the president of FX and Close, within the context of a show review was both clever and comprehensive. Weighing in on the impact of the DVR on ratings, she brought herself back into the piece arguing that the idea that increased DVR usage may mean promising series will not be made was a sobering thought and her wish was that multiple platforms for new media would start to give entertainment companies the types of economic returns they were seeking so that shows that challenged viewers artistically would survive.[47] She ended with a warning: "If the DVR breeds timidity— the kind of timidity that is very much in evidence in the broadcast networks' new shows for fall—that would be a disaster for television." In one piece, Ryan critically analyzed a series and commented on a larger industry issue, all while maintaining an accessible and personable stylistic voice.

Ryan's humor is evident in much of her work, often from the column titles alone. In one *Huffington Post* column from January 7, 2014, she asked: "*Downton Abbey* and *The Walking Dead*: Are They the Same Show? In another from August 6, 2015 titled "*True Detective* Drinking Games That Could Kill You," she poked fun at the second season of the procedural by listing all the ways readers could avoid overindulging if they found themselves in a drinking game based around the show. Don't, she suggested "drink when you start thinking about how the repetitive overhead shots of Los Angeles' highways are a metaphor for the convoluted bowl of spaghetti that is the plot" or "when you wonder whether the entire resolution of the season will amount, more or less, to *a wizard did it*" or when an individual episode seems like it has lasted for several days.[48] The *True Detective* review went on to thoughtfully lay out why the show's second season was a *train wreck* but pointed out one highlight, which for Ryan was episode seven when the actors were able to "underplay and elevate the sometimes overwrought material."

Along with perceptive analysis of characters and performance, Ryan's work also covers the gender politics of television. In 2012, she wrote a long piece on the gender breakdown in the industry, citing a study that reported a sharp drop in the percentage of women writers of prime-time programs on network television.[49] She has written about the lack of representation of women and people of color as TV directors[50] and as creators at subscription channel HBO.[51] Her coverage of *Lost* routinely discussed gender issues. In one episode review, she recapped and revisited her argument about the series' poor representation of women arguing that, with some exceptions, female characters were not in the foreground of the show's narrative. When a female character did appear as a centerpiece to the plot it was "all about how her bitterness, misanthropy and evasions launched centuries of bloodshed. Fabulous."[52]

Ryan commented in an interview with the *Washington Post*, that her viewpoint as a female critic was a significant part of how she understood her role: "I really view my job as, if I'm going to do something valuable, I'd like to open the doors to a discussion as to why the industry is so male-dominated."[53] Her work on the representation of women on the small screen as well as the difficulties women face in the television industry reflects her view on the power of the medium. In a piece for *Variety*, she wrote that no medium was more influential than television, with its enormous growth in scripted programming and the technological ability to follow viewers everywhere. It was for those reasons that its representations mattered more than at any other time in its history. Today's "TV storytellers don't just shape reality, they help create it."[54] Influential and passionate about her work—she has called her job "a lot of damned fun"—Ryan is one of the best writers covering the gender politics of television.[55]

Men might tip the scales in the gender balance of television creation and production but women like Maureen Ryan are increasingly driving the conversation about the small screen. Joining Ryan are critics including Heather Havrilesky, who covered TV for *Salon* until mid–2014 and is a contributor to *New York Times Magazine*; Virginia Heffernan, who was Slate's TV critic from 2001 to 2003 before joining Alessandra Stanley at the *New York Times*; Alyssa Rosenberg who blogs about popular culture for the *Washington Post*'s Opinions section and was previously the culture editor at *ThinkProgress*, and National Public Radio's Linda Holmes, who writes the *Monkey See* blog. Havrilesky recapped *Mad Men* for *Salon*, explored nostalgia television as seen through *Game of Thrones* and discussed the limits of series that heavily rely on a central concept.[56] In clear, strongly supported critiques, Rosenberg has covered film, politics, literature and other topics. Her writing on television often focuses on representations of power, race and sexuality and untangles their meanings within the context of a particular show and the wider culture. Holmes, who recapped shows for *Television Without Pity* and is a regular contributor to MSNBC.com covering various aspects of popular culture, writes knowledgably about television's trends. In her television work for the *Monkey See* blog, she has covered streaming distribution models, diversity, cultural hierarchies, the relationship between ratings and success and fan engagement. She explains concepts and lays out clear arguments. A piece on the state of television diversity noted its scope both in front of and behind the camera as well as in writers' rooms and executive offices before broadening the concept: "It's about the bland and unremarked upon influence of almost all TV families, and the fact that TV doesn't incorporate very many people who go to church, and all the other ways that it historically looks at the population through a keyhole."[57] Holmes' work is informative but not at the expense of her point of view. She educates her readers on the industry's issues and trends but also persuades them to see the larger impact.

In show reviews, Holmes applies a similar explanatory style to her assessment. A review of the ABC miniseries *Madoff* explained the conceit of breaking the fourth wall (having a character speak directly to the camera creates authority, control and intimacy and is, in part, a conspiratorial device) and then analyzed how it worked in *Madoff* with star Richard Dreyfuss' performance in the title role. The series, she argued, used the conceit to serve a slightly different purpose which was to stress the intimate nature of the narrative, giving it meaning: "Without Dreyfuss' powerful central performance, there's surprisingly little to the story of Madoff if you talk about him rather than about the people whose money he took."[58] With an instructional tone, Holmes informed her readers about the complexities of character and narrative.

Similar to Linda Holmes, who got her start recapping shows online, *The New Yorker*'s chief television critic Emily Nussbaum credits her online interactions with kick starting her television-writing career. It all started with *Buffy the Vampire Slayer*, as she explained in an interview, noting that she was an opinionated person and the show made her interested in larger debates about what TV was capable of doing.[59] Nussbaum found an outlet for the broader debates about television in online conversations in which she frequently participated, an activity she found *wildly stimulating* and global in reach.[60] Her work has appeared in the *New York Times*, *Slate*, *Nerve* and *Vulture*. She was *New York* magazine's critic before moving to *The New Yorker*. Her critical voice is funny and conversational. On *Surf*, the blog she wrote for *New York* magazine, she titled a post "Watch *The Middle* or I'll Kill This Dog," and had this to say about the situation comedy: "The structure is straight-up sitcom, with no postmodern mockumentary trappings. But it's well-written, smart, realistic, and funny." The desperation created when a character panicked over the family's credit card debt and broken home appliances, she wrote, seemed authentic rather than exaggerated.[61] Part assessment, part friendly chat, she set herself apart from other critics with her announcement that the show was "unlikely to be a critic's darling," yet maintained her authority by pointing out its strengths and then declaring her interest in the series: "I hope to hell the series sticks around." In another post on *Surf*, she discussed her feelings about several shows in the same conversational, humorous and impassioned way. On *Glee* she wrote: "*Glee*, I know I should love you. The series is practically a rebus of my guilty-pleasure tastes ... yet [it] is working my last nerve."[62] The post ended with her thoughts on Aaron Sorkin's return to television: "I'm downright giddy that Aaron Sorkin will be back.... Not because I liked *Studio 60 on the Sunset Strip*, mind you ... but Sorkin is clearly fascinated by television itself, as well as social networking, as well as Aaron Sorkin, and these are all obsessions I share."

With her move to *The New Yorker*, Nussbaum continued her signature style of witty prose with thoughtful insight into the politics of representation. A review of *Billions*, a series about a hedge fund billionaire and the state's attorney determined to collapse his empire, she described the antihero appeal of the show's main character Bobby "Axe" Axelrod played by Damian Lewis and then offered a sharp and funny analysis. The appeal of Axe, was in part, due to Lewis' good looks and habit of "wandering onscreen in expensive boxer briefs" but the character was also engaging because he was "the most existentially free person in the show's well-drawn universe of ambitious hypocrites." *Billions*, she quipped, "doesn't care about your politics, or abstractions about justice. It knows what you want."[63] Nussbaum combines a sense of playfulness with powerful critique that explores what television's representations mean beyond the pictures on the screen.

Nussbaum's predecessor at *The New Yorker* was Nancy Franklin, whose criticism, like Nussbaum's, was concerned with the politics of representation. *The New Yorker*'s TV critic for thirteen years until she left in 2011, she began her television writing career with a review of *Sex and the City* in 1998 that established her sharp eye for gender politics. Her critical voice was personable and likable and occasionally she poked fun at her choices. When the *Syfy* network changed the spelling of its name from *Sci Fi*, she wrote: "To switch from the noble *Sci Fi*, associated with so many groundbreaking, beloved writers, to something that looks like your Uncle Seymour's screen name—it's enough to make any earthling go berserk."[64] Franklin's funny take on her reaction to a network's rebranding exercise concluded with a close reading of characterization and acting. In another column, she reviewed *The Talk*, a talk show featuring five well-known women hosts and addressed the program's gendered narrative, noting that guests were introduced by their *reproductive status*. The message to mothers, she argued, was clear, "any mistake they make or any act that they or their children commit in public, no matter how inconsiderate to others, is justified, because being a mother is so all-consumingly difficult."[65] An influential voice, Franklin, along with Dorothy Rabinowitz, was arguably the country's most high profile female critic in the late 90s when she turned her attention to television. Writing for *The New Yorker*, one of the most celebrated arts criticism outlets in the United States comes with built-in prestige but Franklin's work stands on its own as a collection of clever and accessible insights into television and the politics of representation.

For Pulitzer Prize winner Mary McNamara, the job of a TV critic is "not just about whether a certain show is good or not, it's about where it fits in the cultural conversation."[66] In her view, the most important stories, while once the purview of film, are now being told on television and the conversations those stories start about how a society sees itself are ones worth paying attention to because they say a lot about individual and communal identity. It is a process she hopes her work facilitates.[67] A features writer and editor at the *Los Angeles Times* since 1991 and the paper's television critic since 2009, McNamara won the Pulitzer Prize in the category of criticism in 2015. She was a finalist for the award in 2013 and 2014.

An overview of McNamara's Pulitzer Prize winning columns reveals an entertaining prose style in both her close readings of character and story and her broader thought pieces about television's contribution to the cultural conversation. A review of *Downton Abbey*, a show she called "that highly addictive meringue of Edwardian couture and socially tolerant politics that has sentimentalized British past beyond all recognition," argued that the death of main character Matthew Crawley (Dan Stevens), rather than being a tragedy, had instead reinvigorated the series. Stevens received heavy criticism for choosing to leave the series during the height of its popularity but McNamara argued that creator Julian Fellowes should in fact, write Steven's "a posthumous check ... never has the death of a character so obviously cleared away the brambles that can choke even a popular show to death."[68] The character, who she referred to as a "walking, talking deus ex machina ... just saying the Absolutely Right Thing," was overshadowing more interesting characters and moving the show away from its original themes. The review was a smart and humorous analysis of the series through its various seasons with an emphasis on how characters impacted story development. Similarly, in a review of *House of Cards*, she explored the appeal of its main character Claire Underwood (Robin Wright) who she described as calm and cold and a character not typically seen on television: "She's a political wife who seems neither scorned nor thwarted, though in actuality she is both of these things. But she is also plagued by doubts, and menopause; her decision to remain childless has seesawed her from one season to the next."[69] A more detailed examination of McNamara's body of work shows that her reviews accomplish several things at once. She summarizes plot, analyzes strengths and weaknesses and often tells a compelling story featuring the show's characters.

In addition to her show reviews, McNamara makes broader connections between television and culture. In a column exploring the relationship between sexism and entertainment, she argued that television had contributed to a troubling situation that made audiences comfortable watching sexism from a distance. Using examples from *Mad Men* and *Masters of Sex*, she pointed out that screen life and real life were not so far apart. *Mad Men*, she commented, "may well overlap with the current news cycle, which hearkens more and more the mid–'80s ... it is dispiriting to see how many of these problems still plague us, and how deeply they have been buried under assumptions they do not."[70] Part of the entertainment industry's responsibility was to accept not only the impact its creative products had on social attitudes but also acknowledging that it shaped those viewpoints in both positive and negative ways: "To argue that entertainment does not impact culture is absurd. Hollywood doesn't get to take credit for breaking ground with ... shows like *Will & Grace* or for that matter *Girls*, only to wash its hands of more destructive attitudes."[71] Significantly, change starts with conversation and television viewers had an important part to play: "Conversation, whether between the early abolitionists, a group of fed-up drag queens at the Stonewall Inn or online fans of Louis C.K., is where change begins."

McNamara's broader TV essays also asked questions, offered theories and proposed solutions for issues facing the industry. In a column on the increase in diversity, she pointed out that while fans of the series *Sleepy Hollow* were impressed with the imaginative storyline what they should have noticed was something far more revolutionary than making Ichabod Crane a modern day figure battling the Four Horsemen of the Apocalypse: The show had four non-white main characters.[72] The essay continued with a discussion of TV's casting diversity before it posed an interesting question: "So why is it that cable, with its more upscale demographic and boutique ratings-tolerance, remains so overpopulated with white men while broadcast, which lives and dies by big numbers, seems to be finally embracing the rainbow?" McNamara answered the question with an analysis that touched on individual influencers and series that failed to cast a diversity of actors. She argued that the problem was larger than the fact that so many of the writers for cable series were white men. It began when those in power decided that television shows could be intelligent and "*The Sopranos* was the only exception to the pat proclamation among the elite that TV was for idiots and shut-ins." Despite the fact that other shows including *The Wire* and *Friday Night Lights* were similarly received, she noted, it was *Mad Men* that began to turn popular opinion.

The progress that broadcast networks made with shows that demonstrated sophisticated writing and performances, however, did not eliminate the snobbish attitude that was inherent to the notion of prestige drama. McNamara argued that terms like prestige and elite were often another way of saying white. The problem, she noted, presented an important opportunity for broadcast networks to differentiate themselves from cable instead of chasing networks like HBO and Showtime by increasing levels of sex, violence and profanity. The solution may lie in telling stories with broad appeal and even taking a cue from a reimagining of *Sleepy Hollow*: "It may turn out that populism is the answer. The stories television, broadcast and cable tells still represent only a narrow band of its audience. But if 200-year-old Ichabod Crane can adapt to a world in which white men aren't the only people whose lives matter, presumably TV can too."[73] A thought provoking response to television's slow move toward racial diversification, the essay urged readers to recognize the better role the medium could play in representing society.

In one of McNamara's most personal essays, she discussed how television impacted her family when her son was injured and had a long recuperation at home. It was a meditation on the healing effects of spending time with an art form that is capable of teaching individuals about themselves. Discussing her son's reaction to the series *Friday Night Lights* and how its characters' stories resonated with that painful time in his life, she wrote that she worried the show's plot would be a painful reminder of what he was no longer capable of doing and "the fragility of even a simple dream."[74] She continued with a striking and beautiful description of what happened instead, as her son spoke to her about his frustration and loss over losing his team and the sport he loved: "Eventually he spoke of his own pain ... without the hours spent practicing and playing to give his day, and his identity, a tangible form. But his voice rang with a passing tense, as if he were describing a place he was leaving even as he left it, the wreckage still visible in the rearview window, but growing smaller with every passing mile." The essay demonstrated McNamara's skill at using storytelling devices to make a compelling argument. She ended the piece by defining television as a form of art and noting that at its best, the medium allowed viewers to be open to "the thoughts and emotions of others, to see different sides of the human story unfurl slowly."

Like McNamara, longtime TV critic David Bianculli finds joy in the experience of watching television, though it's not without some accompanying pain: "You have to watch so much awful TV, it's painful.... At the same time, it makes you appreciate the good stuff.... The thrill is identifying something really good and steering people to it."[75] According to Bianculli, he has been appreciating the good stuff since he was seven years old when he wrote in his diary: "Man was *Alice in Wonderland* good."[76] It was the start of a long career that has taken him from a diary entry that reached an audience of one to an on air role as the TV critic for National Public Radio's *Fresh Air* with Terry Gross program and an audience of millions. Along the way, he wrote TV reviews for *The Gainesville Sun* while he was attending the University of Florida, his first paying job as a TV critic (He earned five dollars for each review). He has contributed TV reviews to *Fresh Air* since 1985 and substitutes for host Terry Gross. His work has appeared in six daily newspapers including the *Philadelphia Inquirer* and he was the *New York Daily News* TV critic from 1993 to 2007. He teaches TV and film history at Rowan University in New Jersey and is the author of three books on television. He founded a website, *TV Worth Watching*, where he blogs short recommendations and serves as editor to various contributors.

Bianculli, who estimated that he watches more than sixty hours of television a week, takes pleasure in the medium despite saying that he gets paid to watch bad TV.[77] For the shows he enjoys, his writing style is often enthusiastic and his reviews demonstrate a broad knowledge of television history. A review of the 2016 six-episode return of *The X-Files* discussed its influences, including a little known 1970s drama featuring similar themes[78] while a review of *Supergirl* outlined television's Superman franchise beginning with the 1950s show *The Adventures of Superman* and gave background on the previous television roles of its main actors.[79] For a piece on the premiere of *30 Rock*, he referenced *Seinfeld*, *The Mary Tyler Moore Show* and *The Jack Benny Program*.[80] Bianculli's historical perspective is combined with a focus on performance and plot. He defines "great TV" as a show that stops him from doing anything else.[81]

If Bianculli finds both pleasures and pitfalls in television, Ken Tucker's writing suggests that he is as equally divided. Surveying his reviews for *Entertainment Weekly* where he was a founding editor and the chief TV critic for twenty-two years until he left in 2013 to join *Yahoo! TV* as its television critic, it is quickly apparent that in all that he finds good and bad about the medium, his opinions challenge readers to think about TV as discourse. His critical voice is authoritative but also casual. During his time with *Entertainment Weekly*, he covered *The X-Files* extensively and was one of the earliest proponents of *Buffy the Vampire Slayer*. His review of a series episode in 1998 began with a line spoken by the main character played by Sarah Michelle Gellar who said: "I told him that I love him and I kissed him and I killed him." The line, Tucker wrote, "was an example of unguarded, unironic emotionalism in a slam-bang series that prides itself on its blithe knowingness and sarcasm and just keeps getting better at juggling hilarity, gothic romance, and horror."[82] What followed was a witty overview of the show as it compared to *Charmed*, a series Tucker called *spike-heeled* to *Buffy's fleet-footed*. The concluding paragraph argued: "no other show balances so many elements as deftly, without a trace of corniness or melodrama. I can admire *Charmed* for its shrewd casting and pop-culture timing, but week in and week out, *Buffy* just slays me." A clear champion of the show, Tucker's full review balanced delight with thoughtful critique. A cultural critic and author of two books, Tucker is also the music critic for NPR's *Fresh Air* and has reviewed films for *New York Magazine* and published book reviews for the *New York Times Book Review* and other publications. He brings a well-rounded perspective to his television writing often concentrating on performance and narrative with close readings of series and an understanding of cultural trends. In a review of *Smash*, he addressed the show's connection to the phrase hate-watching and offered a defense of the pleasures of popular culture, arguing that terms like guilty pleasure and hate watching should be considered meaningless in today's television landscape: "You watch something because it's attracted your attention.... Watching *Smash* in order to wallow in elements you find foolish or unbelievable or laughable? That sounds like a variation on pleasure to me."[83] The act of watching a series was in itself an act of accepting its weaknesses and moreover, finding joy in those limitations. The argument established the idea of an active audience mindfully choosing their viewing experiences.

A prolific writer, Tucker's work was and continues to be influential. He posted over 1800 entries to his blog for *Entertainment Weekly, Ken Tucker's Watching TV* (later called *Ken Tucker's TV*), and Judd Apatow credited his review of *Freaks and Geeks* with saving the show for one last season.[84] In the review, he wrote that the series was "the one ratings-endangered new show this season worth begging viewers to watch" and he was submissively coming to the reader to say "please give this show a shot, because you'll come away from it a better person, or at least a more satisfied TV watcher."[85] Tucker's powerful critical voice was not always well received, however, and his negative reaction to *Family Guy* launched a long-running feud with the show's creator Seth MacFarlane. Tucker had much to say about the animated show, which features dad Peter Griffin, his wife, three children and a talking dog. He accused the series of being *The Simpsons* "as conceived by a singularly sophomoric mind that lacks any reference point beyond other TV shows.... What is laughable is the clunky animation."[86] Later that year, he crowned the series number one in his worst shows list with this description: "Racist, anti–Semitic and AIDS jokes; shoddy animation, stolen ideas. The cartoon as vile swill."[87] MacFarlane responded through his characters. In one episode Peter Griffin wiped his bottom with a page from *Entertainment Weekly* and remarked, "Well, at least that's one problem solved."[88] Similarly, the writers of *Psych* created a psychotic killer doctor for one of the show's episodes. They named him Ken Tucker.[89] In the case of the killer doctor homage, Tucker responded with a sense of humor and said: "It shows you're not wishy-washy. You have strong opinions and people react strongly to them."[90] Robust opinions are a signature of Tucker's work and a goal he set from his first column with *Entertainment Weekly*. Signing off from *Ken Tucker's TV*, he quoted the first post of the blog: "Here's the way I began this blog in 2008: Hello. I'll use this space to: talk about what I watched last night (strong opinions guaranteed); what I think you shouldn't miss tonight; and what's coming up that you should set your DVR for.... I watch TV, you watch TV: Let's share our thoughts and passions, OK?"[91] More than simply watch TV Tucker has cheered its successes and pointed out its failures with a definitive critical voice.

The field of contemporary critics is a full one and this chapter has highlighted many but not all of its most influential voices. To cover everyone is a book in itself but here are a few more in the critical community who are speaking with energy and enthusiasm: Daniel Fienberg and Tim Goodman are doing clever, insightful analysis at *The Hollywood Reporter* as are Donna Bowman and Todd VanDerWerff at *A.V. Club*. Matt Roush and Damian Holbrook keep *TV Guide*'s readers informed and entertained while the critics at *Entertainment Weekly* including Jeff Jensen, Dalton Ross and Dan Snierson cover a wide range of programs and issues. Ryan McGee writes sharp commentary for *HitFix*, *A.V. Club* and his own blog, *Boob Tube Dude*. *Grantland*'s Andy Greenwald and Molly Lambert, Robert Bianco in *USA Today*, Robert Lloyd for the *Los Angeles Times*, Mandi Bierly for *Yahoo!TV*, Brian Lowry at *Variety*, Gail Pennington at the *St. Louis Post-Dispatch*, Michael Ausiello at *TVLine*, Joe Adalian at *Vulture*,

Conclusion

> When television is good, nothing—not the theater, not the magazines
> or newspapers—nothing is better.—NEWTON MINOW

FOR THE CRITICS WHOSE WORK appears throughout the pages of this
book, Minow's words to the National Association of Broadcasters on May
9, 1961, capture why they do their job. For the people who write about the
medium's vast and diverse creative products, it is at its best when its
images and stories offer visual and narrative complexities that not only
prove that television deserves to be on the same level as high art but also
enriches cultures and communities in the process. The best critical voices
bring this belief to their conversations about television and in doing so
shape how society understands its relationship to a pervasive medium.
Throughout their history, journalistic TV critics have taken on various
roles but they have always been more than consumer guides. They raise
questions about television's processes and policies, its social and political
impact, the meaning of its representations and the level of its power. Their
work encourages and creates more critical viewers.

Television's history is the history of its critics and while this book is
not a definitive account of TV's past, it has used a chronological structure
of the medium's development to contextualize the critics' story. With each
decade, television, as an industry, a technology and a social force, experienced important changes that influenced how critics viewed their work
and their profession. In the 1950s technical and aesthetic innovations coa-
lesced to form the medium's first Golden Age and the creative borders of
a new, emerging art form were drawn. Influential critics, including Jack Gould
and John Crosby, found themselves in an informal alliance with industry

leaders who were seeking respectability for the new medium. As television entered the 1960s, Gould and others grew increasingly disappointed with what they saw as homogenous programming designed to support television's bottom line. The industry mandate became less aspirational and more commercial and the once friendly relationship between critics and the industry turned contentious. Critics accused industry decision-makers of sacrificing quality programming for market interests. The industry responded with a campaign to paint critics as out of touch elitists.

By the 1960s, the early critics saw their role shift from program evaluation that influenced policy-makers and industry leaders to program promotion that served network publicity departments. With the advent of previewing, critics could recommend shows before they aired, making them valuable promotional agents. Junkets began and the lavish treatment planned around introducing critics to new programming often resulted in work that was little more than a rewrite of network press releases. It was a trend that alarmed many who called for change and by the late 1970s, the Television Critics Association was formed in an effort to formalize the profession and create institutionalized events. It was the start of an era in which critics, many of whom were trained in journalism rather than in the arts, approached television as a legitimate news beat. Television criticism's push for more respectability was recognized with a Pulitzer Prize for Ron Powers in 1973. Along with Powers, the work of Michael Arlen, John O'Connor, and Les Brown engaged with television in news ways, exploring its cultural and political impact.

While critics formalized and institutionalized their profession in a move designed to free themselves from the role of publicity, technological changes in the 1980s and 1990s ensured that promotion was still part of their job. Satellite and cable technologies turned three networks into many and the multichannel universe fragmented audiences. Critics' columns became tools for audiences to sift through myriad show choices and value came from the promotional possibilities their writing offered. With more to watch, came more to write about and critics had to reassess the criteria they used to choose the shows they covered. William Henry III, Howard Rosenberg, Tom Shales and Dorothy Rabinowitz were among the critical leaders during this time period with Henry, Rosenberg and Shales all awarded a Pulitzer Prize for their work. The multi-channel era also opened the door to more risk-taking and programs appeared that pushed boundaries. As a result, critics began to define certain TV as art, a trend that would continue into the new millennium.

The Internet gave critics new venues and new reach, which expanded their role as cultural agenda setters and meaning-makers. Republication of print columns online and the creation of blogs as a supplement to established columns expanded the critics' audience beyond the geographical range of newspapers. These new communities of readers enhanced the critics' contribution as agenda-setters and eliminated the one-way communication model of newspaper writing.

The online space, along with new distribution models for television programming that allowed on-demand, streaming and delayed viewing, changed how viewers watched and how some critics wrote. The rise of recapping launched interesting debates around episodic versus serialized television and professional versus amateur reviewers. For some critics, even the definition of recap and review was a contested area, as recapping often favored detailed plot summaries while reviewing adhered to more traditional methods of cultural criticism. Some argued that recapping every episode of a series allowed for more creative freedom than traditional methods. Others suggested that it was stifling the profession's creative output as so many rushed to copy the style. Still others used the topic to delve into larger issues emerging from the shift in distribution models. The trend toward serialization, spurred on by the economic benefits of selling long form shows to streaming outlets rather than the traditional model of selling syndicated repeats, effected how individual episodes were written. Single, well-written episodes that stood alone versus episodes that were designed as chapters in a longer story demanded different approaches to reviewing and not all critics were happy about it.

The critical debate continues over the best way to assess shows and serve readers but what most in the profession will agree on is that a vibrant and interactive comment culture has developed as a result of evolving technologies and this community of readers has changed criticism for the better. Ideas and opinions are now shared between critic and reader in long, ongoing conversations that for the most part, are invigorating and revealing.

The men and women who write contemporary criticism including Alan Sepinwall, Matt Zoller Seitz, Maureen Ryan and Emily Nussbaum, among many others, are much more than program advisers. They offer insights into television's sociopolitical impact. They give close readings of shows and provide incisive commentary on programming trends, industry issues and production values. Their work takes the form of detailed run downs, analysis of episodes and seasons, weekly podcasts and occasional essays. Serious or playful, respectful or incendiary, their work is at its finest when it is both a personal response and an informed perspective that captures television at its best and sometimes, at its worst, all with an eye toward revealing how its representations shape life.

Chapter Notes

Introduction

1. Jackie Gleason quoted in Charles Steinberg, "The Compleat Television Critic," *Television Quarterly* 2 (Winter 1974): 6.

2. TV Studies is "more a loose coalition of subfields from many disciplines rather than a singular discipline unto itself." See Janet McCabe, "In Debate: Television Studies in the American Academy," *Critical Studies in Television* 6.1 (May 2011): 99–112.

3. Brooks Atkinson quoted in Ralph Lewis Smith, *A Study of the Professional Criticism of Broadcasting in the United States 1920–1955* (New York: Arno Press, 1979), 109.

4. See Wesley Schrum, *Fringe and Fortune: The Role of Critics in High and Popular Art* (Princeton: Princeton University Press, 1996).

5. Herbert Gans, *Popular Culture and High Culture: An Analysis and Evaluation of Taste* (New York: Basic Books, 1974), 14.

6. See Horace Newcomb, "American Television Criticism, 1970–1985," *Critical Studies in Mass Communication* 3 (1986): 217–288.

7. It can also be argued that as a cultural industry tied to the production of social meaning, television must reach a bigger audience than what is typical for "high art."

8. Hal Himmelstein, *On the Small Screen: New Approaches in Television and Video Criticism* (New York: Praeger, 1981), xi.

9. John Simon quoted in Peter Orlik, *Critiquing Radio and Television Content* (New York: Simon & Schuster, 2008), 15.

10. Paul du Gay, ed., *Production of Culture/Culture of Production* (New York: Sage, 1997).

11. John Fiske, *Television Culture* (New York: Routledge, 1987).

12. Pierre Bourdieu, *Distinction: A Social Critique of the Judgment of Taste* (Cambridge: Harvard University Press, 1983).

13. Jonathan Gray, *Show Sold Separately: Promos, Spoilers and Other Media Paratexts* (New York: New York University Press, 2010), 36.

14. *Ibid.*, 166.

Chapter One

1. Quoted in Gary Edgerton, *The Columbia History of American Television* (New York: Columbia University Press, 2007), 36.

2. *Ibid.*

3. David Sarnoff quoted in Paul Schatzkin, *The Boy Who Invented Television: A Story of Inspiration, Persistence and Quiet Passion* (Silver Spring, MD: Teamcom Books, 2002), 182.

4. Erik Barnouw, *Tube of Plenty: The Evolution of American Television*, 2nd edition (Oxford: Oxford University Press, 1990), 114.

5. Lynne Spigel, *Make Room for TV: Television and the Family Ideal in Postwar*

America (Chicago: University of Chicago Press, 1992), 3.

6. Gary Steiner, *The People Look at TV: A Study of Audience Attitudes* (New York: Knopf, 1963), 17.

7. *Ibid.*

8. Quoted in Edgerton, 95.

9. Steiner, 228.

10. *Ibid.*, 25.

11. Edgerton, 109.

12. *Ibid.*, 85.

13. *Ibid.*

14. *Ibid.*, 86.

15. Marya Mannes, "Channels: Comments on TV," *The Reporter*, February 17, 1953, 35.

16. *Ibid.*

17. Mannes, "Channels: Comments on TV," *The Reporter*, June 6, 1953, 34.

18. Quoted in Richard Butsch, *The Citizen Audience: Crowds, Publics, and Individuals* (New York: Routledge, 2007), 104.

19. Quoted in Bob Pondillo, "Chicago TV's Winter of Violence 1952-53," *Television Quarterly* 34 (Winter 2004): 26.

20. *Ibid.*

21. Edgerton, 55.

22. Harry Castleman and Walter J. Podrazik, *Watching TV: Six Decades of American Television*, 2nd edition (Syracuse: Syracuse University Press, 2010), 91. Due to its popularity, NBC re-stages the production and broadcasts it live again in January 1956.

23. Jack Gould, "The Boys From Boise," *New York Times*, October 8, 1944, 51.

24. He also narrates the series *The Seven Lively Arts*, broadcast on CBS from 1957 to 1958, which covers jazz, ballet and films and shows the first telecast of Tchaikovsky's *The Nutcracker*.

25. Jack Gould, "Telling the Whole Story: TV Discussions and Interviews Are Well and Good but They Cannot Replace Basic Reporting," *New York Times*, July 23, 1961.

26. Quoted in "Critics Views of Hits, Misses," *Broadcasting*, September 19, 1966, 64–65.

27. *Ibid.*

28. Harriet Van Horne, "Out of the Flying Pan and Into the Mire," *New York Magazine*, 1977, 63.

29. *Ibid.*

30. Van Horne, "The Way We Were at Our Worst," *New York Magazine*, 1977, 62.

31. Van Horne, "Truth and Consequences," *New York Magazine*, 1977, 97.

32. Harriet Van Horne, *Never Go Anywhere Without a Pencil* (New York: G.P. Putnam's Sons, 1969,1972), 107.

33. *Ibid.*, 195.

34. *Ibid.*, 196.

35. "Group Profile: The Critics," *Television Magazine* 11 (December 1954): 44.

36. Lewis Gould, ed., *Watching Television Come of Age: "The New York Times" Reviews by Jack Gould* (Austin: University of Texas Press, 2002), 95.

37. Lewis Gould remembers that his father rarely saved letters he received about his columns but in this case he kept all of them. See *Watching Television*, 95.

38. Jack Gould, "*The Play of the Week*: Demise of Drama Series Has Economic Moral," *New York Times*, June 11, 1961, X11.

39. Gould, "Case of Jean Muir: Principles of Fair Play Yield to Pressure," *New York Times*, September 3, 1950, 49.

40. Gould, "A Plague on TV's House: Rigged Quiz Shows Viewed as Symptom of the Age, with Many Guilty Parties," *New York Times*, October 12, 1959, 39.

41. Gould, "Parent-Teacher Organization Issues Its First Appraisal of Programs," *New York Times*, September 13, 1959, X15.

42. Gould, "Stamford Survey: TV Habits of Children Offer Opportunity," *New York Times*, March 12, 1950, X11.

43. John Crosby, "Shows for Kids on the Skids?" *Detroit Free Press*, August 2, 1953, 55.

44. John Crosby, *Out of the Blue: A Book About Radio and Television* (New York: Simon & Schuster, 1952), 284.

45. *Ibid.*, 284–85.

46. Lewis Gould, 76.

47. *Ibid.*

48. Jack Gould, "Edward R. Murrow's News Review 'See it Now' Demonstrates Journalistic Power of Video," *New York Times*, November 19, 1951, 26.

49. Gould, "Murrow's 'This Is Korea' Film over CBS Captures Poignancy and Frustration of Life in Battle," *New York Times*, December 29, 1952, 25.

50. Crosby, *Out of the Blue*, 247.

51. *Ibid.*, 248.

52. *Ibid.*, 249.

53. *Ibid.*

54. Quoted in Barnouw, 237.

55. Crosby, *Out of the Blue*, 241.

56. *Ibid.*, 240.

57. *Ibid.*, 241.

58. *Ibid.*, 242.

59. John Crosby, *With Love and Loathing* (New York: McGraw-Hill, 1963), 73.

60. *Ibid.*, 74.

61. *Ibid.*, 72.

62. *Ibid.*, 75.

63. John Crosby quoted in William Boddy, *Fifties Television: The Industry and Its Critics* (Urbana: University of Illinois Press, 1990), 89.

64. Jack Gould, "Television Debut: Theatre Guild Makes Video Bow on NBC with Production of *John Ferguson*," *New York Times*, November 16, 1947, x11.

65. Jack Gould, "*Julius Caesar*: Worthington Miner's Version in Modern Dress Proves Spectacular Television," *New York Times*, March 13, 1949, x11.

66. Jack Gould, "Live TV Vs. Canned: A Critic Casts a Vote for Live TV and Its 'First Night' Quality," *New York Times*, February 5, 1956, 218.

67. Gilbert Seldes, *Writing For Television* (New York: Doubleday, 1952), 32.

68. Jack Gould, "A Plea for Live Video: Switch to Film for TV Was a Major Mistake," *New York Times*, December 7, 1952, X17.

69. Gilbert Seldes, "A Clinical Analysis of TV," *New York Times Magazine*, November 23, 1954, 60.

70. James Whiteside, "The Communicator I: Athens Starts Pouring In," *New Yorker*, October 16, 1954, 58, 60.

71. Quoted in Boddy, 73.

72. *Ibid.*

73. *Ibid.*, 127.

74. George Lipsitz, *Time Passages: Collective Memory and American Popular Culture* (Minneapolis: University of Minnesota Press, 1990), 41–42 in Gary R. Edgerton, *The Columbia History of American Television* (New York: Columbia University Press, 2007), 130.

75. Gould liked *I Love Lucy*, describing the show as a "piece of hilarious theatre put together with deceptively brilliant know-how" ("Why Millions Love Lucy," March 1,

1953) and called Ball "the outstanding figure in popularity for all TV programs" ("TV's Top Comediennes," *New York Times Magazine* (December 27, 1953) 16–17.

76. Philip Hamburger, "Television," *New Yorker*, January 23, 1954, 89.

77. Robert Lewis Shayon, in Ralph Lewis Smith, *A Study of the Professional Criticism of Broadcasting in the United States 1920–1955* (New York: Arno Press, 1979), 177.

78. John Crosby, "Twilight World on TV Getting Little Mildewed," *St. Petersburg Times*, May 25, 1954, 30.

79. Jack Gould, "TV's Psychodrama: How to Keep 'Em Down on the Couch After They've Written for TV?" *New York Times*, August 7, 1955, 264.

80. Crosby, *Out of the Blue*, 199.

81. Jack Gould, "Mediocrity Is Basis of California Activity: Moment from a Christopher Morley Story," *New York Times*, July 10, 1955, 85.

82. Barnouw, 163.

83. *Ibid.*, 165.

84. Boddy, 189.

85. Barnouw, 213.

86. John Crosby, "Papa Is a Patsy," *Pittsburgh Post-Gazette*, June 9, 1954, 27.

87. Robert Lewis Shayon in Ralph Lewis Smith, *A Study of the Professional Criticism*, 205.

88. John Crosby, "Problems? TV Is Full of Them on Family Night," *Detroit Free Press*, July 22, 1953, 17.

89. Shayon in Smith, 207.

90. *Ibid.*, 220.

91. Mannes, "Comments on TV," *The Reporter*, January 6, 1953, 35.

92. *Ibid.*, 36.

93. Mannes, "Channels: Under the Knife," *The Reporter*, October 21, 1954, 42.

94. Crosby in Smith, 203.

95. Jack Gould, "TV: Tribute to *Omnibus*; Expected Loss of Program Brings Call for Similar Experimental Shows," *New York Times*, July 30, 1959, 55.

96. John Crosby, "TV Kills its Critics," *Detroit Free Press*, August 21, 1958, 33.

97. Crosby, "Press Criticism by TV Welcomed," *Detroit Free Press*, July 7, 1958, 35.

98. Later, he will become a prolific novelist, publishing more than a dozen books.

99. Quoted in Boddy, 240.

Chapter Two

1. Boddy, 244.
2. *Ibid.*, 246.
3. *Ibid.*, 251.
4. One of these detractors was Connecticut Senator Thomas Dodd who, in 1961, held the first in what would be a three year long series of high-profile hearings on television violence and its potential effects on children.
5. In the mid–1960s one network took out a full page ad in the *New York Times* declaring that "nobody likes us but people" See Robert Rutherford-Smith, *Beyond the Wasteland: The Criticism of Broadcasting* (Washington, D.C.: The National Institute of Education, 1976), 8.
6. Boddy, 234.
7. *Ibid.*, 235.
8. *Ibid.*
9. Frank Stanton in "Program Hearings Fail to Orbit," *Broadcasting* 62 (January 29, 1962): 46.
10. Quoted in Boddy, 235.
11. Quoted in William Boddy, "The Seven Dwarfs and the Money Grubbers: The Public Relations Crisis of U.S. Television in the Late 1950s," in Patricia Mellencamp, ed., *Logics of Television: Essays in Cultural Criticism* (Bloomington: Indiana University Press, 1990), 111.
12. "New Wave of Television Criticism," *Television Age*, December 11, 1961, 75 quoted in Boddy, 31.
13. Quoted in Lewis Gould, *Watching Television*, 21.
14. Minow quoted in Barnouw, 300.
15. Minow quoted in James L. Baughman, "Minow's Viewers: Understanding the Response to the 'Vast Wasteland' Address," *Federal Communications Law Journal* 55 (2003): 449.
16. The new wave of television criticism, inspired in part by Minow, continued into 1962. At least six books investigating the industry were in print that year including *TV in America: The Morality of Hard Cash.* See Mary Ann Watson, *The Expanding Vista: American Television in the Kennedy Years* (Durham: Duke University Press, 1994).
17. Watson, *The Expanding Vista*, 23.
18. Quoted in Boddy, 227.
19. *Ibid.*, 228.
20. In 1966, the University of Texas convened a conference called "The Meaning of Commercial Television."
21. Edgerton, 225.
22. During the 1961-1962 season, the three networks aired more than 250 hours of nonfiction programming including several one-hour documentaries on the civil rights movement from the perspective of African Americans. See Edgerton, 238.
23. *Dr. Kildare* is also popular with Gould who wrote: "The education of Dr. Kildare is the education of the set owner. Together they are becoming acquainted with the assorted dimensions of medical life." See Jack Gould, "TV: Hospital Dramas; High Ratings of Drs. Casey and Kildare Reveal Public's Interest In Medicine," *New York Times*, March 12, 1962, 55.
24. Barnouw, 403.
25. *Ibid.*, 381.
26. Michael Arlen, *Living Room War* (New York: Penguin Books, 1982), xiv.
27. Quoted in Barnouw, 381.
28. Arlen, 6.
29. Quoted in Edgerton, 266.
30. Barnouw, 403.
31. See Castleman and Podrazik, Walter, 201.
32. Jack Gould, "TV: An Hour of Smothers: Program That C.B.S. Forced Off the Air Found Topical and Amusing," *New York Times*, April 8, 1969, 95.
33. Lynn Spigel, "The Making of a TV Literate Elite," in Christine Geraghty and David Lusted, *The Television Studies Book* (London: Arnold, 1998), 79.
34. *Ibid.*, 80.
35. Howard Rosenberg quoted in Dennis McLellan, "Cecil Smith Dies at 92: *Times* TV Critic Advocated Literate, High-Quality Shows," *Los Angeles Times*, July 14, 2009, http://www.latimes.com/local/obituaries/la-me-cecil-smith14-2009jul14-story.html.
36. Cecil Smith quoted in McLellan.
37. Dick Van Dyke, *My Lucky Life In and Out of Show Business: A Memoir* (New York: Three Rivers Press, 2012), 93.
38. Cecil Smith, "*The Rebel* Coming with Hit Material," *Los Angeles Times*, July 16, 1959, A12.
39. Cecil Smith, "Voice of Public vs.

Voice of Sponsor," *Los Angeles Times*, February 3, 1960, A6.

40. Sherwood Schwartz, *Inside Gilligan's Island: A Three Hour Tour Through the Making of a Television Classic* (New York: St. Martin's Griffin, 1994), 168–169.

41. *Ibid.*, 169.

42. Hal Humphrey, "What It Takes to Gain TV Favor," *Los Angeles Times*, November 6, 1962, D14.

43. *Ibid.*

44. Hal Humphrey, "TV Should Stop Fitting Viewers in Stereotype," *Los Angeles Times*, June 7, 1964, V27.

45. Harlan Ellison, *The Glass Teat* (New York: Ace Books, 1983), 19.

46. *Ibid.*, 29.

47. *Ibid.*, 151.

48. Spigel, 69.

49. *Ibid.*, 67.

50. Others in this group include Terrance O'Flaherty of the *San Francisco Chronicle*, Paul Malloy of the *Chicago Sun-Times* and the *Chicago Tribune*'s Larry Wolters.

51. Lawrence Laurent, "FCC Chief and Prober Harris Clash Before Broadcasters Over TV Ethics," *Washington Post*, March 1, 1960, A1; "FCC May Ease Cable TV Curbs," May 18, 1970, A1.

52. Laurent, "TV's Controversial Prime Time Access Rule," February 25, 1973, 1, "Better Be Cautious of TV Persuasion," July 31, 1960, G2, "The History, Frustrations and Hopes of Public Television," March 24, 1968, H2.

53. Laurent, "TV Spawns Game of Ennui," June 8, 1966, D14, "About Those Non-Viewers," June 21, 1970, 178; "Disenchanted or Not, Viewers Still Are Losing Ground to TV," October 26, 1962, B9.

54. Laurent, "A Critic Looks at Reviewing," *Journal of Broadcasting* 1 (Winter 1966-1967): 16.

55. Spigel, 66.

56. Laurent, "The Complete Television Critic," in Robert Lewis, *The Eighth Art: Twenty-Three Views of Television Today* (New York: Holt, Rinehart and Winston, 1962), 156.

57. *Ibid.*, 171.

58. Jack Gould, "Poor Judgment: Craftsmen and Viewers Tend to Settle for Mediocrity in TV Programs," *New York Times*, February 6, 1955, x15.

59. Seldes quoted in Smith, 120.

60. Mannes quoted in Smith, 120.

61. Crosby quoted in Smith, 126.

62. Laurent, 156.

63. Mannes in Shayon, *The Eighth Art: Twenty-Three Views of Television Today* (New York: Holt, Rinehart and Winston, 1962), 26.

64. *Ibid.*, 28.

65. Gleason's joke was widely repeated. In 1974, one scholar suggested that following Gleason's analogy, the TV critic might give a different account of the traffic accident than the eyewitness. He then offered another way to think about it: "Alas, the television viewer is somewhat like the victim of the traffic accident. He may not even know what hit him, and the task of the reviewer is to tell him what happened and why." John Wright, "Tune-In: The Focus of Television Criticism," *Journal of Popular Culture* 4 (Spring 1974): 889.

66. Amanda Lotz, "On 'Television Criticism': The Pursuit of the Critical Examination of a Popular Art," *Popular Communication* 6 (2008): 27. In January of 1974, news program *60 Minutes* aired a report on press junkets that showed a critic for the *Pittsburgh Post-Gazette* on a New York junket sponsored by CBS opening an envelope that contained two $10 bills. The network's vice president for press information explained that while the footage looked bad, it was a practice that was adopted because many critics complained that their papers did not reimburse them for minor expenses. See Les Brown, "C.B.S. Junkets Program Stirs Industry," the *New York Times*, January 22, 1974, 78.

67. Ernie Kreiling, "A Critical Critic," *Journal of Broadcasting* 1 (Winter 1966-67): 6–7.

68. *Ibid.*

69. He made a point to exclude Gould, Laurent and Shayon, explaining that "they are not typical of the main body of television commentary" but also that they were not the critics who were read by the "vast majority" of newspaper and magazine readers. See Ernie Kreiling, "The Kreiling Thesis," *The Bulletin of the American Society of Newspaper Editors* (September 1965): 4.

70. Les Brown, "Medium Needs Respected Jury," *Variety*, 1965, 52.

71. Kreiling, "A Critical Critic," 8, 27.

72. Quality in this case referred to the classical role of criticism as a public service practice rather the modern industrial idea of criticism as promotion and public relations.

73. Norman Mark, "TV Junketeers," *Columbia Journalism Review* (July-August 1974): 29.

74. *Ibid.*, 30.

75. *Ibid.*, 31.

76. *Ibid.*, 27.

77. *Ibid.*

78. *Ibid.*, 29.

79. Ron Powers quoted in Mark, 29. Except for a few short excerpts such as this one, the work of Ron Powers is not featured in this book. The *Chicago Sun-Times*, where Powers worked for much of the seventies, is not widely archived and access to his columns was unavailable.

80. Gary Deeb, "TV Critics—The Hack Pack," *Variety*, January 9, 1974, 104.

Chapter Three

1. However, some newspapers, particularly those with smaller circulation, let the networks pick up the tab for their critics into the late 1980s. See Sharon Waxman, "Spoon-fed News," *American Journalism Review* 20.8 (October 1998): 29.

2. Lotz, 28.

3. Alan Sepinwall, "Your Guide to the Television Critics Association Press Tour," Hitfix.com, July 8, 2014, http://www.hitfix.com/whats-alan-watching/your-guide-to-the-television-critics-association-press-tour-2.

4. *Ibid.*

5. Todd VanDerWerff, "Why the Television Critics Association Press Tour Still Matters," AVclub.com, August 7, 2012, http://www.avclub.com/article/why-the-television-critics-association-press-tour-83436.

6. *Ibid.*

7. Waxman, 38.

8. Sepinwall, "Your Guide," http://www.hitfix.com/whats-alan-watching/your-guide-to-the-television-critics-association-press-tour-2.

9. Amanda Lotz, "Seventeen Days in July at Hollywood and Highland," *Journal of Popular Film and Television* 33 (Spring 2005): 29.

10. "TCA: An Anonymous Executive Trashes TV Critics," January 11, 2012, http://www.hollywoodreporter.com/news/tca-2012-television-critics-association-press-tour-280600.

11. Adam Wright, "Non-Anonymous TV Critic Trashes Anonymous Executive (and Publication)," *Huffington Post*, August 27, 2013, http://www.huffingtonpost.com/adam-wright/nonanonymous-tv-critic-tr_b_1202581.html.

12. Waxman, 36.

13. *Ibid.*, 38.

14. Lotz, 27.

15. *Ibid.*, 25.

16. For example, skipping the PBS panel might not indicate lack of interest on the part of a critic but rather recognition that the public broadcaster only has a very small share of the national audience. See Lotz, 25.

17. *Ibid.*, 27.

18. Sepinwall, "Your Guide," http://www.hitfix.com/whats-alan-watching/your-guide-to-the-television-critics-association-press-tour-2.

19. Rena Pederson quoted in Hal Himmelstein, *On The Small Screen*, 34.

20. *Ibid.*

21. David Williamson quoted in Mary Ann Watson, "Television Criticism in the Popular Press," *Critical Studies in Mass Communication* 2 (1985): 70.

22. *Ibid.*

23. Pederson in Himmelstein, 35.

24. *Ibid.*

25. Lotz, 27.

26. Castleman and Podrazik, 217.

27. *Ibid.*, 218.

28. Gary Deeb, "MTM's Parting Turns Out Lights of TV Comedy," *Chicago Tribune*, March 18, 1977, A12.

29. The show will later be regarded as a pioneer of "quality" television in academic scholarship as well. While the show's position in the relevancy programming of the 1970s emerged in retrospect, its significance lied in how it depicted the "feel of a culture undergoing the upheavals of a decade." See Jane Feuer et al., *MTM:*

"Quality Television" (London: British Film Institute, 1984): 8.

30. Jerry Buck, "Archie Bunker's Success Influences New Comedies," *Chicago Tribune*, August 15, 1971, NW1.

31. John O' Connor, "TV Review: 4 Situation Comedies Lined Up on C.B.S.," *New York Times*, September 20, 1971, 53.

32. Quoted in Barnouw, 433.

33. Clarence Petersen, "CBS Debuts Courageous New Comedy," *Chicago Tribune*, January 12, 1971, A9.

34. Gary Deeb, "MTM & Co.: Alive and Doing Well, Though Bruised," *Chicago Tribune*, June 11, 1979, A10.

35. Lawrence Laurent, "Happy Days Opposes Trend to Hostility," *Washington Post*, December 22, 1974, 3.

36. Barnouw, 434.

37. Edgerton, 276.

38. Castleman and Podrazik, 257.

39. Edgerton, 295.

40. *Ibid.*

41. Quoted in Edgerton, 295.

42. Michael Arlen, *Living Room War*, xii.

43. *Ibid.*

44. *Ibid.*

45. Arlen, *Living Room War*, 1969 edition, x.

46. Arlen, *Living Room War*, 1976, 9.

47. Jonh O'Connor quoted in Hal Himmelstein, 41.

48. *Ibid.*, 42.

49. *Ibid.*

50. *Ibid.*, 43.

51. *Ibid.*, 60.

52. *Ibid.*

53. John O'Connor, "Bette Davis and Gena Rowlands Star," *New York Times*, May 11, 1979, C26.

54. O'Connor, *"Live From Lincoln Center* Has Found Its Focus," *New York Times*, July 11, 1076, D21.

55. O'Connor, "There's Gold in That There Trash," *New York Times*, March 28, 1971, D21.

56. *Ibid.*

57. *Ibid.*

58. *Ibid.*

59. O'Connor, "Much of New Schedule Insulting," *The Morning News*, September 28, 1975, 51.

60. O'Connor, "TV: Taxi Rolls Into Su-perior Sit-Com," *New York Times*, June 19, 1979, C21.

61. *Ibid.*

62. O'Connor, "Is Norman Lear in a Rut?" *New York Times*, March 21, 1976, 79.

63. O'Connor, "TV: A Sex Comedy by Innuendo," *New York Times*, March 31, 1977, 73.

64. O'Connor, "Prime-Time Programming: By—and for—Whom?" *New York Times*, April 23, 1972, D75.

65. O'Connor, "The 3-Way Race for Mediocrity," *New York Times*, October 12, 1975, 177.

66. *Ibid.*

67. *Ibid.*

68. O'Connor, "In Pursuit of Quality Programs," *New York Times*, March 18, 1979, D37.

69. O'Connor, "Will They Be Fair Without Being Forced?" *New York Times*, January 9, 1972, D17.

70. O'Connor, "Drama Is Dead, Isn't It?" May 16, 1971, D15; "Will a 'Fourth Network' Work?" July 11, 1971, D17.

71. O'Connor, "Can Public Television Be Bought?" *New York Times*, October 13, 1974, 179.

72. O'Connor, "Catching Up, Taking Notice and Gaining Perspective," *New York Times*, November 20, 1977, D33.

73. *Ibid.*

74. O'Connor, "In Pursuit of Quality Programs," *New York Times*, March 18, 1979, D37.

75. Michael Arlen, *Living Room War*, 1982 edition, 240.

76. *Ibid.*, 178.

77. *Ibid.*, 205.

78. *Ibid.*, 117, 120–121.

79. *Ibid.*, 231.

80. *Ibid.*, 218.

81. *Ibid.*, 250.

82. O'Connor also picked up on the discrepancies and he used his review to discuss the production's claims to factual history, writing that the drama "strays distressingly far from historical truth." It was a serious issue for O'Connor who argued that a program's claim to being a true story should not be casually disregarded in favor of dramatic license: "Excuses are made for productions that are "almost true" or "nearly true." But something cannot be almost

true. Falling short of the mark, it is quite simply false. Keeping the distinction clear is crucial for at least the semblance of social sanity." See "TV View: Historical Dramas—Fact or Fancy?" *New York Times*, May 25, 1975, 127.

83. Arlen, 90.

84. *Ibid.*, 198.

85. *Ibid.*, 3.

86. *Ibid.*, 10–11.

87. *Ibid.*, 34.

88. *Ibid.*, 17.

89. Tom Shales, *On the Air!* (New York: Summit Books, 1982), 11.

90. In 2006, Shales accepts a buyout from the *Washington Post* but remains as a contract writer for the paper. He is replaced as lead TV critic in 2009 but appointed as an at-large cultural critic where his focus remains on television. In an interview in 2010, he claims that the paper tells him they can no longer afford his contract. He leaves the *Post* at the end of the year but not before writing a message on the Facebook page of Donald Graham, chairman of the *Washington Post* Company, announcing his departure. Zeke Turner, "After Almost 40 Years Tom Shales Confirms He's Leaving *Washington Post*," October 22, 2010, http://observer.com/2010/10/after-almost-40-years-tom-shales-confirms-hes-leaving-emwashington-postem/.

91. Shales, 11–12.

92. Tom Shales, "The Great One," *Washington Post*, May 28, 1976, reprinted in *On the Air!*, 21.

93. Shales, "Johnny Carson, a Rolls Not a Chevy," *Washington Post*, August 8, 1976, reprinted in *On the Air!*, 24.

94. Shales, "Carol Burnett," *Washington Post*, April 19, 1979, reprinted in *On the Air!*, 153.

95. Shales, "The Garner File: Marshmallow Macho," *Washington Post*, May 13, 1979, reprinted in *On the Air!*, 162.

96. Shales, "Farrah Fawcett-Majors: 'I Just Laugh,'" *Washington Post*, January 5, 1977, reprinted in *On the Air!*, 37.

97. Shales, "Fast *Feud* with Relish," *Washington Post*, November 29, 1978, reprinted in *On the Air!*, 127.

98. Shales, "Robin Williams Visits Earth," *Washington Post*, November 19, 1978, reprinted in *On the Air!*, 121.

99. Shales, "The Last of the Media Monarchs," *Washington Post*, March 11, 1979, reprinted in *On the Air!*, 139.

100. Shales, "Lou Grant: Just What TV Needs," *Washington Post*, September 20, 1977, reprinted in *On the Air!*, 67.

101. Shales, "Edith Bunker's Ordeal," *Washington Post*, October 16, 1977, reprinted in *On the Air!*, 78.

102. Shales, "Singing Sausages," *Washington Post*, October 5, 1977, reprinted in *On the Air!*, 69.

103. Shales, "Nostalgia for the Future," *Washington Post*, December 31, 1977, reprinted in *On the Air!*, 88.

104. Shales, "From L.A., Heeerre's ... the Newsonality!" *Washington Post*, December 28, 1977, reprinted in *On the Air!*, 92.

105. Shales, "Watching *The Teng Show*," *Washington Post*, February 11, 1979, reprinted in *On the Air!*, 146.

106. Shales, "And Now—the End of the World," *Washington Post*, January 27, 1980, reprinted in *On the Air!*, 193.

107. Lawrence Laurent, "A Critic Looks at Reviewing," 16.

108. Originally a non-profit publication under Brown's direction, *Channels* was bought by TV producer Norman Lear in 1985 and re-launched in 2006 as a for-profit publication with more emphasis on the business side of the industry.

109. Quoted in Holston, "Les Brown: Thinking Inside the Box," 2013, http://www.peabodyawards.com/stories/story/les-brown-thinking-inside-the-box.

110. Responding to Brown's piece, critic Larry Wolters gave the more typical defense. "Well Les," he wrote, "we suspect TV will draw more responsible and respected critics when television does more responsible and worthwhile shows." The comment suggested that Brown's analysis was the more thoughtful one. Wolters, "TV Critic Answers Critic's Criticism," *Chicago Tribune*, August 22, 1965, 12.

111. Brown, "Slick Trappings Versus Claptrap," *Variety*, September 13, 1967, 34.

112. Brown, "No Lack of Controversy in 'PBL's' Non-Bland Brand of Public Video," *Variety*, November 8, 1967, 41.

113. Brown, "Sesame Street: Wunderkind," *Variety*, December 24, 1969, 23.

114. Brown, "Revenue Worries Cut

Prime-Time TV News Special," *New York Times*, October 24, 1973, 94.

115. Brown, "*60 Minutes*: The Knotty Problem of Scheduling," *New York Times*, December 29, 1973, 47.

116. O'Connor, "To the Critics: How Would You Improve Things?" *New York Times*, October 10, 1971, D17.

117. Brown, *Televi$ion: The Business Behind the Box* (New York: Harcourt, Brace Jovanovich, 1971): 61.

118. *Ibid.*, 62.

119. *Ibid.*, 63.

120. *Ibid.*,, 15–16.

121. *Ibid.*, 365.

122. Brown, "Broadcasters, at Convention, Strike Back at Activist Critics," *New York Times*, March 19, 1974, 75.

123. Brown, *Keeping Your Eye on Television* (New York: Pilgrim Press, 1979), 7.

124. Brown, "Remarks to the Iowa TV Critics Conference," *Critical Studies in Mass Communication* 2 (December 1985): 394.

125. *Ibid.*

Chapter Four

1. Edgerton, 296.

2. Castleman and Podrazik, 293.

3. Edgerton, 296.

4. Les Brown, "The Networks Cry Havoc," *New York Times*, February 12, 1978, 166.

5. *Ibid.*

6. Quoted in Les Brown, "Cable and Pay TV on Eve of Technological Revolution," *New York Times*, July 31, 1978, C12.

7. *Ibid.*

8. *Ibid.*

9. Brown, "The TV Audience vs. the Public," *New York Times*, August 19, 1979, D27.

10. N.R. Kleinfield, "ABC Is Being Sold for $3.5 Billion; 1st Network Sale," *New York Times*, March 19, 1985, http://www.ny times.com/1985/03/19/business/abc-is-being-sold-for-3.5-billion-1st-network-sale.html.

11. Edgerton, 298–299.

12. David Lachenbruch, "Television in the '90s: The Shape of Things to Come," *TV Guide*, January 20, 1990, 13.

13. Jane Feuer, *Seeing Through the Eight-*

ies: Television and Reaganism* (Durham: Duke University Press, 1995): 51.

14. O'Connor, "TV View: The 'Hill Street Blues' Lesson," *New York Times*, December 13, 1981, http://www.nytimes.com/1981/12/13/arts/tv-view-the-hill-street-blues-lesson.html.

15. *Ibid.*

16. Tony Schwartz, "How 'Hill Street' Broke the Police-Show Mold," *New York Times*, April 27, 1982, http://www.nytimes.com/1982/04/27/arts/how-hill-street-broke-the-police-show-mold.html.

17. Rosenberg, "The 'Hill Street Blues' Shuffle," *Los Angeles Times*, January 14, 1981, H8.

18. William Henry III, "NBC's Peacock Not So Proud," *Boston Globe*, July 25, 1980.

19. Schwartz, "How 'Hill Street' Broke the Police-Show Mold," *New York Times*, April 27, 1982, http://www.nytimes.com/1982/04/27/arts/how-hill-street-broke-the-police-show-mold.html.

20. Shales, "Hill Street Blues: TV's Embattled Precinct," *Washington Post*, March 8, 1981, M1.

21. Joyce Carol-Oates, "The Best of Television: For Its Audacity, Its Defiantly Bad Taste and Its Superb Character Studies," *TV Guide*, June 1, 1985, 4–7.

22. O'Connor, "The Hill Street Blues Lesson."

23. See Michael Newman and Elana Levine, *Legitimating Television* (Routledge: New York, 2012).

24. Robert Thompson, "Hill Street: An Avenue to Quality Storytelling," *Washington Post*, January 22, 2006, http://www.washingtonpost.com/wp/dyn/content/article/2006/01/17/AR2006011701117.htm l.

25. See Robert Thompson, *Television's Second Golden Age: From "Hill Street Blues" to "ER"* (New York: Syracuse University Press, 1997).

26. Gail Caldwell, "Making Us Squirm..." *Boston Globe*, June 30, 1989, 41.

27. Rosenberg, "New TV Generation Gets Older, Better at *thirtysomething*," *Los Angeles Times*, September 29, 1987, 1.

28. Marvin Kitman, "A Show on the Edge of Reality," *Newsday*, December 13, 1988, 15.

29. Kitman, "A Dramady with a Touch

of Realism," *Newsday*, September 29, 1987, 17.

30. Ed Siegel, "A Superb *St. Elsewhere*," *Boston Globe*, September 25, 1985, 55.

31. Kitman, "The Saddest News of the TV Season," *Newsday*, March 1, 1988, 11.

32. Rosenberg, "NBC's New *L.A. Law*: The Verdict Is Great," *Los Angeles Times*, September 15, 1986, 1.

33. Julie D'Acci, Julie quoted in Edgerton, 315.

34. In 1989, it shared number one with *Roseanne*.

35. O'Connor "TV Reviews: Bill Cosby's Triumph," *New York Times*, May 9, 1985, http://www.nytimes.com/1985/05/09/arts/tv-reviews-bill-cosby-s-triumph.html.

36. Sally Bedell Smith, "Cosby Puts His Stamp on a TV Hit," *New York Times*, November 18, 1984, http://www.nytimes.com/1984/11/18/arts/cosby-puts-his-stamp-on-a-tv-hit.html.

37. Kitman "*Father Knows Best* of the 1980's," *Newsday*, December 15, 1985, 7.

38. Bedell Smith, "Cosby Puts His Stamp on a TV Hit," *New York Times*, November 18, 1984, http://www.nytimes.com/1984/11/18/arts/cosby-puts-his-stamp-on-a-tv-hit.html.

39. O'Connor, "TV Reviews: An Update on The Cosby Show," *New York Times*, January 21, 1988, http://www.nytimes.com/1988/01/21/arts/tv-reviews-an-update-on-the-cosby-show.html.

40. *Ibid.*

41. Edgerton, 353.

42. Comic Roseanne Barr's version of working class married life in the successful sitcom *Roseanne* was still going strong in the nineties while *Grace Under Fire*, a success for ABC when it premiered in 1993, showcased comedian Brett Butler as blue-collar single mom Grace Kelly.

43. The most watched entertainment events up until that point were the 1983 finale of *Mash* (106 million viewers), the "Who Shot J.R.?" episode of *Dallas* in 1980 (83.6 million), the final *Cheers* in 1993 (80.5 million), the 1983 movie *The Day After* (77.4 million) and the last chapter of *Roots* (76.7 million) in 1977. See Brian Lowry, "*Seinfeld's* Finale Ends Up in Sixth Place of All Time," *Los Angeles Times*, May 16, 1998, http://articles.latimes.com/1998/may/16/entertainment/ca-50143.

44. O'Connor, "New York Cops in a Frank Light," *New York Times*, September 21, 1993, http://www.nytimes.com/1993/09/21/arts/review-television-new-york-cops-in-a-frank-light.html.

45. Kitman, "*NYPD's* Censorship Blues," *Newsday*, September 19, 1993, 19.

46. Ed Siegel, "Bochco Hits Bottom with *NYPD Blue*," *Boston Globe*, September 10, 1993, https://www.highbeam.com/doc/1P2-8244430.html.

47. Rosenberg "*Blue*: Color It a Pale Imitation of *Blues*," *Los Angeles Times*, September 21, 1993, http://articles.latimes.com/1993-09-21/entertainment/ca-37382_1_nypd-blue.

48. Kitman, "Too Good to Last," *Newsday*, January 31, 1993, 21.

49. For more on this see Sara Gwenllian-Jones and Roberta Pearson, eds., *Cult Television* (Minneapolis: University of Minnesota Press, 2004) and Matt Hills, "Defining Cult TV: Texts, Inter-Texts and Fan Audiences," in *The Television Studies Book*, ed. Robert C. Allen and Annette Hill (New York: Routledge, 2004).

50. Richard Zoglin, "Like Nothing on Earth," *Time*, April 9, 1990, http://content.time.com/time/magazine/article/0,9171,154191,00.html.

51. Kitman, "Lynch's Powerful Mystery," *Newsday*, April 5, 1990.

52. Frost quoted in Michael Giltz, "*Twin Peaks'* Fever: The Show Ushered in a New Kind of TV in 1990, Paving the Way for *X-Files* and Other Like-Minded Series," *Los Angeles Times*, September 10, 2010.

53. Joyce Millman, "As the Parallel World Turns," *San Francisco Examiner*, July 22, 1990, https://joycemillman.wordpress.com/2014/10/09/from-the-vault-twin-peaks-in-its-time/.

54. Zoglin, "Like Nothing on Earth," *Time*, April 9, 1990, http://content.time.com/time/magazine/article/0,9171,154191,00.html.

55. Jim Jerome, "The Triumph of Twin Peaks," *Entertainment Weekly*, April 6, 1990, lynchnet.com.

56. Caldwell, "Post-Modern Gothic: A Whacked-Out World in *Twin Peaks*, U.S.A.," *Boston Globe*, April 26, 1990, 85.

57. *Ibid.*

58. Zoglin, "Like Nothing on Earth,"

Time, April 9, 1990, http://content.time.com/time/magazine/article/0,9171,154191,00.html.

59. Caldwell, "Post-Modern Gothic: A Whacked-Out World in *Twin Peaks*, U.S.A.," *Boston Globe*, April 26, 1990, 85.

60. Mark Harris, "Why TV Had to Make *Peaks*," *Entertainment Weekly*, April 6, 1990, http://www.ew.com/article/1990/04/06/why-tv-had-make-twin-peaks.

61. Past programs, like those from MTM Productions and its creative alumni, were applauded for their innovation but on an individual basis.

62. Quoted in Newman and Levine, 27.

63. Ed Siegel, "The Lesson is Clear: Differ and Conquer," *Boston Globe*, April 19, 1990, 65.

64. Michael Giltz "*Twin Peaks* Fever: The Show Ushered in a New Kind of TV in 1990, Paving the Way for *X-Files* and Other Like-Minded Series," *Los Angeles Times*, September 10, 2010, D3.

65. Newman and Levine, 27.

66. See Thompson, *Television's Second Golden Age*, 159.

67. Mike Duffy, "HBO Celebrates 25 Years of Fun in Risky Business," *Boston Globe*, November 14, 1997, D16.

68. *Ibid.*

69. The message has been a lasting one. In 2011, a journalist wrote that the "near-miraculous transformation" of television from the "lowliest art form" is "almost entirely" the result of HBO and "its commitment to quality" (Peter Aspden, "It's Not Just TV: How HBO Revolutionized Television," *Financial Times*, September 24, 2011).

70. Rosenberg, "*Sopranos* Still Supreme," *Los Angeles Times*, January 14, 2000, 1.

71. Caryn James, "Addicted to a Mob Family Potion," *New York Times*, March 25, 1999, http://www.nytimes.com/1999/03/25/arts/addicted-to-a-mob-family-potion.html.

72. Kitman, "Here's an Offer You Can't Refuse," *Newsday*, January 10, 1999, D35.

73. David Bianculli, "*Sopranos* Has Makings of a Hit," *New York Daily News*, January 8, 1999, http://www.nydailynews.com/entertainment/tv/sopranos-makings-hit-1999-review-article-1.822131.

74. Rosenberg, "*Providence* Is Flat but *Sopranos* Really Sings," *Los Angeles Times*, January 8, 1999, http://articles.latimes.com/1999/jan/08/entertainment/ca-61442.

75. Vincent Canby, "From the Humble Mini-Series Comes the Magnificent Megamovie," *New York Times*, October 31, 1999, http://www.nytimes.com/1999/10/31/arts/from-the-humble-mini-series-comes-the-magnificent-megamovie.html.

76. Matthew Gilbert, "Bada Bing! The Hits Just Keep Coming as Mob Series *The Sopranos* Returns with all its Operatic, Lowlife Potency," *Boston Globe*, January 14, 2000, D1.

77. James, "Addicted to a Mob Family Potion," *New York Times*, March 25, 1999, http://www.nytimes.com/1999/03/25/arts/addicted-to-a-mob-family-potion.html.

78. Matthew Gilbert, "Mob Hit: *The Sopranos* Is a Killer Series with a Smart Edge," *Boston Globe*, April 2, 1999, F1.

79. Kendall Hamilton and Corrie Brown, "They're Having a Heat Wave," *Newsweek*, June 21, 1999, 68.

80. Newman and Levine, 32.

81. Bill Carter ,"He Engineered a Mob Hit, And Now It's Time to Pay Up; Entering a 2nd Season, *The Sopranos* Has a Hard Act to Follow," *New York Times*, January 11, 2000, http://www.nytimes.com/2000/01/11/arts/he-engineered-mob-hit-now-it-s-time-pay-up-entering-2nd-season-sopranos-has-hard.html.

82. Carter, "A Cable Show Networks Truly Watch," *New York Times*, March 25, 1999, http://www.nytimes.com/1999/03/25/arts/a-cable-show-networks-truly-watch.html.

83. Peter Liguori quoted in David Goetzl, "The Biz: Taking Cue from Cable, Gingerly," *Advertising Age*, March 18, 2002, 63.

84. Quoted in Newman and Levine, 33.

85. For example, television was no longer compared to film as a lower art form because certain shows proved it could be cinematic.

86. Arlen, *The Camera Age* (New York: Penguin, 1981), 10.

87. William Henry quoted in Watson, 71.

88. *Ibid.*, 72.

89. Henry, "Once Upon a Time ... a

Modern Fable," *Boston Globe*, March 5, 1980, 1.

90. Henry, "Here's a Word from the Sponsor," *Boston Globe*, April 2, 1980, 1.

91. Henry, "Please, Optimism Only," *Boston Globe*, June 27, 1980, 1.

92. Henry, "Nothing Very Lovable About This Lucy Show," *Boston Globe*, February 8, 1980, 1.

93. Henry, "Of Hispanics and Cambodia," *Boston Globe*, March 28, 1980, 1.

94. Henry, "Ring Around the Blue Collar," *Boston Globe*, January 16, 1980, 1.

95. Henry, "Glamorizing Gangsters' Lives," *Boston Globe*, August 8, 1980, 1.

96. Henry, "Beyond 60 Minutes," *Boston Globe*, July 9, 1980, 1.

97. Henry, "Reruns Recall Simpler Times," *Boston Globe*, May 13, 1980, 1.

98. Henry, "How TV Reports the Process," *Boston Globe*, August 12, 1980, 1.

99. Henry, "On Racial Harmony," *Boston Globe*, May 17, 1980, 1.

100. Henry, "Goodbye Boston, Hello New York," *Boston Globe*, August 31, 1980, 1.

101. Rosenberg, *Not So Prime Time: Chasing The Trivial on American Television* (Chicago: Ivan R. Dee, 2004), xv.

102. *Ibid.*

103. Covering Rosenberg's large collection of work could be a book in itself. Here, I mainly focus on his columns from 1985, the year he won the Pulitzer Prize.

104. Rosenberg, "Reality: Blowout vs. Being Blown Away," *Los Angeles Times*, March 2, 1981, G9.

105. *Ibid.*, G1.

106. Rosenberg, "TV Takes the Fun Out of Funny," *Los Angeles Times*, February 22, 1985, 1.

107. *Ibid.*

108. Rosenberg, "A Little of the Big House Over HBO," *Los Angeles Times*, February 27, 1985, 10.

109. Rosenberg, "TV Comes to Terms with Disabled," *Los Angeles Times*, October 16, 1985, 1.

110. Rosenberg, "TV Review: Hard to Sit Long for *Stone Pillow*," *Los Angeles Times*, November 5, 1985, 9.

111. Rosenberg, "TV Abuse of the Child-Abuse Issue," *Los Angeles Times*, March 5, 1985, 8.

112. Rosenberg, "The Fall TV Season

America: Welcome to 'Bozovision,'" *Los Angeles Times*, September 25, 1985, 1.

113. Rosenberg, "A Matter of Light and Death," *Los Angeles Times*, November 20, 1985, 1.

114. Rosenberg, "Commercial Break, and All's Well," *Los Angeles Times*, July 24, 1985, 1.

115. Rosenberg, "Gobble, Gobble, Ugh, Ugh, The Turkeys Are Coming Home to TV Roost," *Los Angeles Times*, November 28, 1985, 1.

116. Rosenberg, "TV Respect: As Simple As, Uh, ABC," *Los Angeles Times*, April 29, 1985, 1.

117. Rosenberg, "Contraceptive Issue: Networks on the Spot," *Los Angeles Times*, August 7, 1985, 1.

118. Rosenberg, "Television's March Through Atlantagate," *Los Angeles Times*, February 13, 1985, 1.

119. Rosenberg, "A Miracle! I Can Now Spell 'Pulitzer,'" *Los Angeles Times*, April 26, 1985, 1.

120. Rosenberg, "If You're Not for Yourself, Who Will Be for You?" reprinted in *Not So Prime Time*, 45.

121. Rosenberg, "*A Masterpiece Theatre* of Pomp and Puff," reprinted in *Not So Prime Time*, 250).

122. *Ibid.*, 251.

123. *Ibid.*, 252.

124. Rosenberg, "When the Coverage Is as Senseless as the Tragedy," reprinted in *Not So Prime Time*, 253.

125. *Ibid.*, 255.

126. Rosenberg, "The Death of 'Challenger' Recalled," reprinted in *Not So Prime Time*, 209.

127. *Ibid.*

128. Bob Klapisch, "Newsday Newsie," November 11, 2013, Bergen.com.

129. Marvin Kitman, "A Comatose *Saturday Night Live*," *Newsday*, November 12, 1985, 28.

130. Kitman, "Score One for the Wholesome Contingent," *Newsday*, March 25, 1986, 28.

131. Kitman, "Where's All the Great Trash," *Newsday*, March 2, 1986, 7.

132. Kitman, "A Tragedy Brought Home," *Newsday*, January 29, 1986, 56.

133. *Ibid.*

134. Kitman, "Living the Creative Life

of a Grapefruit," *Newsday*, November 3, 1985, 4.

135. Kitman "People Meters: It's New Wave TV Gadgetry," *Newsday*, September 4, 1987, 9.

136. *Ibid.*

137. Kitman, "The Screen Goes Dark, After 35 Years of Sitting Through the Good, the Bad and the Worst, Newsday's TV Critic Hits the Off Button," *Newsday*, April 3, 2005, C.16.

138. Rabinowitz was also nominated for the Pulitzer Prize for Criticism for her television writing in 1995 and 1998. In 1996, she was nominated in the Commentary category for her columns challenging several cases on alleged child abuse. She won the Pulitzer Prize for Commentary in 2001 for a series of articles published in 2000 on social and cultural trends in the United States.

139. Rabinowitz, "The President and the Polls," *Wall Street Journal*, February 2, 1998, http://www.wsj.com/articles/SB886 371380741548000.

140. Rabinowitz, "A Touch of Early Frost," *Wall Street Journal*, March 30, 1998, http://www.wsj.com/articles/SB8912099 58164059500.

141. Rabinowitz "All Abuse, All the Time," *Wall Street Journal*, August 31, 1998, http://www.wsj.com/articles/SB9045229 54220730500.

142. Rabinowitz "Fiddling With the Fact," *Wall Street Journal*, October 12, 1998, http://www.wsj.com/articles/SB9081565 75286060000.

143. Rabinowitz "Aliens Emerge on the Tube," *Wall Street Journal*, January 19, 1998.

144. Rabinowitz "A Virtuous Brood," *Wall Street Journal*, November 9, 1998, http://www.wsj.com/articles/SB9105700 72363239000.

145. *Ibid.*

146. It should be noted that Joyce Millman is part of the list of influential TV critics during the 1980s and 1990s. Millman was a finalist for the Pulitzer Prize for criticism in 1989 and 1991 for her *San Francisco Examiner* TV columns. In 1995, she left the *Examiner* and was a founding member of Salon.com where she wrote television and pop music criticism. An overview of her work is not included here be-

cause there are no digital archives available for the *Examiner*.

Chapter Five

1. Edgerton, 411.

2. *Ibid.*, 424.

3. See "Netflix Is Now Available Around the World," January 6, 2016, https://media.netflix.com/en/press-releases/netflix-is-now-available-around-the-world.

4. While *Television Without Pity* stopped operating in 2014, its archives are still available on the site.

5. Castleman and Podrazik, 409.

6. Gail Pennington, "Light Up the Tiki Torches, *Survivor* Is a Winner," *St. Louis Post-Dispatch*, June 2, 2000, 49, https://www.newspapers.com/newspage/14262 4324/.

7. Sepinwall, "*Survivor*," *Newark Star-Ledger*, June 2, 2000, 37, http://www.metacritic.com/tv/survivor/critic-reviews and Bianculli, "*Survivor* A Winner," *New York Daily News*, June 1, 2000, http://www.nydailynews.com/archives/entertainment/survivor-winner-article-1.873993.

8. Robert Bianco, "*Lost* Finds Fresh Adventure in Familiar Story," *USA Today*, September 21, 2004, http://usatoday30.usatoday.com/life/television/reviews/2004-09-21-lost-review_x.htm.

9. Ken Tucker, "Review: *Lost*," September 24, 2004, http://www.ew.com/article/2004/09/24/lost.

10. Phil Rosenthal, "*Lost*," *Chicago Sun-Times*, September 22, 2004, 65, http://www.metacritic.com/critic/phil-rosenthal?filter=tvshows.

11. Bryan Lowry, "Review: *Lost*," *Variety*, September 19, 2004, http://variety.com/2004/tv/reviews/lost-6-1200530982/.

12. See Brett Martin, *Difficult Men: Behind the Scenes of a Creative Revolution From "The Sopranos" and "The Wire" to "Mad Men" and "Breaking Bad"* (New York: Penguin, 2014).

13. Lisa Schwarzbaum, "No More Mr. Nice Guys," Sunday Book Review, *New York Times*, July 12, 2013http://www.nytimes.com/2013/07/14/books/review/difficult-men-by-brett-martin.html?_r=0.

14. Jeff Simon, "Let's Put the Smartest TV Critics on Television," *Buffalo News*,

August 20, 2013, http://www.buffalonews.
com/columns/jeff-simon/jeff-simon-lets-
put-the-smartest-tv-critics-on-television-
20130820.

15. Sepinwall, "How Much Good TV Is
Too Much?" April 11, 2013, HitFix.com,
http://www.hitfix.com/whats-alan-watch
ing/how-much-good-tv-is-too-much.

16. Sepinwall, "Peak TV in America: Is
There Really Too Much Good Scripted
Television?" August 18, 2015, HitFix.com,
http://www.hitfix.com/whats-alan-watch
ing/peak-tv-in-america-is-there-really-
too-much-good-scripted-television.

17. Linda Holmes, "Television 2015: Is
There Really Too Much TV?" *NPR.org*, August 16, 2015, http://www.npr.org/sections/
monkeysee/2015/08/16/432458841/tele
vision-2015-is-there-really-too-much-tv.

18. Mary McNamara, "How TV's Age
of Exploration Put Viewers in Control," *Los
Angeles Times*, November 21, 2014, http://
www.latimes.com/entertainment/tv/la-et-
st-tv-critics-exploration-collectible-tv-
20141123-column.html.

19. In 2011, research found that commenting on shows via Twitter increased
362 percent. See Karen Brooks, "When
Twitter Meets Television, Criticism Becomes Fast and Faceless," *Courier-Mail*,
June 20, 2012, http://www.couriermail.
com.au.

20. John Jurgensen, "The TV Recappers:
From *Breaking Bad* to *Honey Boo Boo*," *Wall
Street Journal*, August 16, 2013, http://www.
wsj.com/articles/SB10001424127887324
769704579008593725664338.

21. *Ibid.*

22. Quoted in Jeremy Egner, "The Game
Never Ends: David Simon on Wearying
Wire Love and the Surprising Usefulness
of Twitter," *New York Times*, April 5, 2012,
http://artsbeat.blogs.nytimes.com/2012/
04/05/the-game-never-ends-david-
simon-on-wearying-wire-love-and-the-
surprising-usefulness-of-twitter/.

23. Media scholar Jason Mittell also
published a response on his blog. See "Jus-
tifying David Simon," justtv.wordpress.com,
April 11, 2012.

24. Sepinwall, "Interview: David Simon
Doesn't Want to Tell You How to Watch
The Wire," HitFix.com, April 6, 2012,
http://www.hitfix.com/blogs/whats-alan-

watching/posts/interview-david-simon-
doesnt-want-to-tell-you-how-to-watch-
the-wire.

25. Noel Murray, "Sympathy for Kurt
Sutter (and Veena Sud, and David Simon),"
April 11, 2012, AVclub.com, http://www.
avclub.com/article/sympathy-for-kurt-
sutter-and-veena-sud-and-david-s-72226.

26. One recapper who wrote about
Breaking Bad for the *A.V. Club* received
around 3,000 comments after her post on
the show's first episode of its final season
went on the site. See Jurgensen, "The TV
Recappers."

27. Murray, "Sympathy for Kurt Sutter
(and Veena Sud, and David Simon)," April
11, 2012, AVclub.com, http://www.avclub.
com/article/sympathy-for-kurt-sutter-
and-veena-sud-and-david-s-72226.

28. Emily Nussbaum quoted in Sara
Morrison, "Taking the Seen-It Route," *Columbia Journalism Review* (November/De-
cember 2012): 44.

29. Tucker, "The Masculine Mystique,"
Bookforum, Summer 2013, http://www.
bookforum.com/inprint/020_02/11665.

30. Matt Zoller Seitz, "The Sum and the
Parts: In Defense of TV Recaps," Vulture.
com, April 12, 2002. In this piece, Zoller
Seitz also defines recap and overnight review as two separate types of writing.
http://www.vulture.com/2012/04/matt-
zoller-seitz-in-defense-of-tv-recaps.html.

31. Ryan McGee, "Never Mind the Bol-
locks, Here's the Future of Television Criticism," Boobtubedude.com, November 6,
2011, http://boobtubedude.com/index.php/
2011/11/06/theory/never-mind-the-
bollocks-heres-the-future-of-television-
criticism/.

32. Noel Murray and Scott Tobias, "How
Has the Culture of TV (and TV Watching)
Changed?" AVclub.com, June 18, 2010,
http://www.avclub.com/article/how-has-
the-culture-of-tv-and-tv-watching-
changed-42274.

33. Zoller Seitz, "The Sum and the Parts:
In Defense of TV Recaps," Vulture.com,
April 12, 2002. In this piece, Zoller Seitz
also defines recap and overnight review as
two separate types of writing. http://www.
vulture.com/2012/04/matt-zoller-seitz-in-
defense-of-tv-recaps.html.

34. Murray, "Sympathy for Kurt Sutter

(and Veena Sud, and David Simon)," April 11, 2012, AVclub.com, http://www.avclub.com/article/sympathy-for-kurt-sutter-and-veena-sud-and-david-s-72226.

35. Zoller Seitz, "The Sum and the Parts: In Defense of TV Recaps," Vulture.com, April 12, 2002. In this piece, Zoller Seitz also defines recap and overnight review as two separate types of writing. http://www.vulture.com/2012/04/matt-zoller-seitz-in-defense-of-tv-recaps.html.

36. Murray, "Sympathy for Kurt Sutter (and Veena Sud, and David Simon)," April 11, 2012, AVclub.com, http://www.avclub.com/article/sympathy-for-kurt-sutter-and-veena-sud-and-david-s-72226.

37. Murray and Tobias, "How Has the Culture of TV (and TV Watching) Changed?" AVclub.com, June 18, 2010, http://www.avclub.com/article/how-has-the-culture-of-tv-and-tv-watching-changed-42274.

38. Murray, "Sympathy for Kurt Sutter (and Veena Sud, and David Simon)," April 11, 2012, AVclub.com, http://www.avclub.com/article/sympathy-for-kurt-sutter-and-veena-sud-and-david-s-72226.

39. Sepinwall, "Why Your TV Show Doesn't Have to Be a Novel: In Defense of the Episode," Hitfix.com, November 24, 2015, http://www.hitfix.com/whats-alan-watching/why-your-tv-show-doesnt-have-to-be-a-novel-in-defense-of-the-episode.

40. Alyssa Rosenberg, "Our Relationship with TV Is Messed Up. It's Time for a Change," *Washington Post*, February 26, 2016, https://www.washingtonpost.com/news/act-four/wp/2016/02/26/our-relationship-with-tv-is-messed-up-its-time-for-a-change/.

41. Todd VanDerWerff, "Netflix Is Accidentally Inventing a New Art Form—Not Quite TV and Not Quite Film," Vox.com, July, 29, 2015, http://www.vox.com/2015/7/29/9061833/netflix-binge-new-artform.

42. James Poniewozik, "Streaming TV Isn't Just a New Way to Watch. It's a New Genre," *New York Times*, December 16, 2015, http://www.nytimes.com/2015/12/20/arts/television/streaming-tv-isnt-just-a-new-way-to-watch-its-a-new-genre.html.

43. Josh Levin, "Alan Sepinwall: He Changed TV Criticism. But Can You Be a Rabid Fan and a Thoughtful Reviewer?" Slate.com, February 14, 2011, http://www.slate.com/articles/arts/culturebox/2011/02/the_tv_guide.html.

44. Poniewozik, "Warming: TV Critic Discussing TV Critics Discussing TV Criticism," *Time*, Feb. 14, 2011, http://entertainment.time.com/2011/02/14/warning-tv-critic-discussing-tv-critics-discussing-tv-criticism/.

45. Sepinwall, "In Which I Talk About Slate Talking About Me," Hitfix.com, February 14, 2011, http://www.hitfix.com/blogs/whats-alan-watching/posts/in-which-i-talk-about-slate-talking-about-me.

46. Myles McNutt, "The Critic in (Online) Society: An Alternate History of 21st Century Television Criticism," Cultural-learnings.com, February 15, 2011, https://cultural-learnings.com/2011/02/15/the-critic-in-online-society-an-alternate-history-of-21st-century-television-criticism/.

47. Complicating this is the fact that episodic coverage is usually of interest to dedicated fans who may be more attracted to praise about their favorite show than condemnation.

Chapter Six

1. Sepinwall "In Which I Talk About...," http://www.hitfix.com/blogs/whats-alan-watching/posts/in-which-i-talk-about-slate-talking-about-me.

2. Sepinwall says he does not write recaps. In his first *What's Alan Watching?* blog for *Hitfix* he writes: "These are not recaps I'm writing, though of course a good chunk of the plot can and will be discussed. My goal is to figure out whether an episode worked or didn't, talk about why, and in the cases of some shows that go deeper (*Lost*, *Treme*) talk about theme and hidden meaning and the rest." See http://www.hitfix.com/blogs/whats-alan-watching/posts/glad-to-see-me-i-guess-we-re-in-the-next-blog#boU5ekwTHDk2J0cv.99.

3. Sepinwall, "*Chuck*: An Open Letter to NBC to Save It," *Star-Ledger*, April 20, 2009 http://www.nj.com/entertainment/tv/index.ssf/2009/04/chuck_an_open_letter_to_nbc_to.html.

4. Sepinwall, "*Chuck*: Talking Renewal

with Ben Silverman and Chris Fedak," *Star-Ledger*, May 19, 2009, http://www.nj. com/entertainment/tv/index.ssf/2009/05/ chuck_talking_renewal_with_ben.html.

5. Levin, "Alan Sepinwall: He Changed TV Criticism...," http://www.slate.com/ articles/arts/culturebox/2011/02/the_tv_ guide.html.

6. *Ibid.*

7. Sepinwall, "In Which I Talk About...," http://www.hitfix.com/blogs/whats-alan-watching/posts/in-which-i-talk-about-slate-talking-about-me.

8. *Ibid.* Sepinwall received so much reader backlash on his negative reviews of *Modern Family* that he stopped covering the show. He claimed that due to the amount of shows he wrote about, getting so much angry feedback on a show that he liked but didn't love was not worth it and he was better off using that time to cover what he still enjoyed writing about. He added that he would still cover shows he didn't like or ones where he disagreed with his readers but the *Modern Family* situation "had gone too far."

9. Sepinwall, "*Chuck*, 'Chuck vs. the Role Models': Lady or the Tiger," *What's Alan Watching?* May 3, 2010, http://sepinwall. blogspot.com/2010/05/chuck-chuck-vs-role-models-lady-or.html.

10. Sepinwall, "*Friday Night Lights*, 'Thanksgiving': Pride of the Lions," *What's Alan Watching?* February 10, 2010, http:// sepinwall.blogspot.com/2010/02/friday-night-lights-thanksgiving-pride.html.

11. Sepinwall, "*The Wire*: Scrubbing Bubbles," *What's Alan Watching?* January 13, 2008, http://sepinwall.blogspot. com/2008/01/wire-scrubbing-bubbles. html.

12. Sepinwall in Myles McNutt, "The Critic in (Online) Society...," https://cul tural-learnings.com/2011/02/15/the-critic-in-online-society-an-alternate-history-of-21st-century-television-criticism/.

13. *Ibid.*

14. Matt Zoller Seitz, "*Glee* Has a Judy Garland Christmas," Salon.com, December 14, 2011, http://www.salon.com/2011/12/ 14/glee_has_a_judy_garland_christmas/.

15. Zoller Seitz, "*Boardwalk Empire* Does Not Want Your Forgiveness," Salon. com, December 12, 2011, http://www.salon.

com/2011/12/12/boardwalk_empire_does_ not_want_your_forgiveness/.

16. Zoller Seitz, "The Awful Brilliance of *American Horror Story*," Salon.com, November 2, 2011, http://www.salon.com/ 2011/11/02/the_awful_brilliance_of_ american_horror_story/.

17. Zoller Seitz, "*Hannibal* Redefined How We Tell Stories on Television," Vulture. com, April 31, 2015, http://www.vulture. com/2015/08/hannibal-redefined-how-we-tell-stories-on-tv.html.

18. Zoller Seitz, "Dear HBO: Renew *Enlightened*," Salon.com, December 13, 2011, http://www.salon.com/2011/12/13/dear_ hbo_renew_enlightened/.

19. Zoller Seitz, "In Prime-Time, Big Brother Watches Everything," Salon.com, November 6, 2011, http://www.salon.com/ 2011/11/06/in_prime_time_big_brother_ watches_everything/.

20. Zoller Seitz, "Reality TV: A Blood Sport That Must Change," Salon.com, August 18, 2011, http://www.salon.com/2011/ 08/18/reality_tv_blood_sport/. Russell Armstrong, who at the time of his death was the estranged husband of Taylor Armstrong, a star of *The Real Housewives of Beverly Hills*, committed suicide in 2011. Friends noted that the pressure of having his marriage examined on national TV along with the financial hardship of having to keep up with the other participants on the show contributed to his emotional breakdown.

21. Zoller Seitz, "The Radical Humanism of David Simon," Vulture.com, August 13, 2015, http://www.vulture.com/2015/ 08/david-simons-radical-humanism.html.

22. Zoller Seitz, "Meet *Vulture's* New TV Critic, Matt Zoller Seitz," Vulture.com, January 11, 2012, http://www.vulture.com/ 2012/01/vulture-tv-critic-matt-zoller-seitz.html.

23. *Tuned In* became a column in *Time's* print edition in 2006.

24. James Poniewozik, "*True Detective*, *Louie*, and the Limits of TV Auteurism," *Time*, August 10, 2015, http://time.com/ 3990805/true-detective-finale-louie-tv-auteurs/.

25. Poniewozik, "Review: Housing Drama *Show Me a Hero* Hits Us Where We Live," *Time*, August 13, 2015, http://time.com/

3994783/review-show-me-a-hero-hbo-david-simon/.

26. Poniewozik "Review: *The People v. O.J. Simpson*, Seen This Time in Double Vision," *New York Times*, February 1, 2016, http://www.nytimes.com/2016/02/02/arts/television/tv-review-people-vs-oj-simpson-american-crime-story.html?_r=0.

27. Poniewozik, "How *South Park* Perfectly Captures Our Era of Outrage," *New York Times*, December 8, 2015, http://www.nytimes.com/2015/12/09/arts/television/south-park-sketches-grander-satire-themes.html.

28. Poniewozik, "Review: *I Am Cait* Shows What It's Like to Come Out with the Kardashians," *Time*, July 22, 2015, http://time.com/3967543/i-am-cait-review-caitlyn-jenner-e-reality-show/.

29. Poniewozik, "Donald Trump Is a Conundrum for Political Comedy," *New York Times*, February 16, 2016, http://www.nytimes.com/2016/02/17/arts/television/donald-trump-is-a-conundrum-for-political-comedy.html.

30. Poniewozik, "When TV Turns Itself Off," *New York Times*, November 17, 2015, http://www.nytimes.com/2015/11/18/arts/television/after-bloodshed-tv-can-be-cathartic-or-insensitive.html.

31. Poniewozik, "Why 'Diverse TV' Matters: It's Better TV. Discuss," *New York Times*, February 10, 2016, http://www.nytimes.com/2016/02/14/arts/television/smaller-screens-truer-colors.html.

32. Alessandra Stanley, "Mom Brakes for Drug Deals," *New York Times*, August 5, 2005, http://query.nytimes.com/gst/fullpage.html?res=9402E3D81F3FF936A3575BC0A9639C8B63.

33. Stanley, "The New Modern Woman, Ambitious and Feeble," *New York Times*, May 5, 2007, http://www.nytimes.com/2007/05/05/arts/television/05grey.html.

34. Stanley, "Travelogues to the Nine Circles and Back," *New York Times*, May 6, 2010, http://mobile.nytimes.com/2010/05/09/arts/television/09stanley.html.

35. Stanley, "Where Alcoholism Drinks in the Laughs," *New York Times*, December 2, 2010, http://www.nytimes.com/2010/12/03/arts/television/03watch.html.

36. Stanley, "Female Stars Step Off the Scale," *New York Times*, October 11, 2012, http://www.nytimes.com/2012/10/14/arts/television/women-on-tv-step-off-the-scale.html.

37. Stanley, "The Final Story for a Paean to Journalism," *New York Times*, December 14, 2014, http://www.nytimes.com/2014/12/15/arts/the-newsroom-ends-its-final-season-on-hbo.html.

38. Stanley, "Travelogues…," http://mobile.nytimes.com/2010/05/09/arts/television/09stanley.html.

39. Stanley, "Cooking Up Redemption, With a Dollop of Denial," *New York Times*, June 26, 2013, http://www.nytimes.com/2013/06/27/arts/television/cooking-up-redemption-with-a-dollop-of-denial.html.

40. Stanley, "Wrought in Rhime's Image," *New York Times*, September 18, 2014, http://www.nytimes.com/2014/09/21/arts/television/viola-davis-plays-shonda-rhimess-latest-tough-heroine.html.

41. Rhimes is executive producer.

42. Margaret Sullivan, "An Article on Shonda Rhimes Rightly Causes a Furor," *New York Times*, September 22, 2014, http://publiceditor.blogs.nytimes.com/2014/09/22/an-article-on-shonda-rhimes-rightly-causes-a-furor/.

43. *Ibid.*

44. Maureen Ryan, see moryan.tumblr.com.

45. Along with Alan Sepinwall, she was also among the critics who urged their readers to save *Chuck* from cancellation. She said she was "not going to sit back and passively accept that *Chuck* may not come back" because it was "just the kind of well-crafted escapism that people need in these trying times." See "Please Help Save *Chuck*: The Campaign to Get a Nerd Third," *Chicago Tribune*, April 13, 2009, http://featuresblogs.chicagotribune.com/entertainment_tv/2009/04/chuck-nbc-save.html

46. Ryan, "The Gripping Mysteries of *Damages* and the Dangers of the DVRs," *Chicago Tribune*, October 19, 2007, http://featuresblogs.chicagotribune.com/entertainment_tv/2007/10/the-gripping-my.html.

47. *Ibid.*

48. See: http://www.huffingtonpost.com/entry/true-detective-drinking-games-season-2_us_55c23e51e4b0138b0bf4ae4f.

49. Ryan, "Why Is Television Losing Women Writers? Veteran Producers Weigh In," *Huffington Post*, April 11, 2012, http://www.huffingtonpost.com/2011/09/08/women-writers-television_n_1418584.html.

50. Ryan, "Peak Inequality: Investigating the Lack of Diversity Among TV Directors," *Variety*, November 10, 2015, http://variety.com/2015/tv/news/diversity-directors-tv-amc-fx-hbo-netflix-showtime-1201633122/.

51. Ryan, "Who Creates Drama at HBO? Very Few Women or People of Color," *Huffington Post*, March 6, 2014, http://www.huffingtonpost.com/2014/03/06/hbo-diversity_n_4899679.html.

52. Ryan, "Let's Talk *Lost*: Motherload," *Chicago Tribune*, May 12, 2010, http://featuresblogs.chicagotribune.com/entertainment_tv/2010/05/lost-across-the-sea.html.

53. Quoted in Anna Holmes, "TV's Best Criticism Now Has Women Behind the Words," *Washington Post*, December 9, 2011, https://www.highbeam.com/doc/1P2-30279987.html.

54. Ryan, "It's Up to Men in Power to Take the First Step Toward Diversity in TV," *Variety*, October 6, 2015, http://variety.com/2015/voices/news/tv-diversity-women-men-in-power-1201610583/.

55. Ryan, "How to Be a TV Critic," *Huffington Post*, December 14, 2011, http://www.huffingtonpost.com/maureen-ryan/how-to-be-a-tv-critic_b_1146322.html.

56. Heather Havrilesky, see "The Nostalgia-Industrial Complex: What *Game of Thrones* Teaches Us About TV's Obsession With the Past," *Salon*, June 16, 2014, http://www.salon.com/2014/06/16/the_nostalgia_industrial_complex_what_game_of_thrones_teaches_us_about_tvs_obsession_with_the_past/ and "*The Leftovers* Reveals the Limits of Concept-Driven TV," *Salon*, June 26, 2014, http://www.salon.com/2014/06/26/ the_leftovers_ reveals_ the_limits_ of_concept_ driven_tv/.

57. Linda Holmes, "Television 2015: Hammering On the Door of Diversity," *NPR*, August 21, 2015, http://www.npr.org/sections/monkeysee/2015/08/21/433214404/television-2015-hammering-on-the-door-of-diversity.

58. Holmes, "*Madoff* Tells Its Tale to the Camera," *NPR*, February 2, 2016, http://www.npr.org/sections/monkeysee/2016/02/02/465306451/madoff-tells-its-tale-to-the-camera.

59. Lisa French, "Speaking With: *The New Yorker* TV Critic Emily Nussbaum," *The Conversation*, August 18, 2014, http://theconversation.com/speaking-with-the-new-yorker-tv-critic-emily-nussbaum-30033.

60. *Ibid.*

61. Emily Nussbaum, "Watch *The Middle* or I'll Kill This Dog," *New York Magazine*, October 8, 2009, http://nymag.com/daily/tv/2009/10/watch_the_middle_or_ill_kill_t.html.

62. Nussbaum, "Static: *Glee* Hate, *Dexter* Love and I Dream of Aaron Sorkin," *New York Magazine*, November 18, 2009, http://nymag.com/daily/tv/2009/11/static_glee_hate.html.

63. Nussbaum, "Waiting on the Man," *New Yorker*, February 22, 2016, http://www.newyorker.com/magazine/2016/02/22/vinyl-and-billions-reviews.

64. Nancy Franklin, "Odd Bods," *New Yorker*, August 1, 2011, http://www.newyorker.com/magazine/2011/08/01/odd-bods.

65. Nancy Franklin, "Yackety-Yak," *New Yorker*, December 20 and 27, 2010, http://www.newyorker.com/magazine/2010/12/20/yackety-yak.

66. Mary McNamara quoted in Brett Lake, "Q&A: Westminster Native Reflects on Being Name Pulitzer Prize Finalist," *Carroll County Times*, June 8, 2013, http://www.carrollcountytimes. com/cct-arc-5de67a3a-7dad-56bf-b570-80896e482cf0-20130610-story.html.

67. *Ibid.*

68. McNamara, "Matthew's Death May Inject Some Life Into *Downton Abbey*," *Los Angeles Times*, January 3, 2014, http://www.latimes.com/entertainment/tv/showtracker/la-et-st-downton-abbey-review-story.html.

69. McNamara, "*House of Cards* Plays New Hand with Brutal, Clear Resolve," *Los Angeles Times*, February 14, 2014, http://articles.latimes.com/2014/feb/14/entertainment/la-et-st-house-of-cards-review-20140214.

70. McNamara, "Fresh Spate of Sexism, Violence Ominously Familiar," *Los Angeles Times*, May 31, 2014, http://www.latimes.com/entertainment/la-et-critics-note book-women-20140531-column.html.

71. *Ibid.*

72. McNamara, "Broadcasting the Big Strides in TV Diversity," *Los Angeles Times*, March 29, 2014, http://articles.latimes.com/2014/mar/29/entertainment/la-et-st-broadcast-tv-diversity-20140329.

73. *Ibid.*

74. McNamara, "Binge Watching, That Great American Pastime, Can Also Be Good Medicine," *Los Angeles Times*, July 4, 2014, http://www.latimes.com/entertainment/tv/la-et-st-binge-watching-20140704-column.html. McNamara's son Danny, in high school at the time of writing, had a back operation and recovered but could no longer play football. *Friday Night Lights*, in part, deals with a high school football player who suffers an injury that permanently ends his days on the field.

75. Quoted in Tom Wilk, "The Watchman," *New Jersey Monthly*, July 12, 2010, http://www.tvworthwatching.com/Blog PostDetails.aspx?postId=45.

76. *Ibid.*

77. *Ibid.*

78. Bianculli, "*X-Files* Reboot Brings Back Mulder, Scully and the Search for the Truth," *NPR*, January 22, 2016, http://www.npr.org/2016/01/21/463901978/an-x-files-reboot-brings-back-mulder-scully-and-the-search-for-truth.

79. Bianculli, "CBS' *Supergirl* Struggles to Get off the Ground," *NPR*, October 26, 2016, http://www.npr.org/2015/10/26/451 861531/cbs-supergirl-struggles-to-get-off-the-ground.

80. Bianculli, "*SNL* Alums 'Rock' in New Sitcom," *New York Daily News*, October 11, 2006, http://www.nydailynews.com/enter tainment/tv/nbc-30-rock-premieres-2006-article-1.617709.

81. Wilk, "The Watchman," *New Jersey Monthly*, July 12, 2010, http://www.tvworth watching.com/BlogPostDetails.aspx?post Id=45.

82. Ken Tucker, "*Buffy the Vampire Slayer*," *Entertainment Weekly*, November 6, 1998, http://www.ew.com/article/1998/11/06/buffy-vampire-slayer.

83. Tucker, "*Smash* Season Premiere Review: Jennifer Hudson, More of a 'Bombshell' than Katharine McPhee? Plus, Why 'Hate-Watching' Should be Mothballed," *Entertainment Weekly*, February 5, 2013, http://www.ew.com/article/2013/02/05/smash-season-2-jennifer-hudson-review.

84. See Jess Cagle's memo reprinted in Alexander Kaufman, "Ken Tucker Leaving *Entertainment Weekly*," *The Wrap*, February 13, 2013, http://www.thewrap.com/entertainment-weekly-tv-critic-ken-tucker-leaving-magazine-77536/.

85. Tucker, "*Freaks and Geeks*," *Entertainment Weekly*, November 19, 1999, http://www.ew.com/article/1999/11/19/freaks-and-geeks.

86. Tucker, "*Family Guy*," *Entertainment Weekly*, April 9, 1999, http://www.ew.com/article/1999/04/09/family-guy.

87. Tucker, "The Worst/TV: 1999," *Entertainment Weekly*, December 24, 1999, http://www.ew.com/article/1999/12/24/worsttv-1999.

88. Claire Hoffman, "No. 1 Offender," *New Yorker*, June 18, 2012, http://www.new yorker.com/magazine/2012/06/18/no-1-offender.

89. Amy Chozick, "Revenge of the TV Writers," *Wall Street Journal*, August 20, 2010, http://www.wsj.com/articles/SB10 0014240527487045541045754355315525 25078.

90. *Ibid.*

91. Tucker, "Goodnight and a Few More Opinions and Recommendations," *Entertainment Weekly* February 16, 2013, http://www.ew.com/article/2013/02/16/ken-tucker-hbo-amc-cbs-abc-nbc-pbs.

Bibliography

Adler, Richard, ed. *Television as a Social Force: New Approaches to TV Criticism.* New York: Praeger, 1975.

Arlen, Michael. *The Camera Age: Essays on Television.* New York: Penguin, 1982.

____. *Living Room War.* New York: Viking Press, 1969.

____. *The View from Highway 1.* New York: Farrar, Straus & Giroux, 1976.

Barnouw, Erik. *Tube of Plenty: The Evolution of American Television.* 2nd edition. New York: Oxford University Press, 1990.

Baughman, James L. "Minow's Viewers: Understanding the Response to the "Vast Wasteland" Address." *Federal Communications Law Journal* 55 (2003): 449–458.

Berman, Marc. "One Lonely Critic." *MediaWeek* 14 (March 22, 2004): 34.

Bielby, Denise, Molly Moloney and Bob Q. Ngo. "Aesthetics of Television Criticism: Mapping Critics' Reviews in an Era of Industry Transformation." *Research in the Sociology of Organizations* 23 (2005): 1–43.

Bielby, Denise. "Who's to Say? Why Television Criticism Is Complicated." *Flow,* May 5, 2014.

Boddy, William. *Fifties Television: The Industry and Its Critics.* Urbana: University of Illinois Press, 1990.

____. "Loving a Nineteen-Inch Motorola: American Writing on Television." In *Regarding Television: Critical Approaches, An Anthology,* ed. E. Ann Kaplan, 1–11.

Los Angeles: American Film Institute, 1983.

Brooks, Karen. "When Twitter Meets Television, Criticism Becomes Fast and Faceless." *Courier-Mail,* June 20, 2012.

Brown, Les. *Keeping Your Eye on Television.* New York: Pilgrim Press, 1979.

____. "Remarks to the Iowa TV Critics Conference." *Critical Studies in Mass Communication* 2 (December 1985): 390–395.

____. *Televi$ion: The Business Behind the Box.* New York: Harcourt Brace Jovanovich, 1971.

Carden, John. "A Conversation with John. J. O'Connor of the Times." *Television Quarterly* 2 (Winter 1974): 13–18.

Castleman, Harry, and Walter J. Podrazik. *Watching TV: Six Decades of American Television.* 2nd edition. Syracuse, New York: Syracuse University Press, 2010.

Cawelti, John G. "With the Benefit of Hindsight: Popular Culture Criticism." *Critical Studies in Mass Communication* 2 (1985): 363–379.

Chapel, Gage William. "Television Criticism: A Rhetorical Perspective." *Western Speech Communication* (Spring 1975): 81–91.

Christians, Clifford. "Professional Criticism." *Critical Studies in Mass Communication* 2 (1985): 65–85.

Cole, Barry, ed. *Television Today: A Close-Up View.* Oxford: Oxford University Press, 1981.

Crosby, John. *Out of the Blue: A Book About Radio and Television*. New York: Simon & Schuster, 1952.

Deming, Caren J. "On the Becoming of Television Criticism." *Critical Studies in Mass Communication* 1 (September 1984): 324–326.

Edgerton, Gary R. *The Columbia History of American Television*. New York: Columbia University Press, 2007.

Ellison, Harlan. *The Glass Teat*. New York: Ace, 1970.

Feuer, Jane. *Seeing Through the Eighties: Television and Reaganism*. Durham: Duke University Press, 1995.

Flannery, Gerald. "Television Criticism: A Technical Approach." *Journal of Applied Communications Research* 8 (November 1980): 69–77.

Frank, Reuven. "When a Critic Counted." *The New Leader* (November-December 2002): 54–56.

Gans, Herbert. *Popular Culture and High Culture: An Analysis and Evaluation of Taste*. New York: Basic Books, 1974.

Gosling, Nigel. "The Critical Tightrope." *Twentieth Century* 174 (1967): 11–12.

Gould, Lewis L. "The TV Critic." *Quill* 84 (December 1996): 11–14.

____, ed. *Watching Television Come of Age: The New York Times Reviews by Jack Gould*. Austin: University of Texas Press, 2013.

Gray, Jonathan. *Show Sold Separately: Promos, Spoilers and Other Media Paratexts*. New York: New York University Press, 2010.

Gray, Rebecca. "Covering the Company's TV Station." *American Journalism Review* 22 (May 2000): 16–17.

Gronbeck, Bruce E. "The Academic Practice of Television Criticism." *Quarterly Journal of Speech* 74 (1988): 334–347.

Haberski, Raymond J., Jr. *It's Only a Movie! Films and Critics in American Culture*. Lexington: University Press of Kentucky, 2001.

Himmelstein, Hal. *On the Small Screen: New Approaches in Television and Video Criticism*. New York: Praeger, 1981.

Holmes, Anna. "TV's Best Criticism Now Has Women Behind the Words." *Washington Post*, December 9, 2011.

Krampner, Jon. "Mom Always Liked Them Best: The Smothers Brothers Story Revisited." *Television Quarterly* 29 (1998): 62–71.

Kreiling, Ernie. "A Critical Critic." *Journal of Broadcasting* 11 (Winter 1966-67): 3–8.

Laurent, Lawrence. "A Critic Looks at Reviewing." *Journal of Broadcasting* 11 (1966-1967): 16.

Lichty, Lawrence. "What Does a Television Critic Write About?" *Journal of Broadcasting* 7 (1962-1963): 353–358.

Littlejohn, David. "Thoughts on Television Criticism." In *Television as a Cultural Force*, ed. Richard Adler and Douglas Cater, 147–173. New York: Praeger, 1976.

Lotz, Amanda. "On 'Television Criticism': The Pursuit of the Critical Examination of a Popular Art." *Popular Communication* 6 (2008): 20–36.

____. "Seventeen Days in July at Hollywood and Highland: Examining the Television Critics Association Tour." *Journal of Popular Film and Television* 33 (Spring 2005): 22–28.

____. *The Television Will Be Revolutionized*. New York: New York University Press, 2014.

Mark, Norman. "TV Junketeers." *Columbia Journalism Review* (July-August 1974): 27–31.

Mayeux, Peter. "Three Television Critics: Stated vs. Manifest Functions." *Journal of Broadcasting* 14 (1969-1970): 25–35.

McCabe, Janet. "In Debate: Television Studies in the American Academy." *Critical Studies in Television* 6 (May 2011): 99–112.

McGrath, J.B., and Margette Nance. "Television Reviewing: A Search for Criteria." *Journal of Broadcasting* 11 (1966-1967): 57–61.

Montgomery, Katherine. "Writing About Television in the Popular Press." *Critical Studies in Mass Communication* 2 (1985): 75–80.

Newcomb, Horace. "American Television Criticism, 1970–1985." *Critical Studies in Mass Communication* 3 (1986): 217–228.

____, ed. *Television: The Critical View*. New York: Oxford University Press, 1976.

Newman, Michael Z., and Elana Levine. *Legitimating Television: Media Conver-*

gence and Cultural Status. New York: Routledge, 2012.

Orlik, Peter. *Critiquing Radio and Television Content*. Needham, MA: Allyn and Bacon, 1988.

Pondillo, Bob. "Chicago TV's Winter of Violence 1952-53." *Television Quarterly* 34 (Winter 2004): 24–29.

Rixon, Paul. *TV Critics and Popular Culture: A History of British Television Criticism*. London: I.B. Tauris, 2011.

Rosenberg, Howard. *Not So Prime Time: Chasing the Trivial on American Television*. Chicago: Ivan R. Dee, 2004.

Rossman, Jules. "The TV Critic Column: Is it Influential?" *Journal of Broadcasting* 19 (Fall 1974): 401–411.

____. "What Do Reviewers Actually Review?" *Journal of Broadcasting* 9 (1964-1965): 167–175.

Scher, Saul N. "The Role of the Television Critic: Four Approaches." *Today's Speech* (Summer 1974): 1–6.

Seldes, Gilbert. *The Public Arts*. New York: Simon & Schuster, 1956.

Shales, Tom. *On the Air!* New York: Summit Books, 1982.

Shayon, Robert Lewis. *The Eighth Art*. New York: Holt, Rinehart and Winston, 1962.

____. *Open to Criticism*. Boston: Little, Brown, 1971.

Shelby, Maurice, Jr. "Criticism and Longevity of Television Programs." *Journal of Broadcasting* 17 (1973): 277–285.

____. "Patterns in Thirty Years of Broadcast Criticism." *Journal of Broadcasting* 11 (1966-1967): 27–40.

Shrum, Wesley Monroe Jr. *Fringe and Fortune: The Role of Critics in High and Popular Art*. Princeton: Princeton University Press, 1996.

Smith, Cecil. "Changing Portrait of the TV Critic." *Television Quarterly*. 2 (Winter 1974): 29–31.

Smith, Ralph Lewis. *A Study of the Professional Criticism of Broadcasting in the United States 1920–1955*. New York: Arno Press, 1979.

Smith, Robert Rutherford. *Beyond the Wasteland: The Criticism of Broadcasting*. Falls Church, VA: Speech Communication Association, 1976.

Sopkin, Charles. *Seven Glorious Days, Seven Fun-Filled Nights*. New York: Ace, 1968.

Spigel, Lynn. "The Making of a TV Literate Elite." In *The Television Studies Book*, ed. Christine Geraghty and David Lusted, 63–85. London: Arnold, 1998.

Steinberg, Charles. "The Compleat Television Critic." *Television Quarterly* 2 (Winter 1974): 5–12.

Steiner, Gary A. *The People Look at Television: A Study of Audience Attitudes*. New York: Alfred A. Knopf, 1963.

Thompson, Robert J. "Television's Second Golden Age: The Quality Shows." *Television Quarterly* 28 (1996): 75–81.

Thompson, Robert. "Reality and the Future of Television." *Television Quarterly* 31 (Winter 2001): 20–25.

Turow, Joseph. *Media Systems in Society*. New York: Longman, 1992.

Van Horne, Harriet. *Never Go Anywhere Without a Pencil*. New York: G.P. Putnam's Sons, 1969.

Vande Berg, Leah, Lawrence Wenner and Bruce Gronbeck. "Media Literacy and Television Criticism: Enabling an Informed and Engaged Citizenry." *The American Behavioral Scientist* 48 (2004): 219–228.

Vincent, Richard. "The Evolution of Television Criticism in the *New York Times*: 1949–1977." *Journalism Quarterly* 57 (Winter 1980): 647–676.

Watson, Mary Ann. "Television Criticism in the Popular Press." *Critical Studies in Mass Communication* 2 (March 1985): 66–75.

Waxman, Sharon. "Spoon-Fed News." *American Journalism Review* 20 (October 1998): 36–39.

Wright, John L. "The Focus of Television Criticism." *Journal of Popular Culture* 7 (Spring 1974): 887–895.

Young, Elizabeth. "One Medium: Two Critics, Two Views." *Journal of Broadcasting* 11 (1966-1967): 41–55.

Index